Best of the Best

The best recipes from the 25 best cookbooks of the year chosen by the editors of FOOD & WINE magazine

FOOD&**WINE**

FOOD & WINE BEST OF THE BEST VOL. 8

Editor Kate Heddings
Art Director Ethan Cornell
Senior Editor Rachael Shapiro
Designer Nancy Blumberg
Copy Editor Lisa Leventer
Assistant Editor Melissa Rubel
Reporters Tracey Gertler, Sonali Laschever, Jennifer Murphy, Ann Pepi

FOOD & WINE MAGAZINE

Editor in Chief Dana Cowin
Creative Director Stephen Scoble
Managing Editor Mary Ellen Ward
Executive Editor Pamela Kaufman
Executive Food Editor Tina Ujlaki
Art Director Patricia Sanchez

AMERICAN EXPRESS PUBLISHING CORPORATION

Senior Vice President, Chief Marketing Officer Mark V. Stanich
Vice President, Books and Products Marshall Corey
Senior Marketing Manager Bruce Spanier
Corporate Production Manager Stuart Handelman
Senior Operations Manager Phil Black
Business Manager Thomas Noonan

Cover
Photograph by James Baigrie
Prop Styling by Alistair Turnbull

Flap Photographs
Dana Cowin portrait by Andrew French
Kate Heddings portrait by Andrew French

ISBN 1-932624-04-X
ISSN 1524-2862

Published by American Express Publishing Corporation
1120 Avenue of the Americas, New York, New York 10036

Manufactured in the United States of America

Best of the Best

The best recipes from the 25 best cookbooks of the year chosen by the editors of FOOD & WINE magazine

FOOD&WINE
BOOKS

American Express Publishing Corporation, New York

Contents

Best of the Best Exclusives Recipe titles in orange are brand-new dishes appearing exclusively in *Best of the Best*.

Contents

Recipes

Hors d'Oeuvres

First Courses

Pasta & Risotto

Fish & Shellfish

Foreword

To find the year's top 25 cookbooks for *Best of the Best,* we tested over 200. We were pleased that so many were terrific, even though it made the task of narrowing down the list a challenge. We were especially gratified by the chef cookbooks—finally, chefs seem to have figured out that home cooks want recipes that they can do without a kitchen brigade. The Simple Roast Chicken in Thomas Keller's *Bouchon* and the Alpine Baked Pasta from Michael Lomonaco's *Nightly Specials* were easy to prepare and completely delicious.

We noticed another trend: retro desserts. Two of the best were the Lemon Chiffon Pie with Pretzel Crust from Abigail Johnson Dodge's *The Weekend Baker* and the Chocolate Whoopie Pie from *The King Arthur Cookie Companion* (indeed, the ubiquitous whoopie pie seems to be this year's "it" dessert).

Beyond providing great recipes, many of the year's best cookbooks are also great reads. In *Les Halles Cookbook,* Anthony Bourdain's irreverent, sometimes profane, always engaging personality comes through loud and clear. Marcella Hazan's warm, authoritative voice permeates *Marcella Says...* as she recounts lessons from the intimate master classes she taught in Venice for 20 years. Grace Young's evocative *Breath of a Wok* belongs as much on your night table as it does on your kitchen counter.

As always, the recipes in *Best of the Best* appear exactly as they do in their original volumes. But we've added tips throughout the book to share a few things we discovered while trying these recipes in the FOOD & WINE Test Kitchen. And we're excited to introduce two new extras this year. One is a special book-buyer's code that will provide access to FOOD & WINE's Web site, foodandwine.com, where you'll find more recipes by many of the authors. The other is almost two dozen never-before-seen recipes, one from nearly every author, published exclusively in *Best of the Best.* We swooned over Emeril Lagasse's Crabmeat Fettuccine Carbonara and Jamie Oliver's Chicken Noodle Stir-Fry.

Do any of the recipes in *Best of the Best* make *you* swoon? We'd love to know. Please e-mail us at cookbookcomments@aexp.com.

Dana Cowin
Editor in Chief
FOOD & WINE MAGAZINE

Kate Heddings
Editor
FOOD & WINE COOKBOOKS

Hot Chickpea
Puree, PAGE 18

The Middle Eastern Kitchen

by Ghillie Başan

**Published by Hippocrene Books,
240 pages, color photos, $29.50**

"There's something incredibly sumptuous about the food of the Middle East, teasing the palate with exotic and tantalizing flavors—delicate and spicy, aromatic and fragrant, scented and syrupy," declares Ghillie Başan in this follow-up to her *Classic Turkish Cookery*. This guide to the foods of Iran, Turkey, Syria, Lebanon, Saudi Arabia and beyond explores 75 ingredients, from quince and cumin to less familiar flavorings like sumac and orchid root. Each chapter offers a detailed description of the ingredient—how it grows, buying and storing tips—followed by a few recipes.

Featured Recipes Iranian Baked Rice; Baklava; Hot Chickpea Puree

Best of the Best Exclusive Couscous with Roasted Eggplant and Cherry Tomatoes

13

Iranian Baked Rice

Tahcheen

Literally translated as "laid on the bottom," *tahcheen* is a classic Persian dish served on special occasions like weddings and festive days. Traditionally, the dish was made in a wide-bottomed pan that was placed in the hot coals of a baker's oven, where it would bake for many hours so that a thick, crusty layer formed on the bottom. Lamb or chicken can be used in this recipe.

PREPARATION TIME: APPROXIMATELY 30 MINUTES (+ 1 HOUR SOAKING THE RICE AND 1 HOUR MARINATING THE CHICKEN)
COOKING TIME: 30 TO 40 MINUTES
4 TO 6 SERVINGS

- 2 pinches saffron fronds
- A sprinkling of sugar
- ¾ cup yogurt
- 2 eggs
- 1 onion, grated
- Salt and freshly ground black pepper
- 1 small roast chicken, the meat stripped off and cut into pieces
- 2½ cups long-grain rice, washed and soaked in salted water for about 1 hour
- Roughly ½ cup olive oil
- Roughly ¼ cup butter, cut into pieces

In a small bowl, grind the saffron with the sugar. Add a few drops of boiling water and mix well.

Mix the yogurt and eggs together, beat in the grated onion, and season with salt and pepper. Stir the saffron mixture into the yogurt, and marinate the chicken pieces in it for 1 to 2 hours.

Meanwhile, fill a large saucepan with water and bring it to a boil with a little salt. Toss in the drained rice and cook for about 5 minutes, until the grains are soft on the outside but firm in the middle. Drain and rinse under lukewarm water.

Remove the chicken from the marinade, then mix half of the cooked rice with the remaining yogurt mixture. Heat the oil in the bottom of a heavy-based pan and spread the rice and yogurt mixture across the base and up the sides. Lay the chicken on top, followed by the rest of the rice, or arrange the rice and chicken in alternate layers. Dot the butter on top.

Poke a few holes through the rice, then cover the pan with a clean dish towel and the lid. Keep it on a high heat for a minute or two, then reduce to the lowest heat and leave the rice to steam for about 30 minutes. Alternatively, bake it in a low oven, about 325°F, for 30 to 40 minutes.

Spoon the cooked rice onto a serving dish and arrange the chicken on it with thick wedges of crispy bottom. If you prefer, you can turn the pan upside down onto a serving dish to present the rice in a mound.

The Middle
Eastern Kitchen
Ghillie Başan

Baklava

A legacy of the Ottoman Empire, baklava is arguably the grandest of the Middle Eastern syrupy pastries. Certainly, it is the best known and the most misunderstood. The magnificent creation of the pastry chefs in the Topkapı Palace, the classic baklava was made with eight layers of a special pastry dough, clarified butter, and seven layers of nuts.

In the Middle East, baklava is generally associated with celebrations, such as births, weddings, festivals, the Jewish bar mitzvah, and the Muslim Ramadan. As vast quantities are consumed, most people buy their baklava from the specialty pastry stores, where they will be enticed by other syrupy pastries too. However, if you use sheets of phyllo pastry, a straightforward baklava is easy to prepare at home. Pistachios are often regarded as the most prestigious filling, but walnuts are traditional.

PREPARATION TIME: 30 MINUTES
COOKING TIME: APPROXIMATELY 1 HOUR
8 TO 12 SERVINGS

- ¾ cup clarified or ordinary butter
- ½ cup sunflower oil
- 1 pound phyllo pastry
- 4 cups finely chopped walnuts
- 1 teaspoon ground cinnamon

FOR THE SYRUP

- 2 cups sugar
- 1 cup + 2 tablespoons water

Juice of ½ lemon, or 2 tablespoons rose water

Preheat the oven to 325°F.

Melt the butter with the oil in a pan and brush a little of it on the base and sides of a 12-inch baking pan. Place a sheet of phyllo pastry in the bottom and brush with the melted butter and oil. Do the same with half the quantity of phyllo pastry, easing them into the corners and trimming the edges if they flop over the rim.

Spread the chopped walnuts over the top sheet and, if you like, sprinkle with cinnamon. Continue with the phyllo pastry, brushing each layer with the melted butter and oil. Brush the top and, using a sharp-pointed knife, cut parallel lines

Test Kitchen Tip

Clarified butter is a traditional ingredient in Middle Eastern cooking. In this recipe it adds a subtle nutty flavor. To make it, slowly melt the butter over moderate heat. Remove from the heat and set aside until white milk solids settle to the bottom of the pan. Use a ladle or spoon to remove just the clear, clarified butter on top, leaving the milk solids behind.

The Middle
Eastern Kitchen
Ghillie Başan

right through all the layers to the bottom, making small diamond shapes. Then pop it in the oven for about 1 hour. If the top is not golden brown at the end of the hour, turn the oven up to 400°F for a few minutes.

Meanwhile, make the syrup. Put the sugar and water into a pan and bring to a boil, stirring all the time. Stir in the lemon juice, reduce the heat, and simmer for 10 to 15 minutes—if using rose water, add it at this stage. Leave the syrup to cool.

Take the golden baklava out of the oven and pour the cold syrup over the hot pastry. You can zap it back into the oven for 5 minutes if you like, to help the pastry absorb the syrup, or just let it cool. Once cooled, lift the diamond-shaped pieces out of the pan and arrange on a serving dish.

The Middle
Eastern Kitchen
Ghillie Başan

Hot Chickpea Puree

Sicak Hummus

Test Kitchen Tip
If you have trouble finding Middle Eastern red pepper (also called Aleppo pepper), you can substitute the same amount of crushed red pepper flakes.

This recipe is a specialty from the east of Turkey, particularly popular with the people who live in the mountains, where the air is cold. It is served by itself or as part of a hot *meze* spread, with plenty of fresh bread to scoop it up.

PREPARATION TIME: 10 MINUTES (IF USING AN ELECTRIC MIXER) + 8 HOURS
    SOAKING THE CHICKPEAS AND 1½ HOURS COOKING
COOKING TIME: 25 MINUTES
4 TO 6 SERVINGS

2¼ cups dried chickpeas, soaked, cooked,
    and drained with skins removed
Roughly ½ cup olive oil
Juice of 2 lemons
  2 to 3 cloves garlic, crushed
  1 to 2 teaspoons cumin seeds
  2 tablespoons light or dark tahini
Roughly 2 cups thick, strained yogurt
Salt and freshly ground black pepper

FOR THE TOP
  2 tablespoons pine nuts
Roughly 3 tablespoons butter
  1 teaspoon Middle Eastern red pepper

Preheat the oven to 400°F.

Pounding the chickpeas by hand is laborious, so if you have a liquidizer or food processor, whiz all the hummus ingredients together. Season well and spoon into an ovenproof dish.

In a flat heavy-based pan, roast the pine nuts until they are brown. Quickly add the butter and allow it to melt before stirring in the red pepper. Spoon the melted butter over the top of the hummus and bake it in the oven for about 25 minutes, until it has risen slightly and most of the butter has been absorbed. Serve hot with lots of crusty or flat bread.

The Middle
Eastern Kitchen
Ghillie Başan

Couscous with Roasted Eggplant and Cherry Tomatoes

ACTIVE: 15 MIN; TOTAL: 45 MIN
4 SERVINGS

- 2 medium eggplants (about 1 pound), halved lengthwise, then crosswise, each quarter cut into 4 wedges
- 16 cherry tomatoes
- 2 garlic cloves, finely chopped
- 1 long red chile, seeded and finely chopped
- ⅓ cup extra-virgin olive oil
- 2 teaspoons sugar
- 2 teaspoons kosher salt
- 1 cup couscous
- 1 tablespoon sunflower oil
- 1 tablespoon unsalted butter
- 2 cups boiling water
- ¼ cup coarsely chopped flat-leaf parsley
- 1 lemon, cut into wedges

Plain yogurt and *harissa,* for serving

1. Preheat the oven to 400°. In a 9-by-13-inch baking dish, toss the eggplant with the tomatoes, garlic, chile, olive oil, sugar and 1 teaspoon of salt. Pop the dish in the oven for about 40 minutes, turning occasionally, until the vegetables are tender and nicely browned.

2. Meanwhile, in a medium bowl, combine the couscous with the sunflower oil, the butter and the remaining 1 teaspoon of salt. Stir in the boiling water, cover with plastic wrap and let stand until the water is absorbed, about 15 minutes.

3. Fluff the couscous with a fork and transfer to a serving platter. Spoon the roasted eggplant and any juices over the couscous, allowing the flavored roasting juices to soak in. Sprinkle with the parsley and serve with lemon wedges, yogurt and *harissa.*

Editor's Note

Başan is so passionate about eggplants that she hopes to write her next cookbook about them. This dish, in which the eggplant roasts with tomatoes, chile and garlic until it's soft and juicy, is a great accompaniment to roast lamb.

The Middle
Eastern Kitchen
Ghillie Başan

Tomato
Goat Cheese
Strata, PAGE 23

Fresh Food Fast
by Peter Berley

And Melissa Clark, published by ReganBooks, 304 pages, color photos, $34.95

Peter Berley, author of *Fresh Food Fast* and former executive chef of New York City's vegetarian Angelica Kitchen, knows just how to make meat-free food taste great. The book is divided into spring, summer, autumn and winter sections; each offers 12 menus working with seasonal produce and spanning casual to fancy dishes. Every menu clearly lays out exactly what you need—groceries, equipment—and comes with a game plan. Recipes rely on flavorful ingredients rather than lengthy techniques to ensure that they are both speedy and satisfying.

Featured Recipes Bibb Lettuce and Radish Salad with Crème Fraîche Citronette; Tomato Goat Cheese Strata; Pita Pizza with Green Olives, Monterey Jack, and Chopped Salad; White Bean and Arugula Salad with Lemon Dill Vinaigrette

Best of the Best Exclusive Grilled Shrimp in Harissa with Polenta and Grape Tomatoes

Bibb Lettuce and Radish Salad with Crème Fraîche Citronette

Berley on Radishes

Radishes are one of the first vegetables to mature in the spring. Young and tender radish greens are an excellent source of iron and are a component of traditional spring tonics.

Crème fraîche makes this dressing ultra creamy, but you can substitute sour cream or whole-milk yogurt.

4 SERVINGS

FOR THE DRESSING

½ garlic clove

⅓ cup crème fraîche

1 tablespoon freshly squeezed lemon juice

½ teaspoon coarse sea salt or kosher salt

1 tablespoon extra-virgin olive oil

1 tablespoon chopped fresh chives

Freshly milled black pepper

10 ounces Bibb lettuce leaves, separated (about 10 cups)

3 to 4 red radishes, thinly sliced

1. Rub the inside of a salad bowl vigorously with the garlic clove half. Add the crème fraîche, lemon juice, and salt; whisk to combine. Whisk in the olive oil and chives and season with black pepper.

2. Add the lettuce and radishes and toss. Serve immediately.

Fresh Food Fast
Peter Berley

For more recipes by Peter Berley go to foodandwine.com/berley. To access the recipes, log on with this code: **FWBEST05**. Effective through December 31, 2006.

Tomato Goat Cheese Strata

I like to describe this dish, one of my favorites, as a savory bread pudding with cheese.

4 SERVINGS

- 6 large eggs
- 1 cup heavy cream
- 3 tablespoons minced fresh flat-leaf parsley
- 1 medium onion, thinly sliced
- 2 tablespoons extra-virgin olive oil
- 2 large garlic cloves, roughly chopped
- 1 tablespoon minced fresh sage
- ½ teaspoon crushed red pepper flakes
- 1 (28-ounce) can diced tomatoes with their juice
- 1 teaspoon coarse sea salt or kosher salt
- ½ pound day-old artisanal bread, cut into 1-inch cubes (about 6 cups)
- ¼ pound fresh goat cheese
- ¼ cup freshly grated Parmesan or Grana Padano cheese

1. Set a rack on the middle shelf of the oven and preheat to 450°F.

2. In a medium bowl, whisk together the eggs, cream, and parsley and set aside.

3. Place a 10-inch ovenproof sauté pan or 3-quart brazier over high heat. When the pan is hot, add the onion. Cook until lightly browned, about 2 minutes. Add the oil, garlic, sage, and red pepper flakes and sauté, stirring, for 1 more minute. Add the tomatoes and salt and bring to a simmer.

4. Stir the bread into the tomatoes. Crumble the goat cheese over the bread, then pour the egg and cream mixture over all and sprinkle with the Parmesan cheese. Bake until the strata has set and is golden on top, about 25 minutes. Lest rest for 5 minutes before serving.

Fresh Food Fast
Peter Berley

Pita Pizza with Green Olives, Monterey Jack, and Chopped Salad

Pocketless pita bread makes a convenient pizza base. You could also use any other tender, chewy flat bread, such as lavash.

4 SERVINGS

FOR THE CHOPPED SALAD

- 1 garlic clove, peeled and halved
- 2 tablespoons balsamic vinegar
- 1 small red onion, halved and very thinly sliced
- ¼ cup extra-virgin olive oil
- Coarse sea salt or kosher salt and freshly milled black pepper
- 3 hearts of romaine, coarsely chopped (about 8 cups)
- 4 medium Kirby cucumbers, quartered lengthwise and cut into bite-sized pieces
- 2 medium tomatoes, cored, seeded, and diced (about 1 cup)
- 1 ripe avocado, diced
- 5 fresh basil leaves, torn into pieces
- 8 to 10 fresh mint leaves, torn into pieces

FOR THE PIZZAS

- 4 (7-inch) rounds of pocketless pita bread
- 8 ounces Monterey Jack cheese, coarsely grated
- ½ cup pitted and roughly chopped green olives
- 2 jalapeño peppers, minced, or 1 teaspoon crushed red pepper flakes
- Freshly milled black pepper
- Shaved Parmesan cheese for garnish

1. Place a pizza stone or an inverted rimmed baking sheet in the upper third of the oven and preheat the oven to 450°F.

2. To prepare the salad, vigorously rub the inside of a large bowl with the garlic. Add the vinegar and red onion and set aside for 5 minutes. Whisk in the oil and season with salt and pepper. Add the lettuce, cucumbers, tomatoes, avocado, basil, and mint and toss well.

3. Bake the pitas, in batches if necessary, on the heated pizza stone or pan for 3 minutes.

4. In a small bowl, combine the cheese, olives, and jalapeños. Divide this mixture among the 4 pitas.

5. Return the pitas to the oven, 2 at a time, and bake until the cheese is bubbling and lightly browned, about 5 minutes.

6. Mound the salad on top of the pizzas, sprinkle with freshly milled black pepper and Parmesan cheese, and serve.

Fresh Food Fast
Peter Berley

White Bean and Arugula Salad with Lemon Dill Vinaigrette

Berley on His Favorite Fast Recipe

My favorite quick recipe uses vine-ripe tomatoes, and I mean real ones, *not* the kind you get at the supermarket. I like to serve them over grilled bread with anchovies and capers plus some torn cilantro or basil.

This substantial salad, served simply with good crusty bread, is great for lunch. Use a vegetable peeler to shave the Parmesan cheese.

4 SERVINGS

⅓ cup extra-virgin olive oil

3 tablespoons freshly squeezed lemon juice

1 tablespoon minced fresh dill

1 small garlic clove, finely chopped

Coarse sea salt or kosher salt and freshly milled black pepper

3 bunches arugula, trimmed and roughly chopped (6 to 7 cups)

1 (15-ounce) can white beans, such as cannellini or Great Northern, drained

1 yellow bell pepper, halved, seeded, and thinly sliced

Shaved Parmesan cheese for garnish

1. In a large bowl, whisk together the oil, lemon juice, dill, garlic, and salt and pepper. Add the arugula, beans, and yellow pepper and toss to combine.

2. Garnish the salad with shaved Parmesan cheese and serve.

Fresh Food Fast
Peter Berley

Grilled Shrimp in Harissa with Polenta and Grape Tomatoes

4 SERVINGS

 2 teaspoons cumin seeds, finely ground

½ teaspoon caraway seeds, finely ground

½ teaspoon fennel seeds, finely ground

½ teaspoon cayenne pepper

Kosher salt and freshly ground black pepper

 4 garlic cloves, minced

¼ cup plus 5 tablespoons extra-virgin olive oil, plus more for drizzling

¼ cup lemon juice

 1 pound large shrimp, peeled and deveined

 1 ear of corn, kernels cut off the cob

 1 cup instant polenta

 2 tablespoons unsalted butter

½ teaspoon crushed red pepper

 2 pints grape tomatoes

 5 tablespoons coarsely chopped basil, flat-leaf parsley and oregano

Freshly grated Parmesan cheese

1. Light a grill. In a bowl, whisk the ground spices with the cayenne, 1 teaspoon of salt, a pinch of black pepper, 2 minced garlic cloves, 5 tablespoons of the oil and the lemon juice. Toss in the shrimp. Let stand for 15 minutes. Grill the shrimp for 2 minutes per side, or until cooked through.

2. Meanwhile, in a medium saucepan, bring 3 cups of water to a boil. Add 2 teaspoons of salt and the corn and bring back to a boil. Slowly add the polenta and cook over moderately low heat, stirring constantly with a wooden spoon, until thick, about 5 minutes. Stir in the butter, cover and remove from the heat.

3. In a large skillet, heat ¼ cup of olive oil. Add the remaining garlic and the crushed red pepper and cook over moderately high heat until fragrant, about 30 seconds. Add the tomatoes and cook, stirring occasionally, for 4 minutes. Stir in the herbs, season with salt and pepper and cook for 1 minute longer.

4. Spoon the polenta into shallow bowls; top with the shrimp, tomatoes and their juices. Drizzle with olive oil, sprinkle with Parmesan cheese and serve.

Editor's Note

This recipe is a perfect midweek meal—it's light, fast and tasty. Instant polenta is easier to use than regular polenta because it's made from finely (rather than coarsely) ground cornmeal, so it takes about 5 minutes to cook instead of 30. The shrimp are a good addition if you are serving this as a main course, although even without them the dish is delicious as a vegetarian entrée.

Fresh Food Fast
Peter Berley

Blanc et Noir, PAGE 30

Pure Chocolate

by Fran Bigelow

With Helene Siegel, published by Broadway Books, 248 pages, color photos, $35

Fran Bigelow, owner of Fran's Chocolates in Seattle, admits that she was attracted to chocolate-making because the precision required reminded her of one of her favorite subjects in school, math. In this, her first cookbook, Bigelow applies an almost scientific approach to chocolate desserts—giving cocoa-solid percentages for every type of chocolate she uses, for instance, and specifying the exact temperatures at which different kinds of chocolate should be stored. While this may seem clinical, recipes like Princess Pudding and Pure Chocolate-Chunk Cookies are voluptuous, extravagant and (another of Bigelow's trademarks) not too sweet.

Featured Recipes Blanc et Noir; Chocolate Hazelnut Cheesecake; Pure Chocolate-Chunk Cookies; Princess Pudding

Best of the Best Exclusive Peanut Butter Cup Tart

Blanc et Noir

With its sharp corners and graphic black-and-white design, this modern layer cake is an elegant showstopper. For such a sophisticated-looking cake, the Blanc et Noir is surprisingly user friendly. It freezes well, cuts easily into thin clean slices, and is a melt-in-your-mouth delight. Each bite is like biting into a perfect baked truffle.

Even those who don't normally like white chocolate love the white-chocolate ganache between its layers. It's much lighter than a buttercream and the taste is all chocolate, rather than the cloying sugary sensation you often get with fillings. It's worth shopping for a good-quality white chocolate like Valrhona. It makes all the difference.

12 TO 16 SERVINGS

WHITE-CHOCOLATE GANACHE FILLING

- ½ cup heavy cream
- 8 ounces white chocolate, finely chopped

NOIR CAKE LAYERS

- 8 ounces semisweet chocolate, finely chopped
- 1 stick (8 tablespoons) unsalted butter, room temperature
- 5 large eggs, separated
- ½ cup plus 1 tablespoon sugar
- 1 recipe Dark-Chocolate Ganache Glaze (recipe follows)

WHITE CHOCOLATE FOR WRITING

- 2 ounces white chocolate, roughly chopped
- 2 teaspoons vegetable oil

TO MAKE THE FILLING

In a saucepan, heat the cream over medium-high heat just until it begins to boil. Remove from the heat and add the white chocolate, stirring until the chocolate is smooth and melted. Pour into a small bowl and cover with plastic wrap touching the surface to prevent a skin from forming. Let the ganache set up at least 12 hours or overnight at room temperature.

TO MAKE THE CAKE

Position a rack in the middle of the oven and preheat the oven to 300°F.

Lightly butter a 9-by-13-inch or quarter-sheet pan and line with parchment paper. Then lightly butter the parchment paper.

Pure Chocolate
Fran Bigelow

In a double boiler melt the chocolate over low heat. Remove the boiler top when the chocolate is nearly melted and continue stirring until completely smooth. Add the softened butter in 3 parts, stirring until no visible traces of butter remain. (If the butter begins to melt and separate, stop and allow the chocolate more time to cool.) The finished mixture should be glossy and smooth. Set aside to cool until the mixture is the consistency of softened butter. Briefly return to the double boiler if it begins to thicken too much.

In a mixer fitted with the whisk attachment, whip the egg yolks with half the sugar at medium-high speed, increasing to high speed until pale yellow and tripled in volume, 5 to 6 minutes.

Remove the bowl from the mixer. With a rubber spatula fold in the melted chocolate mixture. The mixture should be smooth and glossy.

Clean the whisk and in another clean bowl begin whipping the egg whites on medium-high speed, increasing the speed and allowing them to become quite frothy. Slowly add the remaining sugar and continue whipping until the peaks are stiff and creamy.

Lighten the chocolate mixture by quickly folding in a quarter of the whites until smooth and no traces of white remain. Then gently fold in the remaining whites in 3 parts, trying not to overmix and lose the volume. Evenly spread the batter into the prepared pan. The pan will be two-thirds full.

Bake for 20 to 25 minutes. The cake will rise above the edges of the pan, and a light crust will form on top. A cake tester inserted in the center will have a few moist crumbs.

Let the cake cool in the pan at room temperature for 10 minutes. Then chill until thoroughly cold, 4 hours or overnight. Wrap tightly with plastic wrap if chilling for longer than 4 hours. (The layer can be wrapped in plastic once cooled and placed in the freezer up to a week prior to assembly.)

TO ASSEMBLE THE CAKE
Have ready the White-Chocolate Ganache Filling.

To remove the well-chilled cake from the pan, run a thin-bladed knife around the edges. Place the bottom of a baking sheet over the cake and invert. Remove the parchment paper.

Bigelow on Cooking with Chocolate
It's the farmer that grows the cocoa beans, harvests them, roasts them and then shells and conches them. All we're doing is bringing out that flavor. We're just melting chocolate and making it into something fabulous.

Pure Chocolate
Fran Bigelow

Place the filling in a mixing bowl. It should be the consistency of softened butter. (If not thick enough, stir and let sit longer to thicken.) With a whisk attachment or using a hand mixer, mix on high speed until the ganache is lighter in color and texture and soft peaks form, 2 to 4 minutes. Stop several times and scrape down the side of the bowl.

Using a ruler and the tip of a paring knife, mark the cake in thirds across its width. Cut the cake with a serrated blade into 3 approximately 4-inch-wide sections.

Place one chilled layer of the cake on the serving plate or on a 4-by-8-inch cardboard cake board. With a metal spatula, spread half of the white ganache filling on the layer. Top with the second chilled cake layer and spread with the remaining filling. Top with the last chilled cake layer.

Using a thin-bladed knife, trim the sides of the cake. Let set in the refrigerator at least 1 hour.

TO FINISH THE CAKE
Make the Dark-Chocolate Ganache Glaze.

Pour about ¼ cup of the glaze into a small bowl and place in the refrigerator to chill for approximately 25 minutes. Set aside the remaining ganache to cool about 30 minutes, gently stirring occasionally until it thickens and ribbons off the end of the spatula, 80–85°F.

Meanwhile, make the White Chocolate for Writing.

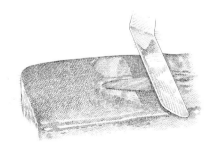 

Glazing and decorating the Blanc et Noir

Pure Chocolate
Fran Bigelow

In a small bowl over simmering water, melt the chocolate. Remove from the heat, add the vegetable oil, and stir with a spatula until smooth. Set aside.

With an offset spatula, thinly coat the top and sides of the finished cake with the ¼ cup chilled ganache glaze. Transfer to a cooling or pouring rack positioned over a rimmed baking sheet.

Slowly and evenly pour some of the glaze around the sides of the cake, being careful to cover all the corners. Then pour the remaining glaze down the center using a metal spatula to spread the glaze evenly over the top, letting the excess run down the sides. Before the glaze sets, decorate.

Pour the writing chocolate into a small parchment paper cone. Pipe 3 thin white parallel lines, ¼ inch apart, lengthwise, down the center of the cake over the soft glaze. Working quickly, with a toothpick, draw small figure eights crosswise through the ganache and white stripes all along the cake's length.

Chill for 1 to 2 hours to set. Remove half an hour before serving. Can be stored in the refrigerator for up to 3 days.

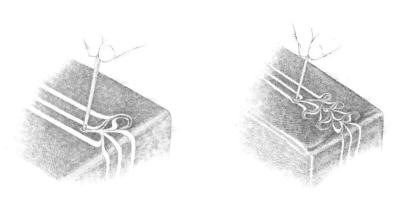

Pure Chocolate
Fran Bigelow

Dark-Chocolate Ganache Glaze

This traditional ganache gives cakes a lovely dark-chocolate velvet finish. The only techniques you need to remember are to start with a well-chilled cake and not to incorporate any air as you gently stir. A resilient ganache such as this one can be gently reheated and used again as a glaze, sauce, or filling. And it does not lose its sheen with refrigeration. You may halve the recipe for a single 9-inch round layer.

MAKES ENOUGH FOR 1 DOUBLE-LAYER 9-INCH ROUND OR QUARTER-SHEET-PAN LAYER CAKE

- 8 ounces semisweet chocolate, finely chopped
- 1 cup heavy cream

Place the chopped chocolate in a stainless-steel mixing bowl.

In a small saucepan heat the cream over medium-high heat until it begins to boil. Remove from the heat and pour over the chocolate. Let sit 1 minute and then start gently stirring with a rubber spatula from the center out, until smooth. Cool at room temperature about 30 minutes, uncovered, stirring occasionally, until the ganache thickens enough to ribbon off the end of the spatula when lifted. The ideal pouring temperature is 80–85°F.

If a recipe calls for a thin coating or masking prior to glazing, chill one-quarter of the mixture for about 25 minutes. The purpose of masking is to seal in the filling and crumbs and give the glaze a smooth surface to stick to. This step is always optional but will give your cakes a professional high-gloss look. Use an offset spatula and a firm hand with constant pressure to apply a thin layer of ganache on all exposed surfaces before pouring the room-temperature glaze.

Pure Chocolate
Fran Bigelow

Chocolate Hazelnut Cheesecake

I created this cheesecake for milk-chocolate lovers. It has just the right balance of tang from the cream cheese and added flavor from the nuts to avoid one-note sweetness. If you prefer your chocolate taste pure, simply skip the nuts and use 14 ounces of milk chocolate—the darkest you can find. Glazing with silky dark chocolate, though not absolutely necessary, adds yet another chocolate dimension. In spite of how it may sound, this creamy cheesecake is not overly rich.

16 SERVINGS

- 14 ounces gianduja, finely chopped, or 9 ounces 36–46% cacao milk chocolate, finely chopped, and 5 ounces hazelnut paste
- 4 ounces semisweet chocolate, finely chopped
- 1½ pounds cream cheese, room temperature
- ½ cup sugar
- 5 large eggs, room temperature
- 3 tablespoons heavy cream
- 3 tablespoons Frangelico or Amaretto liqueur
- Dark-Chocolate Ganache Glaze (facing page; optional)

Position a rack in the middle of the oven and preheat the oven to 300°F. Butter a 9-inch round cake pan and line with parchment paper.

In a double boiler over low heat, melt the gianduja (or milk chocolate with hazelnut paste) and semisweet chocolate. Remove the top of the boiler when the chocolate is nearly melted and continue stirring until smooth. Let the chocolate cool to 90°F, stirring occasionally.

In a mixer fitted with the paddle attachment, beat the cream cheese at medium-high speed until smooth, about 2 minutes. Add the sugar and continue beating for an additional 3 minutes, until the sugar is dissolved and the mixture is light, fluffy, and lump-free. Stop several times to scrape down the sides of the bowl.

In a small bowl whisk together the eggs. Turn the mixer speed to low and slowly add half of the eggs. Stop, scrape down the sides of the bowl, and continue mixing, adding the remaining eggs. Pour in the cream and Frangelico, and thoroughly mix on low.

Bigelow on Hazelnut Paste

Stirring the hazelnut paste before you measure it out is really important. The sort of paste that you get in the store will usually have an oil layer on top of it. If you haven't mixed it really carefully and incorporated all the oil back into it, you'll end up with too much oil in your recipe.

Pure Chocolate
Fran Bigelow

Remove the bowl from the mixer and with a rubber spatula fold in the melted chocolate. Continue folding until no traces of the cream cheese remain. The mixture will thicken as you fold in the chocolate.

Pour into the prepared pan, smoothing the top. The pan will be about three-quarters full. Place on a rimmed baking sheet and place in the oven. Pour about ½ inch of simmering water into the baking sheet for a bain-marie. Bake for 1 hour and 10 minutes, until the top is smooth and slightly dull. The edges should start to pull away from the sides of the pan.

Let cool at room temperature for 2 to 4 hours.

To remove the cake, run a thin knife around the edges to loosen. Place a piece of parchment or waxed paper over the top of the cake and invert it onto a plate. Remove the parchment paper round from the bottom and turn the cake right side up onto its serving plate. Remove the paper from the top.

If you are adding the glaze, set the room-temperature cake on a cake board. Place on a rack over a baking sheet. Have the glaze ready.

When the glaze reaches 80–85°F, beginning 1½ inches from the edge of the cake, slowly and evenly pour some of the glaze around the rim, making sure that the sides are sufficiently covered. Then pour the remaining glaze onto the center of the cake. Working quickly, using a metal offset spatula, spread the glaze evenly over the top, letting the excess run down the sides.

Let set at room temperature until the glaze is slightly firm, about 20 minutes. Once set, slide an offset spatula under the board, rotating the spatula to release any spots where the glaze has stuck to the rack. Carefully lift the cake and, supporting the bottom with your free hand, slide it onto its serving plate. May be stored in the refrigerator as long as 1 week.

Pure Chocolate
Fran Bigelow

Pure Chocolate-Chunk Cookies

If traditional chocolate-chip cookies just don't do it for you these days, these dark-chocolate cookies may be just what you're looking for. They're soft, chewy, and chocolate through and through, without a nut in sight to sully their sheer chocolatey-ness.

MAKES 3 DOZEN BIG COOKIES

- 12 ounces semisweet chocolate, finely chopped
- 1½ ounces unsweetened chocolate, finely chopped
- 1 stick plus 2 tablespoons unsalted butter, room temperature
- ¾ cup plus 2 tablespoons brown sugar
- ⅔ cup sugar
- 1½ teaspoons pure vanilla extract
- 3 large eggs
- 1¾ cups cake flour, sifted then measured
- 8 ounces bittersweet chocolate, cut in ¼-inch chunks

Position a rack in the middle of the oven and preheat the oven to 325°F. Line 2 cookie sheets with parchment paper or Silpats. In a double boiler, melt the semisweet and unsweetened chocolates over low heat. Remove the top part of the boiler when the chocolate is nearly melted and stir until smooth, about 100°F. Set aside.

In a mixer fitted with a paddle attachment, beat together the butter, two sugars, and vanilla until light and very fluffy, 3 to 5 minutes. Beat in the eggs, one at a time, stopping several times to scrape the bowl. Pour in the melted chocolate and mix to combine. Fold in the sifted flour by hand until no traces of white remain. Fold in the bittersweet chocolate chunks. The batter will be quite thick. Chill for 1 hour.

Using a scoop or large spoon, scoop 2 tablespoons of dough for each cookie and drop onto the lined cookie sheets, leaving about 2 inches of space between the cookies. (The cookies will spread to about 3 inches in diameter.) Slightly flatten with your fingers and immediately place in the oven. The cookie dough should still be cold when baked.

Bake for 12 to 14 minutes, or until cracked and puffed on top. The insides should remain moist. Let cool on sheets about 10 minutes. Transfer to racks to completely cool. Store in an airtight container as long as 1 week.

Bigelow on Chocolate Chunks

I prefer cutting my own chunks of chocolate instead of using chips for these cookies. You can really personalize the cookies that way. Each time you make these cookies, experiment with different types of chocolate. You'll be surprised how the results change.

Pure Chocolate
Fran Bigelow

Princess Pudding

Bigelow on Vanilla

I love the taste that vanilla bean imparts to this custard, but you can use vanilla extract, too. Just make sure that it's good-quality vanilla extract and not vanilla essence.

When I was invited to teach a class with nothing more than a hot plate as equipment, I came up with this unbelievably rich, pure chocolate pudding, a miracle of simplicity. It can be made on the stovetop in under 15 minutes. My friend Julie named it because it is a pudding fit for a princess, or some very lucky guests.

It's gorgeous served in elegant demitasse cups or mounded in martini glasses and topped with a dollop of whipped cream. The pudding can also be poured into baked miniature tart shells.

8 SERVINGS

1¼ cups heavy cream

½ cup sugar

½ vanilla bean, split lengthwise

5 large egg yolks

7 ounces semisweet chocolate, finely chopped

Cappuccino Whipped Cream (recipe follows) for serving

Pure Chocolate
Fran Bigelow

In a small saucepan, combine the cream and sugar. Using the back of a paring knife, scrape the vanilla bean seeds into the mixture. Toss in the bean. Place over medium heat and bring just to a simmer. Remove from the heat.

In a mixing bowl, whisk the egg yolks until frothy. Slowly pour one-third of the cream into the yolks, whisking constantly. Pour the mixture back into the pan and return to low heat. Cook, stirring constantly, until the mixture coats the back of a spoon (about 160°F).

Remove from the heat. Remove and discard the vanilla bean. Add the finely chopped chocolate and whisk until melted and smooth.

While the mixture is still warm, pour into a serving bowl or into 8 individual demitasse cups. Let cool slightly, then top with loosely whipped cappuccino cream and serve.

Princess Pudding is best served at room temperature, to bring out the chocolate flavor. It can be refrigerated as long as 2 days.

Cappuccino Whipped Cream

The combination of coffee and chocolate is one of the foolproof marriages of the dessert world.

MAKES 3½ CUPS

¼ cup plus 2 tablespoons sugar

3 tablespoons brewed espresso or 2 tablespoons water mixed with 2 tablespoons instant coffee (preferably freeze-dried)

2 cups heavy cream, chilled

Either by hand or using a mixer, whisk together the sugar and coffee until frothy. The sugar will begin to dissolve. Add the cream and whisk until thoroughly combined and soft peaks form. Take care not to overwhip the cream as it may begin to lose its creamy texture. Store in the refrigerator.

Test Kitchen Tip
When testing the whipped cream recipe here, we found that it made more than we really needed. Cut the recipe in half if you don't want leftovers.

Pure Chocolate
Fran Bigelow

Best of the Best Exclusive
Peanut Butter Cup Tart

Editor's Note

This is the ultimate dessert for fans of chocolate and peanut butter. It's like a Reese's Peanut Butter Cup for adults. The white chocolate gives the filling extra smoothness, while the crunchy sea salt sprinkled on top highlights the sweetness of the filling.

MAKES ONE 9-INCH TART

CRUST

- 6 tablespoons unsalted butter, at room temperature
- ½ cup sugar
- ⅓ cup Dutch-process cocoa, sifted
- 1 large egg
- ½ teaspoon pure vanilla extract
- ½ cup plus 2 tablespoons all-purpose flour

FILLING AND TOPPING

- 6 ounces white chocolate, chopped (1¼ cups)
- ¾ cup creamy peanut butter
- ¼ teaspoon kosher salt
- ½ cup heavy cream
- 4 ounces semisweet chocolate, chopped (¾ cup)
- ½ teaspoon coarse sea salt, for sprinkling

1. MAKE THE CRUST In a large bowl, using an electric mixer with the paddle attachment, beat the butter with the sugar at medium-high speed until pale and fluffy, about 2 minutes. Add the cocoa and beat at low speed until blended. Beat in the egg and vanilla at medium-high speed. Add the flour and beat just until the dough begins to come together. Form the dough into a ball and wrap in plastic. Chill until firm, at least 2 hours.

2. Preheat the oven to 350°. On a lightly floured surface, roll out the dough to an 11½-inch round about ⅛ inch thick. Transfer to a 9-inch fluted tart pan with a removable bottom. Trim the excess dough and patch any holes. Prick the bottom of the tart shell with a fork and refrigerate until chilled, about 30 minutes.

3. Set the chilled tart shell on a baking sheet and bake for 25 minutes, until the crust is blistered and dry. Transfer to a rack to cool completely.

4. MAKE THE FILLING AND TOPPING In a medium heatproof bowl set over a pan of simmering water, begin to melt the white chocolate. When nearly melted, remove from the heat and stir until smooth. Let cool. Stir in the peanut butter and

Pure Chocolate
Fran Bigelow

kosher salt. Pour the filling into the cooled tart shell, spreading it to the edges in an even layer. Refrigerate until set, about 30 minutes.

5. In a small saucepan, bring the cream to a simmer. Remove from the heat. Add the semisweet chocolate and stir until smooth. Spread the chocolate topping over the peanut butter filling and chill until set, about 45 minutes. Sprinkle the tart with sea salt and serve.

MAKE AHEAD This tart can be refrigerated for up to 3 days. Bring to room temperature and sprinkle with sea salt before serving.

Bigelow on Salt

After being around chocolate all day I crave salt. Potato chips or tortilla chips—just give me something with salt on it and get me off the sweets!

Pure Chocolate
Fran Bigelow

Les Halles restaurant,
New York City

Anthony Bourdain's Les Halles Cookbook
by Anthony Bourdain

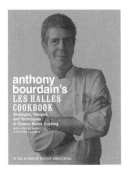

With José de Meirelles and Philippe Lajaunie, published by Bloomsbury, 304 pages, color and black-and-white photos, $34.95

"I said I'd never do a cookbook," admits Anthony Bourdain, the charismatic, globe-trotting, profanity-spouting author of *Kitchen Confidential,* a memoir. "But I found a way to write one that wasn't bogus—to speak to readers the same way I train cooks." And that's exactly what he does, in classic French bistro recipes like deeply savory beef bourguignon and silky crème brûlée from Les Halles, the New York City restaurant that is his home base. Sometimes he offers a friendly "Don't sweat it, amigo"; other times he berates you for being a "useless screwhead." In fact, his enthusiasm and irreverence come straight through in the snappy tips and conversational recipes.

Featured Recipes Onion Soup Les Halles; Moules Normandes; Rôti de Porc au Lait; Poulet Basquaise

Best of the Best Exclusive Marinated Grilled Hanger Steak Sandwich

Onion Soup Les Halles

Bourdain on Making Onion Soup
The caramelization of the onion is very important. And you don't want to use old, stinky onions or red ones; you need good white onions. This recipe is so simple, I could train a chimp to make it.

The better and more intense your stock, the better the soup's going to be. This soup, in particular, is a very good argument for making your own.

8 SERVINGS

- 6 ounces butter
- 8 large onions (or 12 small onions), thinly sliced
- 2 ounces port
- 2 ounces balsamic vinegar
- 2 quarts dark chicken stock
- 4 ounces slab bacon, cut into ½-inch cubes
- 1 bouquet garni (see Note)

Salt and pepper

- 16 baguette croutons (sliced and toasted in the oven with a little olive oil)
- 12 ounces grated Gruyère cheese (real, imported Gruyère!)

EQUIPMENT

Large, heavy-bottomed pot; wooden spoon; ladle; 8 ovenproof soup crocks (restaurant supply shops sell these by the hundreds; be sure to use ovenproof); propane torch (optional; see Note)

PREPARE THE BROTH

In the large pot, heat the butter over medium heat until it is melted and begins to brown. Add the onions and cook over medium heat, stirring occasionally with the wooden spoon, until they are soft and browned (about 20 minutes). Onion soup, unsurprisingly, is *all about the onions*. Make damn sure the onions are a nice, dark, even brown color.

Increase the heat to medium high and stir in the port and the vinegar, scraping all that brown goodness from the bottom of the pot into the liquid. Add the chicken stock. Add the bacon and bouquet garni and bring to a boil.

Reduce to a simmer, season with salt and pepper, and cook for 45 minutes to an hour, skimming any foam off the top with the ladle. Remove the bouquet garni.

Anthony Bourdain's Les Halles Cookbook
Anthony Bourdain

THE CROUTONS AND CHEESE

When the soup is finished cooking, ladle it into the individual crocks. Float two croutons side by side on top of each. Spread a generous, even heaping amount of cheese over the top of the soup. You *want* some extra to hang over the edges, as the crispy, near-burnt stuff that sticks to the outer sides of the crocks once it comes out from under the heat is often the best part.

Place each crock under a *preheated,* rip-roaring broiler until the cheese melts, bubbles, browns, and even scorches slightly in spots. The finished cheese should be a panorama of molten brown hues ranging from golden brown to dark brown to a few black spots where the cheese blistered and burned. Serve immediately—and *carefully.* You don't know pain until you've spilled one of these things in your lap.

If your broiler is too small or too weak to pull this off, you can try it in a preheated 425°F oven until melted. A nice optional move: Once the mound of grated cheese starts to flatten out in the oven, remove each crock and, with a propane torch, blast the cheese until you get the colors you want.

HALF-ASSED ALTERNATIVE

Your broiler sucks. Your oven isn't much better. Can't find those ovenproof crocks anywhere. And you ain't ponying up for a damn propane torch, 'cause your kid's got pyromaniac tendencies. You can simply toast cheese over the croutons on a sheet pan, and float them as garnish on the soup. Not exactly classic—but still good.

NOTE ON THE BOUQUET GARNI 1 sprig of flat parsley, 2 sprigs of fresh thyme, and 1 bay leaf tied together with string and used for flavoring (usually in stews or sauces). Tying the bundle in cheesecloth makes it easier to retrieve from the pot.

NOTE ON THE PROPANE TORCH This is a very handy-dandy piece of equipment, especially if your stove is not the greatest. Nearly all professional kitchens have them; they're not very expensive and they can be used for a variety of sneaky tasks, such as easily caramelizing the top of crème brûlée or toasting meringues.

Bourdain on Why He Wrote the Book

Traveling for so long made me miss my restaurant. I traveled around the world and saw what's great about food in other countries, and that reconnected me to what's enduringly great about French food and what I've been cooking all along.

Anthony Bourdain's Les Halles Cookbook
Anthony Bourdain

Moules Normandes

Bourdain on Buying Mussels

My advice is that you should really buy mussels the day you're serving them. Ideally, you want superfresh mussels—they should be fighting you when you pick them up.

4 SERVINGS

 4 ounces slab bacon, cut into ½-inch cubes
 4 tablespoons butter
 1 shallot, thinly sliced
 6 small white mushrooms, thinly sliced
½ apple, cored, peeled, and cut into small dice or chunks
 3 ounces good Calvados
 1 cup heavy cream
Salt and pepper
 6 pounds mussels, scrubbed and debearded (just before cooking)

EQUIPMENT

 Small pot, large pot with lid, wooden spoon

In the small pot, cook the bacon over medium-high heat until the meat is brown and the fat has been rendered, about 10 minutes, stirring occasionally to avoid sticking. Discard the fat and reserve the meat.

In the large pot, heat the butter until it foams. Add the shallot and cook until soft, about 3 minutes. Add the mushrooms and the apple and cook for 5 minutes, then stir in the Calvados, scraping the bottom of the pot with the wooden spoon to dislodge any good brown stuff that might be clinging there. Stir in the cream and season with salt and pepper.

Once the mixture has come to a boil, add the mussels and cover. Cook for 10 minutes, or until all of the mussels have opened. Shake. Cook for another minute. Shake again. Serve immediately, sprinkled with the bacon.

Anthony Bourdain's
Les Halles Cookbook
Anthony Bourdain

Rôti de Porc au Lait

Bourdain on Shopping for Pork
Choose a cut that looks healthy and pink. It should smell fresh, and it should not be slimy or gray. The fattier the better. The notion that fat is bad has really been harmful to the enjoyment of pork.

6 SERVINGS

3 pounds boneless pork loin roast

Salt and pepper

2 tablespoons olive oil

1 tablespoon butter

1 medium onion, chopped

1 carrot, finely chopped

1 leek, white part only, finely chopped

1 garlic clove, finely chopped

1 tablespoon flour

2 cups whole milk

1 bouquet garni (see Note on page 45)

EQUIPMENT

Dutch oven, large plate, wooden spoon, strainer, small pot, hand blender, carving knife or other very sharp knife, serving platter

COOK THE PORK

Season the pork with salt and pepper. Heat the oil in the Dutch oven. When the oil is hot, add the butter. Brown the roast on all sides, 6 to 7 minutes total. Remove the roast from the pan and set aside on the large plate. Add the onion, carrot, leek, and garlic and stir over high heat until soft and caramelized, about 10 minutes. Stirring constantly with the wooden spoon, add the flour and cook for 2 minutes, then add the milk and the bouquet garni. Bring to a boil and cook over high heat for 5 minutes. Add the pork and any juices that have collected on the plate. Reduce the heat to a simmer. Cover and cook over low heat for 1 hour, making sure to periodically rotate the pork (the sugars in the milk can cause sticking and scorching). Remove the pork and allow to rest for 15 minutes.

FINISH THE SAUCE AND SERVE

Remove and discard the bouquet garni. Strain the cooking liquid into the small pot and bring to a boil. Using the hand blender, purée the sauce until foamy. Adjust the seasoning as needed. Carve the pork and arrange on the serving platter. Spoon the sauce over and around and serve immediately.

Anthony Bourdain's
Les Halles Cookbook
Anthony Bourdain

Poulet Basquaise

4 SERVINGS

 1 whole chicken, about 4 pounds, cut into 8 pieces

Salt and black pepper

Pinch of cayenne pepper or piment d'Espelette

 2 tablespoons olive oil

 1 tablespoon butter

 2 red bell peppers, cut into fine julienne

 2 green bell peppers, cut into fine julienne

 1 onion, thinly sliced

16 ounces canned Italian plum tomatoes

½ cup white wine

½ cup water

½ cube chicken bouillon or ½ cup light chicken stock or
    broth (this is one dish that can handle a bouillon cube)

 3 sprigs of flat parsley, finely chopped

EQUIPMENT

 Large pot with cover, tongs, plate, wooden spoon, serving platter

Season the chicken all over with salt, black pepper, and cayenne. Heat the large pot over medium-high heat and add the oil. When the oil is hot, add the butter. When the butter has foamed and subsided, add the chicken, skin side down, and brown on that side *only*. Remove the chicken with the tongs and set aside on the plate. Add the peppers and the onion to the pot and reduce the heat to medium low. Cook for about 10 minutes, then add the tomatoes and cook until the liquid is reduced by half. Stir in the wine with the wooden spoon, scraping, scraping—as always—to get the good stuff up. Cook until the wine is reduced by half, then add the water and the bouillon (or the ½ cup of chicken stock). Return the chicken to the pot, making sure to add all the juice that's accumulated on the plate while it rested. Cover the pot and allow to cook on low heat for about 25 minutes, then remove the chicken to the serving platter.

Crank up the heat to high and reduce the sauce for 5 minutes. Season with salt and pepper and add the parsley. Pour the sauce over the chicken and serve immediately, with rice pilaf.

Marinated Grilled Hanger Steak Sandwich

4 SERVINGS

- ½ cup plain yogurt
- 2 teaspoons harissa
- 1 garlic clove, finely chopped
- 1 teaspoon chopped cilantro
- ½ teaspoon finely grated fresh ginger
- ½ teaspoon chopped thyme
- ¼ teaspoon ground cumin
- 1 bay leaf

Two 8-ounce hanger steaks

Kosher salt and freshly ground black pepper

- 2 tablespoons extra-virgin olive oil
- 1 green bell pepper, thinly sliced
- 1 medium red onion, thinly sliced
- 2 tablespoons mayonnaise
- 4 cumin-flavored flat breads or pocketless pita breads, warmed

1. In a medium glass baking dish, mix the yogurt with 1 teaspoon of the harissa and the garlic, cilantro, ginger, thyme, cumin and bay leaf. Add the hanger steaks and turn to coat. Cover with plastic wrap and refrigerate overnight. Remove the steaks from the refrigerator 30 minutes before grilling.

2. Light a grill. Season the steaks with salt and pepper. Grill over a medium-hot fire for 4 minutes per side for medium rare. Cover the steaks with foil and let rest for 10 minutes.

3. Meanwhile, in a large skillet, heat the olive oil. Add the bell pepper and onion and cook over moderately high heat, stirring frequently, until softened, about 6 minutes; season with salt and pepper.

4. In a small bowl, combine the remaining 1 teaspoon of harissa with the mayonnaise. Thinly slice the steaks diagonally across the grain and mound on the flat breads. Top with the pepper and onion mixture, slather with the harissa mayonnaise, fold in half and serve.

Bourdain on Being a Chef

I'm not sure what I'd be doing if I wasn't a chef. The restaurant business saved my life. I was headed in a bad direction; I was a bad seed. I shudder at the thought. The values and discipline I have learned in restaurants saved me. If I wasn't doing this, I'd probably be a petty thief. Nothing good would have come of my life.

Anthony Bourdain's Les Halles Cookbook
Anthony Bourdain

A slice of
Sicilian
street life

The Flavors of Southern Italy

by Erica De Mane

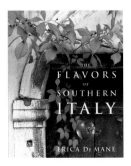

Published by Wiley, 464 pages, $29.95

While the focus of the Italian cookbook canon is the north, this book takes you south to Campania, Puglia and Sicily. Erica De Mane, author of three cookbooks, maps out the essential ingredients of southern Italian cuisine—among them olives, tomatoes, fennel and lemons—devoting a short chapter to each. She also explains the region's fascination with flavors that are sweet-and-sour, bitter and salty. The 250 recipes reflect these flavors, from Rigatoni with Spicy Pork and Fennel Ragù to Baked Lemon Ricotta with Raspberry Sauce. A book for those who want to venture into the lesser-known pleasures of regional Italian cuisine.

Featured Recipes Baked Salmon with Gremolata Crust; Rigatoni with Spicy Pork and Fennel Ragù; Risotto with Arugula Pesto and Mussels

Best of the Best Exclusive Spaghettini with Shrimp, Grape Tomatoes and Star Anise

Baked Salmon with Gremolata Crust

Salmon is not native to southern Italy, but it has become somewhat trendy there, and I've sampled it at upscale restaurants in Sicily and Naples. The southern Italian chef bathes salmon in southern Mediterranean flavors, which makes sense for such a rich, oily fish. Here, I've taken the classic gremolata mix of garlic, lemon zest, and parsley, which is traditionally sprinkled over osso buco (veal shank), and used it for a crust for the fish. The salmon fillets are baked at a high temperature to make them crisp but moist inside, and finished with tomatoes and olives.

4 MAIN-COURSE SERVINGS

GREMOLATA

Grated zest of 2 large lemons

  2 **garlic cloves, minced**

½ **cup chopped fresh flat-leaf parsley**

Leaves from 3 or 4 large thyme sprigs, chopped

  3 **tablespoons homemade dry bread crumbs (see Making Dry Bread Crumbs on facing page)**

Handful of pine nuts, ground in a food processor

  3 **tablespoons extra-virgin olive oil**

Salt and freshly ground black pepper to taste

Four 6- or 8-ounce salmon fillets, cut from the thickest section, skin and pin bones removed

  2 **tablespoons extra-virgin olive oil**

  4 **scallions, including tender green parts, cut into thin rounds**

  2 **cups sweet cherry tomatoes**

  2 **tablespoons dry white wine**

Salt and freshly ground black pepper to taste

Handful of fresh flat-leaf parsley leaves

Leaves from 1 or 2 thyme sprigs, chopped

Preheat the oven to 500°F.

TO MAKE THE GREMOLATA

In a small bowl, combine all the ingredients. Mix well to make a nice, oily paste. (You could grind everything together in a food processor, but I like the hand-chopped texture better; it's less mushy and tends to crisp better when cooked.)

Press the gremolata onto the top of the salmon pieces so it adheres. Lightly coat a nice-looking baking dish (one you can bring to the table) with about a tablespoon of olive oil and place the salmon in it (they shouldn't fit too snugly—you want a little air between the slices so they will bake evenly). Place in the oven to bake until barely translucent in the center, 12 to 15 minutes, depending on the thickness of the fish. (The point of this blasting method is to cook the fish quickly so it sears on the surface, sealing in moisture.)

WHILE THE SALMON IS BAKING, COOK THE TOMATOES
Heat a medium skillet over high heat. Add the remaining tablespoon of olive oil and heat to almost smoking. Add the scallions and tomatoes and sear quickly just until skins crack. This will take only a minute or two. Add the white wine and let it bubble for a few seconds, leaving a little liquid in the pan. Season with salt and pepper.

Remove the salmon from the oven. Add the parsley leaves and thyme to the tomatoes and stir them in. Pour the tomatoes, with all their skillet juices, around (not on) the salmon. Serve right away.

NOTE Farmed salmon is what I generally find in my markets and it's fine, but from late spring into summer wild Alaskan salmon comes into season, and its rich taste and velvety texture can be amazing. Look for Nootka Sound wild salmon or the even richer Copper River king salmon. I also sometimes find wild king, white king, or wild sockeye salmon as well.

MAKING DRY BREAD CRUMBS Use day-old crusty Italian bread. If the inside is still moist, rip it into chunks and put them in a low oven until they're nice and dry. Pulse the chunks in a food processor to make not-too-fine dried crumbs. (The bread crumbs you buy in cans not only taste like cardboard but are too finely ground and can turn to mush. Stale bread makes stale-tasting bread crumbs, so never use bread that's more than a few days old. Ground *taralli*, by the way, make excellent dry bread crumbs. Just throw a few in the food processor and pulse them a few times until they're reduced to a not-too-fine crumb.)

De Mane on Quick Cooking
My favorite superfast recipe is tossing pasta—penne, say—with fresh ricotta that has been thinned with some of the pasta cooking water. I add a little nutmeg, some chopped parsley and basil, some pecorino cheese—and there you have it!

The Flavors of Southern Italy
Erica De Mane

Rigatoni with Spicy Pork and Fennel Ragù

De Mane on Picking a Pasta

You can use other pastas with this ragù, not just rigatoni. Since the sauce is rustic and chunky, I'd use a sturdy pasta that has substance and will stand up to the sauce. Ziti and penne are fine, but I'd stay away from fettuccine and spaghetti.

They like to blend pork, fennel, and hot chiles in Basilicata, and I've borrowed the combination to fashion a simple ragù with bold flavors. Aglianico del Vulture is Basilicata's most famous red wine. It is dry, intense, and spicy, and one of my favorites from anywhere in the South. Use a big glass of it to give this ragù an authentic southern flavor, and drink the rest with dinner.

4 MAIN-COURSE SERVINGS

- 2 tablespoons extra-virgin olive oil
- 2 thin slices pancetta, finely diced
- 1 pound boneless pork shoulder, cut into 1-inch cubes
- 2 sweet Italian pork sausages, removed from casings and crumbled

Pinch of sugar

- 1 large onion, finely diced
- 1 fennel bulb, trimmed, cored, and finely diced (fronds reserved and chopped)
- 2 garlic cloves, thinly sliced
- 2 bay leaves, preferably fresh

Small palmful of fennel seeds

Salt to taste

- 2 small dried red chiles, broken in half
- 1 cup dry red wine, Aglianico del Vulture if available, otherwise another strong, dry red

One 35-ounce can plum tomatoes, finely chopped, with juice

Handful of fresh basil leaves, chopped

- 1 tablespoon balsamic vinegar
- 1 pound rigatoni pasta
- 1 chunk aged pecorino cheese for grating

In a large Dutch oven or flameproof casserole with a lid, heat the olive oil over medium heat. Add the pancetta, pork shoulder, sausage, and sugar (to help the meat brown). Sauté until the meat is lightly browned all over, at least 10 minutes (this is important for adding flavor to ragù, so try not to skimp on this step). Add the onion, fennel and fronds, garlic, bay leaves, fennel seeds, a pinch of salt, and the chiles. Sauté until the vegetables start to soften, about

The Flavors of Southern Italy

Erica De Mane

another 5 minutes. Reduce the heat at any time if the skillet bottom gets too dark. Add the red wine and let it bubble for a few minutes. Add the tomatoes and bring everything to a boil. Reduce the heat to low, cover the pot, and simmer for about 2 hours, or until the ragù has good body and the meat is starting to shred. You might need to skim the surface once or twice during cooking, depending on the fattiness of your meat. Add the basil and a splash of balsamic vinegar (this will sharpen all the flavors). Taste for seasoning, adding more salt, if needed. Set aside and keep warm.

In a large pot of salted boiling water, cook the rigatoni until al dente. Drain, reserving about ½ cup of the cooking water. Transfer the pasta to a warmed large serving bowl. Pour on the ragù and toss, adding a little pasta cooking water, if needed, to loosen the texture. Serve hot, bringing the chunk of pecorino to the table for grating.

Test Kitchen Tip

This luscious sauce keeps beautifully for up to three days in the refrigerator. Making the sauce ahead can even enhance its flavor. Before serving, remember to remove the bay leaves.

The Flavors of
Southern Italy
Erica De Mane

Risotto with Arugula Pesto and Mussels

Risotto with a pesto of stinging nettles is a dish I was served in Campania several years ago. It has a grassy, herby taste and bright green color. I occasionally see nettles at my green market in the early summer, but I've found arugula makes an interesting pesto alternative, without having to deal with the sting.

6 FIRST-COURSE SERVINGS, 4 MAIN-COURSE SERVINGS

PESTO

½ cup whole blanched almonds

1 large garlic clove

1 large bunch arugula, stemmed

½ cup extra-virgin olive oil

½ cup grated grana padano cheese

Salt and freshly ground black pepper to taste

3 pounds small mussels, scrubbed and debearded, if necessary

½ cup dry white wine

Generous drizzle of extra-virgin olive oil, plus 2 tablespoons

Freshly ground black pepper to taste

4 cups Homemade Chicken Broth (recipe follows)

1 cup water, plus hot water if needed

3 shallots

1½ cups risotto rice (see De Mane on Rice for Risotto on facing page)

TO MAKE THE PESTO

In a food processor, process the almonds until finely ground. Add the garlic, arugula, and olive oil and process briefly to make a coarse purée. Add the grana padano and process a few seconds to blend. Season with salt and pepper. Transfer the mixture to a small bowl and cover it with plastic wrap. You can make the pesto in the morning and refrigerate it, but make sure to bring it back to room temperature before adding it to your risotto.

Discard any mussels that don't close when you tap them with your finger. Put the mussels in a large pot. Pour on the wine and a drizzle of olive oil. Season with a few grindings of pepper. Turn the heat to high and cook, uncovered,

The Flavors of Southern Italy
Erica De Mane

stirring occasionally, until the mussels open, about 4 minutes. Using a large strainer spoon, transfer to a bowl. Strain the mussel cooking liquid through a fine-mesh sieve into a small bowl. Shell about half the mussels, leaving the smallest ones in their shells.

Pour the chicken broth into a saucepan. Add the 1 cup water and bring it to a boil (I like diluting the broth for this dish so the chicken taste doesn't compete too much with the mussels). Turn the heat to low and keep the broth at a low simmer.

In a wide, low-sided, heavy saucepan, heat 2 tablespoons olive oil over medium heat. Add the shallots and sauté until softened, about 4 minutes. Add the rice and stir it for 2 to 3 minutes to coat it well with oil and to toast it very lightly. Add the mussel cooking broth and let it cook down to almost nothing, stirring the rice often.

Start adding the chicken broth a few ladles at a time, stirring the rice almost constantly. The heat should be at an even low boil throughout the cooking (if the heat is too low, the rice may become mushy; what you want is a steady evaporation and absorption of the broth). Keep adding broth as the pan gets dry. Continue adding broth and stirring until the rice is creamy but the kernels still have a nice bite. The entire cooking time will be about 20 minutes. If you run out of broth, add ladles of very hot water.

When the rice is just about ready, add all the mussels and any broth they have given off. Add the pesto and toss everything well. Taste for seasoning. These additions will probably thicken your risotto, so add an extra ladle of broth or water to ensure a nice, loose texture. Serve right away.

Homemade Chicken Broth

MAKES ABOUT 5 CUPS

In a large saucepan, brown about 2 dozen chicken wings in a little olive oil, along with a chopped carrot, a piece of celery, a chopped small onion, and a bay leaf. Add about 8 cups of water and bring it to a boil. Reduce the heat and simmer, uncovered, for about 1½ hours. Strain, skim off the fat, and add salt.

De Mane on Rice for Risotto

Carnaroli, Vialone Nano and Arborio are the three main short-grain risotto rice varieties used in Italy. Arborio is the easiest to find in the United States, and it makes a good risotto, but it can sometimes become gummy if even slightly overcooked. You won't have that problem with Carnaroli, which has an excellent balance between bite and creaminess. Vialone Nano produces a firmer and slightly looser risotto, which I especially like for southern Italian–style seafood risotto, as it produces a cleaner texture.

The Flavors of Southern Italy
Erica De Mane

Spaghettini with Shrimp, Grape Tomatoes and Star Anise

4 SERVINGS

1½ pounds large shrimp, shelled and deveined, shells reserved

¼ cup extra-virgin olive oil

1 tablespoon chopped thyme

1 teaspoon crushed red pepper

2 tablespoons unsalted butter

1 whole star anise pod

⅛ teaspoon sugar

⅓ cup dry white wine

1½ cups chicken stock or low-sodium broth

2 pints grape tomatoes

Kosher salt

3 garlic cloves, thinly sliced

1 large shallot, finely chopped

1 pound spaghettini

½ cup coarsely chopped basil leaves

1. In a medium bowl, toss the shrimp with 1 tablespoon of the olive oil and half of the thyme and crushed red pepper. Cover and refrigerate.

2. In a medium saucepan, melt the butter over moderately high heat. Add the shrimp shells, star anise and sugar and cook, stirring occasionally, until the shells turn pink, about 2 minutes. Add the wine and cook until reduced by half, about 1 minute. Add the stock and simmer for 10 minutes. Strain the shrimp broth into a small, deep bowl. Return the star anise pod to the broth and discard the shrimp shells.

3. In a very large skillet, heat 2 tablespoons of the olive oil over moderately high heat. Add the tomatoes and a pinch of salt and cook undisturbed for 1 minute. Reduce the heat to moderate. Add the garlic and the remaining thyme and crushed red pepper and cook, stirring occasionally, until the tomatoes begin to burst, about 4 minutes. Add ¾ cup of the shrimp broth and the star anise and simmer for 1 minute. Remove from the heat.

The Flavors of
Southern Italy
Erica De Mane

4. In a large skillet, heat the remaining 1 tablespoon of olive oil over moderately high heat. Add the shrimp and shallot and cook until the shrimp are pink and curled, about 2 minutes per side. Season with salt. Add the remaining shrimp broth to the skillet and cook, scraping up any browned bits from the bottom of the pan. Add the shrimp and the broth to the tomato mixture and season generously with salt.

5. Meanwhile, in a large pot of boiling salted water, cook the spaghettini until al dente. Drain the pasta and add it to the skillet with the shrimp and tomatoes. Cook over moderate heat, tossing constantly, until the pasta is coated and the sauce has thickened slightly, about 3 minutes. Discard the star anise pod. Add the basil and season with salt. Transfer the pasta to plates and serve right away.

Editor's Note

It might seem surprising to find star anise, an Asian spice, in this Italian recipe. The star-shaped fruit, grown in southwestern China and Vietnam, lends a subtle anise note to the sauce—a flavor that works well with shellfish. The addition is De Mane's twist on a dish packed with traditional Italian flavors.

The Flavors of
Southern Italy
Erica De Mane

Coconut All-Star Custards, PAGE 64

The Weekend Baker
by Abigail Johnson Dodge

Published by Norton, 384 pages, color photos, $30

"If you're a lapsed home baker, I'm here to show you how to head back to the kitchen despite a time-pressed schedule," declares Abigail Johnson Dodge in *The Weekend Baker,* her fifth book. Broken up into three sections—recipes that are quick to make, ones that can be prepared ahead of time and those that are big-production numbers—the book is easy to use. Recipes like 10-Minute Mocha Pots de Crème and Emergency Blender Cupcakes are perfect for cooks in a hurry. Those with a little more time can try Classic Crumb Cake or Lemon Chiffon Pie with Pretzel Crust. With 150 recipes plus clever ideas for shortcuts and variations, this is a great book whether you're preparing for a fancy dinner party or a school bake sale.

Featured Recipes Coconut All-Star Custards; Crunchy Berry Summer Crisp; Lemon Chiffon Pie with Pretzel Crust; Classic Crumb Cake

Best of the Best Exclusive Spiced Raspberry Linzer Bars

Coconut All-Star Custards

Test Kitchen Tip

This recipe includes a technique in Step 3 called tempering: pouring hot liquids slowly into cold liquids to prevent curdling or breaking. For the custards here, be sure to add the hot coconut milk and cream to the egg mixture very slowly to avoid scrambling the eggs.

A custard is different from a pot de crème or a crème brûlée. Think firmer texture and a less rich, slightly eggier taste. The flavors and sweetness are so gentle and soft that you'll be soothed and satisfied with every spoonful.

8 SERVINGS

- 1 can (14 fluid ounces) unsweetened coconut milk
- 1½ cups (12 fluid ounces) heavy cream
- 4 large eggs
- ⅔ cup (5¼ ounces) granulated sugar
- ¼ teaspoon table salt

GO-WITHS

Toasted coconut or chopped walnuts (see Toasting Nuts and Coconut on facing page), blueberries, or raspberries for garnish (optional)

1. Position the oven rack on the middle rung. Heat the oven to 325 degrees. Arrange eight ¾-cup ramekins in a large baking pan with 3-inch sides.

2. Select a medium saucepan. Pour the coconut milk and cream into the pan. Heat until very warm and steamy (no need to bring to a boil). Alternatively, use a 4-cup Pyrex measure and the microwave to heat the liquid.

3. Select a medium bowl. Combine the eggs, sugar, and salt in the bowl. Whisk until well blended. Slowly pour in the hot liquid while whisking constantly. Using a spoon, skim off any bubbles and foam from the surface.

4. Pour the custard into the ramekins. (I like to pour the custard into a 4-cup Pyrex measure and pour it from there into the ramekins—the spout makes pouring easy.) Carefully fill the baking pan with hot water to come halfway up the sides of the ramekins. Bake until the custards wiggle like Jell-O when the ramekins are nudged, 25 to 35 minutes, depending on the thickness of the ramekin walls. Transfer the baking pan to a rack, carefully lift out the ramekins, and set on a rack to cool completely. Cover with plastic wrap and refrigerate until ready to serve.

The Weekend Baker
Abigail Johnson Dodge

• The unbaked custard can be prepared through step 3. Let cool completely and cover with plastic wrap. Refrigerate for up to 1 day before proceeding with the recipe. Please note that the chilled custard will take a few more minutes to bake.

• The baked custards can be prepared through step 4 and refrigerated for up to 2 days.

TOASTING NUTS AND COCONUT Heat the oven to 350 degrees and spread the nuts or coconut on a rimmed baking sheet in a single layer. Toast, shaking the pan occasionally to ensure even browning, until the nuts or coconut are fragrant and lightly browned. Depending on the type and quantity of nuts or coconut, this takes at least 8 minutes. Immediately transfer the nuts or coconut to a plate to cool (they'll keep browning after you've removed them from the oven).

Alternatively, to toast nuts on the stovetop, put them in a dry skillet in a single layer and toast over medium heat, shaking the pan frequently to ensure even browning, until the nuts are fragrant and lightly browned, 8 to 12 minutes. Immediately transfer the nuts to a plate to cool.

The Weekend Baker
Abigail Johnson Dodge

Crunchy Berry Summer Crisp

Dodge on Winter Berries

If you make this dish during the winter, when berries are less sweet and a bit flat-tasting, I recommend adding a little more lemon juice—the acidity will intensify the flavors. And you might want to add a smidge more salt.

As this berry crisp bakes, its intoxicating fragrance floats through your kitchen on the summer breeze. (My kids say that it smells like sunshine.)

My technique for topping a crisp is a bit unusual. I start with softened butter. This way it is much easier to incorporate the other ingredients and to achieve a more even distribution of flavors. Then I tuck the topping into the fridge while I prepare the filling, so it hardens up enough to crumble nicely on top of the berries.

8 SERVINGS

FOR THE TOPPING

- 8 tablespoons (4 ounces) unsalted butter, at room temperature
- ½ cup (4 ounces) firmly packed light brown sugar
- ¼ teaspoon ground cinnamon
- ¼ teaspoon table salt
- ⅔ cup (2 ounces) old-fashioned rolled oats (not instant)
- ½ cup (2¼ ounces) all-purpose flour
- ⅓ cup (1½ ounces) coarsely chopped pecans (no need to toast)

FOR THE FILLING

- ⅔ cup (5¼ ounces) firmly packed light brown sugar
- ¼ cup (1¼ ounces) all-purpose flour
- ¼ teaspoon table salt
- 3 pints (30 ounces/about 6 cups) assorted fresh berries, rinsed and well dried
- 1 teaspoon finely grated lemon zest (optional)
- 1 teaspoon lemon juice

GO-WITHS

Sweetened Whipped Cream (recipe follows) or vanilla ice cream

1. Position the oven rack on the middle rung. Heat the oven to 375 degrees. Have ready a shallow 10-cup baking dish. (I like to use a ceramic oval.)

The Weekend Baker
Abigail Johnson Dodge

2. **TO MAKE THE TOPPING** In a medium bowl, combine the butter, brown sugar, cinnamon, and salt. Mix with a spoon until blended. Add the oats, flour, and pecans. Stir until well blended. Refrigerate while preparing the fruit filling. (At this point, the topping can be covered and refrigerated for up to 2 days or frozen for up to 1 month before using.)

3. **TO MAKE THE FILLING** In a large bowl, combine the brown sugar, flour, and salt. Stir with a rubber spatula until blended. Add the berries, lemon zest (if using), and lemon juice and toss gently until the fruit is evenly coated. Pile the berry filling into the baking dish and spread evenly.

4. Remove the topping from the refrigerator. Using your fingers, crumble the topping and scatter it evenly over the fruit. Bake until the filling is bubbling and the topping is browned, about 30 minutes. Transfer to a rack and let cool at least 15 minutes. The crisp is best when served warm from the oven. Serve with a dollop of whipped cream or a generous scoop of vanilla ice cream, if desired.

STORAGE Cover the cooled crisp with plastic wrap and store at room temperature for up to 1 day.

Sweetened Whipped Cream

MAKES 2 CUPS

- 1 cup (8 fluid ounces) heavy cream
- 2 tablespoons granulated sugar
- ½ teaspoon pure vanilla extract

Pinch of table salt

Chill the bowl and beaters if your kitchen is hot. In a medium bowl, combine the cream, sugar, vanilla, and salt. Beat with an electric mixer (a handheld is the right size) on medium-high speed or with a hand whisk until medium-firm peaks form. Serve immediately, or cover and refrigerate for up to 2 hours.

DO AHEAD

- The ingredients can be combined in the bowl, covered, and refrigerated up to 3 days before beating and serving.

The Weekend Baker
Abigail Johnson Dodge

Lemon Chiffon Pie
with Pretzel Crust

I earned my first stripes as a food editor on the staff of *Woman's Day* magazine. The brilliant, gracious Elizabeth Alston was one of my most influential mentors. She headed up a staff full of talented people from whom I learned much—including how important it is to listen to readers. The inspiration for this pretzel crust comes from a *Woman's Day* recipe. It's been 20 years, but I still remember how the salty, buttery crust played against the citrus filling. The textural combination of the soft, billowy lemon chiffon and the crunchy, salty crust is addictive. You'll notice that I don't use egg yolks, just the whites, and that I call for ricotta in the filling instead of heavy cream. So, except for the butter in the crust, this dessert is almost lo-cal. Well, at the least, it's less rich than classic versions. I like to garnish each serving with a mini-pretzel or two. It gives guests a hint of what to expect.

MAKES ONE 9-INCH PIE, OR 8 SERVINGS

FOR THE CRUST

3½ cups (4½ ounces) salted mini-pretzels

¼ cup (2 ounces) granulated sugar

12 tablespoons (6 ounces) unsalted butter, melted and cooled slightly

FOR THE FILLING

1 packet (2¼ teaspoons) unflavored powdered
    gelatin (see What Is It? on page 71)

¾ cup (6 fluid ounces) lemon juice

1¼ cups (10 ounces) ricotta cheese (part-skim or whole is fine)

1 cup (8 ounces) granulated sugar

Pinch of table salt

1 tablespoon finely grated lemon zest

4 whites from large eggs (½ cup/4 fluid ounces)

GO-WITHS

Lemon slices, mini-pretzels, mint sprigs, or Sweetened Whipped Cream
    (page 67) for garnish (optional)

1. TO MAKE THE CRUST Have ready a 9-inch pie plate (I use Pyrex). Combine the pretzels and sugar in a food processor and process until the pretzels are medium-fine crumbs (some small chunks are okay, as they add crunch). Add the melted butter and process briefly until the crumbs are evenly moist.

Test Kitchen Tip

To be sure that the gelatin fully dissolves in Step 3, add the lemon juice to the blender first and then sprinkle the gelatin evenly over it.

The Weekend Baker
Abigail Johnson Dodge

2. Dump the crumbs into the pie plate and cover with a large sheet of plastic wrap. Place your hands on the plastic wrap and spread the crumbs to coat the bottom evenly. (The plastic wrap will keep the crumbs from sticking to your hands.) Once the crumbs are in place, and with the plastic wrap in place, use your fingers to pinch and press some of the crumbs around the inside edge and on the rim of the plate to cover evenly and completely. Redistribute the remaining crumbs evenly over the bottom of the pie plate, and press down firmly to make a compact layer. I like to use a metal measuring cup with straight sides and a flat bottom for this task. Set aside.

3. **TO MAKE THE FILLING** Sprinkle the gelatin in the bottom of a blender, making sure that it's all off the blades. Pour about ⅓ cup of the lemon juice over the gelatin and let stand until the gelatin is no longer dry looking and has softened, about 5 minutes.

4. In a small saucepan, bring the remaining lemon juice just to a boil. (This can also be done in the microwave.) Carefully pour it into the blender to cover the gelatin. Let stand for 2 minutes. Cover the blender and blend until the gelatin is dissolved, about 1 minute. Dip a spoon or spatula into the liquid. It should look clear and feel smooth to the touch.

5. Add the ricotta, ¾ cup (6 ounces) sugar, and the salt. Cover and blend until the mixture is smooth, about 45 seconds. Pour into a medium bowl and stir in the lemon zest. Refrigerate, stirring frequently, until the mixture is cooled and beginning to thicken, about 15 minutes.

6. Once the lemon mixture is thickened (it should be as thick as unbeaten egg whites), remove it from the fridge. The mixture should mound slightly. If it's too thick, heat it gently in a double boiler (see What Is It? on facing page) until it's more liquid and repeat the chilling process.

7. In a large bowl, beat the egg whites with an electric mixer (stand mixer fitted with the whisk attachment or handheld mixer) on medium-high speed until they hold soft peaks. Continue beating while gradually sprinkling the remaining ¼ cup (2 ounces) sugar. When all the sugar has been added, increase the speed to high and beat until firm, glossy peaks form. Using a rubber spatula, stir about one-fourth of the whites into the chilled lemon mixture. Add the remaining whites and fold together gently but thoroughly until blended.

The Weekend Baker

Abigail Johnson Dodge

8. Pour the filling into the crust and allow it to mound in the center. Cover and refrigerate until well chilled and set, at least 4 hours. To serve, use a sharp, pointed knife to cut the pie into 8 wedges.

DO AHEADS

• The crust can be prepared through step 2, covered with plastic wrap, and stored in the refrigerator for up to 1 day or frozen for up to 1 month before proceeding with the recipe.

• The lemon mixture can be prepared through step 5, covered, and refrigerated for up to 2 days before gently softening the mixture to the correct consistency and proceeding with the recipe.

• The pie can be prepared through step 8 and stored in the fridge for up to 3 days before serving.

WHAT IS IT? (UNFLAVORED GELATIN) Most often found in powdered form, unflavored gelatin is a thickener that helps give body to mousses and puddings. It's a great invisible helper, as it imparts neither color nor flavor to the finished product. Gelatin first needs to be softened in a small amount of cold liquid. The granules will swell and expand. Once dissolved, combine it with more liquid to unleash its thickening powers. On the other hand, you must never allow it to come to a boil, as its holding power will be reduced.

WHAT IS IT? (DOUBLE BOILER) A double boiler provides the gentle heat you need when melting chocolate or cooking custards or other egg-based mixtures. These mixtures are more likely to scorch or curdle over the direct heat of a stove burner. You can buy a double boiler, but it's easy to construct one with a saucepan and a stainless-steel bowl that will rest securely in the top of the pan. Fill the saucepan with about 2 inches of water and place the bowl on top. Check the water level before positioning the bowl. The water must not touch the bottom of the bowl. Set the pan and bowl over medium-high heat and bring the water to a boil. Reduce the heat to low and proceed as directed.

Dodge on Baking with Ricotta

I used ricotta cheese in this dish because I was going for something a little lighter... I'm not your low-fat girl, but ricotta gives you dairy richness without making the pie too heavy.

The Weekend Baker
Abigail Johnson Dodge

Classic Crumb Cake

Dodge on Time-Saving

Melting all the butter you need for the cake and the crumb topping in one pan shaves off a bit of time. Before I use it in the recipe, I give the butter a good stir, and then I pour off the ¾ cup (6 fluid ounces) for the cake before continuing with the remainder for the crumb topping.

When I was growing up in Brooklyn Heights, an unbelievably delicious store-bought crumb cake was a special breakfast treat on weekends. I was especially (if not obsessively) partial to the crumb topping, picking off every last bit before discarding the cake and moving on to my next piece. I can't begin to tell you how that irritated my brothers. In this recipe the cake is every bit as delicious as its topping.

The crumb topping is lightly sugared and spiced and is prepared first, so that it has time to cool and will be easy to crumble over the batter. When the cake is fresh from the oven, the crumb topping is slightly crunchy—a lovely contrast to the soft, moist cake. Over the next day or so, the crumbs soften and the cinnamon-nutmeg flavor becomes more pronounced.

MAKES ONE 9-BY-13-INCH CAKE, OR 12 SERVINGS

FOR THE TOPPING

16 tablespoons (8 ounces) unsalted butter, cut into 6 pieces

½ cup (4 ounces) granulated sugar

¾ cup (6 ounces) firmly packed light brown sugar

1½ teaspoons ground cinnamon

¼ teaspoon ground nutmeg

Pinch of table salt

2⅔ cups (12 ounces) all-purpose flour

FOR THE CAKE

3 cups (13½ ounces) all-purpose flour

1¼ cups (10 ounces) granulated sugar

1½ teaspoons baking powder

½ teaspoon table salt

2 large eggs

1 cup (8 fluid ounces) whole milk

12 tablespoons (6 ounces) unsalted butter, melted and cooled slightly

2 teaspoons pure vanilla extract

GO-WITH

Confectioners' sugar for dusting (optional)

The Weekend Baker
Abigail Johnson Dodge

1. TO MAKE THE TOPPING In a large saucepan, melt the butter over medium heat. Slide the pan from the heat and add the granulated sugar, brown sugar, cinnamon, nutmeg, and salt. Stir with a rubber spatula, pressing when necessary, until there are no lumps of sugar. Add the flour and mix until well blended and pasty. Set aside.

2. TO MAKE THE CAKE Position an oven rack on the middle rung. Heat the oven to 350 degrees. Lightly grease the bottom and sides of a 9-by-13-inch baking pan or dish.

3. In a large bowl, combine the flour, granulated sugar, baking powder, and salt. Whisk until well blended. In a medium bowl, combine the eggs, milk, melted butter, and vanilla. Whisk until well blended.

4. Pour the wet ingredients over the dry ingredients and gently stir with a rubber spatula just until blended. Scrape the batter into the prepared pan and spread evenly. Break up the topping mixture with your fingers into medium-sized pieces and sprinkle evenly over the cake batter to form a generous layer.

5. Bake until the cake springs back when lightly pressed in the center and a toothpick or cake tester inserted in the center comes out clean, about 40 minutes. Transfer the pan to a rack to cool. Serve warm or at room temperature. Before serving, sift some confectioners' sugar over the top, if desired.

DO AHEADS

• The crumb topping can be prepared through step 1 up to 1 day ahead. Cover with plastic wrap and store at room temperature.

• The dry ingredients and the wet ingredients, except the butter, can be prepared as directed in step 3 up to 1 day ahead. Keep the dry ingredients covered and at room temperature and the wet ingredients covered and in the fridge. Melt the butter just before continuing with the recipe.

• The cake can be prepared through step 5, covered with plastic wrap, and stored at room temperature. It holds beautifully for up to 4 days, and I think it tastes better than it does fresh from the oven. This isn't the type of cake that greatly benefits from being served when still warm, so there's no need to wake up at the crack of dawn to bake it.

The Weekend Baker
Abigail Johnson Dodge

Spiced Raspberry Linzer Bars

MAKES 20 BARS

  1 cup hazelnuts (5 ounces)

2⅓ cups all-purpose flour

  2 tablespoons unsweetened cocoa powder

  1 teaspoon cinnamon

½ teaspoon salt

¼ teaspoon ground cloves

  2 sticks (8 ounces) unsalted butter, at room temperature

1½ cups packed light brown sugar

  2 large eggs

  1 teaspoon pure vanilla extract

  1 cup seedless raspberry preserves

Confectioners' sugar, for dusting

1. Preheat the oven to 325°. Lightly grease a 9-by-13-inch baking pan. In a food processor, pulse the hazelnuts until they are finely ground. In a medium bowl, mix the hazelnuts with the flour, cocoa powder, cinnamon, salt and cloves.

2. In a large bowl, using an electric mixer, beat the butter and brown sugar at medium speed for 2 minutes. Beat in the eggs and vanilla, then beat in the dry ingredients just until combined.

3. Transfer two-thirds of the dough to the prepared pan and spread it in an even layer. Top with the raspberry preserves. Drop tablespoons of the remaining dough over the preserves, spacing them evenly. With lightly floured fingertips, flatten the dough topping; it will not cover the entire surface. Bake for 50 minutes, or until a toothpick inserted in the center comes out clean. Transfer the pan to a wire rack and cool completely, about 1½ hours. Cut into bars, dust lightly with confectioners' sugar and serve.

MAKE AHEAD The uncut bars can be covered with foil and stored at room temperature in the baking pan for up to 5 days.

Editor's Note

These linzer bars are a Dodge family favorite. The secret ingredient, Dodge says, is the cocoa powder. It's not traditional, but it really blends well with the spices, creating a rich, flavorful dough that pairs well with the tart raspberry filling.

The Weekend Baker
Abigail Johnson Dodge

Author Ina Garten in the famous
Poilâne bakery in Paris

Barefoot in Paris

by Ina Garten

Published by Clarkson Potter, 240 pages, color photos, $35

"Americans think of French food as fancy food, as special-occasion food. But what I love is simple, country French food," declares Ina Garten in the introduction to *Barefoot in Paris,* her fourth book. Garten adds her own twist by simplifying and streamlining the classics—soufflés never seemed easier. She also gives tips on where to snag great food, kitchenware and produce in Paris, if the book inspires a trip. *Barefoot in Paris* is a perfect book for those who want to explore French cooking for the first time and need a friendly hand to guide them through.

Featured Recipes Boeuf Bourguignon; Lentil Sausage Soup; Blue Cheese Soufflé

77

Boeuf Bourguignon

Garten on Frozen Baby Onions

I like using frozen baby onions for this recipe— you save yourself time and effort because you don't have to peel them, and they taste just fine!

I never really liked beef bourguignon. After cooking for three hours, the meat was stringy and dry and the vegetables were overcooked. So, I tried to solve the problem and came up with a delicious stew that cooks in an hour and a half. The good news is that it's even better the second day, so it's great for entertaining.

6 SERVINGS

1 tablespoon good olive oil

8 ounces good bacon, diced

2½ pounds beef chuck cut into 1-inch cubes

Kosher salt

Freshly ground black pepper

1 pound carrots, sliced diagonally into 1-inch chunks

2 yellow onions, sliced

2 teaspoons chopped garlic (2 cloves)

½ cup Cognac or good brandy

1 (750-ml) bottle good dry red wine, such as Burgundy

2 to 2½ cups canned beef broth

1 tablespoon tomato paste

1 teaspoon fresh thyme leaves

4 tablespoons (½ stick) unsalted butter, at room temperature, divided

3 tablespoons all-purpose flour

1 pound frozen small whole onions

1 pound mushrooms, stems discarded, caps thickly sliced

FOR SERVING

Country bread, toasted or grilled

1 garlic clove, cut in half

½ cup chopped fresh flat-leaf parsley (optional)

Preheat the oven to 250 degrees.

Heat the olive oil in a large Dutch oven, such as Le Creuset. Add the bacon and cook over medium heat for 8 to 10 minutes, stirring occasionally, until the bacon is lightly browned. Remove the bacon with a slotted spoon to a large plate.

Barefoot in Paris
Ina Garten

Dry the beef cubes with paper towels and then sprinkle them with salt and pepper. In batches in single layers, sear the beef in the hot oil for 3 to 5 minutes, turning to brown on all sides. Remove the seared cubes to the plate with the bacon and continue searing until all the beef is browned. Set aside.

Toss the carrots, onions, 1 tablespoon of salt, and 2 teaspoons of pepper into the fat in the pan and cook over medium heat for 10 to 12 minutes, stirring occasionally, until the onions are lightly browned. Add the garlic and cook for 1 more minute. Add the Cognac, *stand back,* and ignite with a match to burn off the alcohol. Put the meat and bacon back into the pot with any juices that have accumulated on the plate. Add the wine plus enough beef broth to almost cover the meat. Add the tomato paste and thyme. Bring to a boil, cover the pot with a tight-fitting lid, and place it in the oven for about 1¼ hours, or until the meat and vegetables are very tender when pierced with a fork. Remove from the oven and place on top of the stove.

Combine 2 tablespoons of the butter and the flour with a fork and stir into the stew. Add the frozen onions. In a medium pan, sauté the mushrooms in the remaining 2 tablespoons of butter over medium heat for 10 minutes, or until lightly browned, and then add to the stew. Bring the stew to a boil, then lower the heat and simmer uncovered for 15 minutes. Season to taste.

Rub each slice of bread on one side with garlic. For each serving, spoon the stew over a slice of bread and sprinkle with parsley.

IF THE SAUCE IS TOO THIN, you can add more of the butter and flour mixture.

TO MAKE IN ADVANCE, cook the stew and refrigerate. To serve, reheat to a simmer over low heat and serve with the bread and parsley.

Barefoot in Paris
Ina Garten

Lentil Sausage Soup

In Paris, I make this soup with French sausage with truffles and pistachios, which has a much finer texture than the Italian sausage we can find here. However, when I'm home, it's also delicious made with kielbasa and it's so much easier to find.

MAKES 4 QUARTS; 8 TO 10 SERVINGS

- 1 pound French green lentils such as du Puy
- ¼ cup olive oil, plus extra for serving
- 4 cups diced yellow onions (3 large)
- 4 cups chopped leeks, white and light green parts only (2 leeks)
- 1 tablespoon minced garlic (2 large cloves)
- 1 tablespoon kosher salt
- 1½ teaspoons freshly ground black pepper
- 1 tablespoon minced fresh thyme leaves
- 1 teaspoon ground cumin
- 3 cups medium-diced celery (8 stalks)
- 3 cups medium-diced carrots (4 to 6 carrots)
- 3 quarts Homemade Chicken Stock (recipe follows) or canned broth
- ¼ cup tomato paste
- 1 pound kielbasa, cut in half lengthwise and sliced ⅓ inch thick
- 2 tablespoons dry red wine or red wine vinegar

Freshly grated Parmesan cheese, for serving

In a large bowl, cover the lentils with boiling water and allow to sit for 15 minutes. Drain.

In a large stockpot over medium heat, heat the olive oil and sauté the onions, leeks, garlic, salt, pepper, thyme, and cumin for 20 minutes, or until the vegetables are translucent and tender. Add the celery and carrots and sauté for another 10 minutes. Add the chicken stock, tomato paste, and drained lentils, cover, and bring to a boil. Reduce the heat and simmer uncovered for 1 hour, or until the lentils are cooked through and tender. Check the seasonings. Add the kielbasa and red wine and simmer until the kielbasa is hot. Serve drizzled with olive oil and sprinkled with grated Parmesan.

Homemade Chicken Stock

MAKES 6 QUARTS

- 3 (5-pound) chickens
- 3 large onions, unpeeled and quartered
- 6 carrots, unpeeled and halved
- 4 celery stalks with leaves, cut in thirds
- 4 parsnips, unpeeled and cut in half (optional)
- 20 sprigs of fresh flat-leaf parsley
- 15 sprigs of fresh thyme
- 20 sprigs of fresh dill
- 1 head of garlic, unpeeled and cut in half crosswise
- 2 tablespoons kosher salt
- 2 teaspoons whole black peppercorns

Place the chickens, onions, carrots, celery, parsnips, parsley, thyme, dill, garlic, salt, and peppercorns in a 16- to 20-quart stockpot with 7 quarts of water and bring to a boil. Skim the surface as needed. Simmer uncovered for 4 hours. Strain the entire contents of the pot through a colander, discarding the chicken and vegetables, and chill. Discard the hardened fat, and then pack the broth in quart containers.

Barefoot in Paris
Ina Garten

Blue Cheese Soufflé

This really has the WOW! factor. I was a little afraid to attempt a soufflé (think Audrey Hepburn in *Sabrina*), but after you've made this once, you'll agree that it's really easy and so delicious.

2 TO 3 SERVINGS

- 3 tablespoons unsalted butter, plus extra for greasing the dish
- ¼ cup finely grated Parmesan cheese, plus extra for sprinkling
- 3 tablespoons all-purpose flour
- 1 cup scalded milk

Kosher salt and freshly ground black pepper

Pinch of cayenne pepper

Pinch of nutmeg

- 4 extra-large egg yolks, at room temperature
- 3 ounces good Roquefort cheese, chopped
- 5 extra-large egg whites, at room temperature
- ⅛ teaspoon cream of tartar

Preheat the oven to 400 degrees. Butter the inside of an 8-cup soufflé dish (7½ inches in diameter by 3¼ inches deep) and sprinkle evenly with Parmesan.

Melt the butter in a small saucepan over low heat. With a wooden spoon, stir in the flour and cook, stirring constantly, for 2 minutes. Off the heat, whisk in the hot milk, ½ teaspoon salt, ¼ teaspoon black pepper, the cayenne, and nutmeg. Cook over low heat, whisking constantly, for 1 minute, until smooth and thick.

Off the heat, while still hot, whisk in the egg yolks, one at a time. Stir in the Roquefort and the ¼ cup of Parmesan and transfer to a large mixing bowl.

Put the egg whites, cream of tartar, and a pinch of salt in the bowl of an electric mixer fitted with the whisk attachment. Beat on low speed for 1 minute, on medium speed for 1 minute, then finally on high speed until they form firm, glossy peaks.

Whisk one-quarter of the egg whites into the cheese sauce to lighten and then fold in the rest. Pour into the soufflé dish, then smooth the top. Draw a large circle on top with the spatula to help the soufflé rise evenly, and place in the middle of the oven. Turn the temperature down to 375 degrees. Bake for 30 to 35 minutes (don't peek!), until puffed and brown. Serve immediately.

Garten on Cooking Ahead

To make this in advance, prepare the recipe through adding the cheeses up to 2 hours ahead. Keep covered at room temperature and then proceed with the recipe just before baking.

Barefoot in Paris
Ina Garten

Grilled Lamb Chops with Yogurt
and Indian Spices, PAGE 86

The Olive Harvest Cookbook

by Gerald Gass

With Jacqueline Mallorca, published by Chronicle Books, 180 pages, color photos, $35

"I encourage you to taste, touch, smell, and feel the food you are preparing," writes Gerald Gass in his first book, *The Olive Harvest Cookbook*. Gass, the private chef at the McEvoy Ranch in Marin County, California, an organic olive-oil producer, has a remarkable kitchen garden that would be the envy of any cook. That may explain why his California-meets-Mediterranean recipes emphasize gorgeous produce (and olive oil) rather than heavy sauces and difficult techniques. You don't have to be an olive oil fanatic to love this book, just a fan of superfresh food.

Featured Recipes Grilled Lamb Chops with Yogurt and Indian Spices; Celery Salad with Pecorino Cheese; Coriander-Crusted Pork Tenderloin with Roasted New Potatoes

Best of the Best Exclusive Applesauce Spice Cake

85

Grilled Lamb Chops with Yogurt and Indian Spices

Gass on Frenching Lamb Chops

To "french" a lamb chop means to scrape the bone clean of all fat and gristle down as far as the tender little nut of meat. You can ask your butcher to do it, or you can do it yourself using a small knife with a thin, rigid blade. Grasp the chop by the meat end and rest the tip of the bone on a cutting board to steady the chop. Using the back of the knife blade, scrape the bone to remove any remaining fat and tissue, turning the chop as you go to clean all sides.

In India, cooks don't use "curry powder." Instead, they make a *masala*, or spice mixture, that is carefully adjusted according to the main ingredient and can range from subtle, like this one, to fiery hot. I like to serve these chops with raita and an herbed cherry tomato salad and with warmed pita bread and/or a rice pilaf.

4 SERVINGS

SPICE MIXTURE

- 1 tablespoon peppercorns
- 1 tablespoon cumin seeds
- 1 tablespoon coriander seeds
- 1 teaspoon cardamom seeds (removed from husks)
- 1 teaspoon small cinnamon stick pieces
- ¾ teaspoon ground turmeric
- 1 teaspoon paprika
- ½ teaspoon red pepper flakes
- 1½ teaspoons ground ginger

LAMB

- 1 large clove garlic, sliced
- 1 shallot, sliced
- 2 teaspoons spice mixture (above)
- 2 teaspoons extra virgin olive oil
- ¼ cup plain yogurt
- 2 teaspoons grated lemon zest
- 1 tablespoon fresh lemon juice
- 8 lamb rib chops, each 1¼ inches thick, frenched
- ¾ teaspoon sea salt or kosher salt

EGGPLANTS

- 6 small Japanese eggplants, each about 5 inches long
- 1 tablespoon reserved spice mixture (above)
- 2 tablespoons extra virgin olive oil
- ¾ teaspoon sea salt or kosher salt

The Olive
Harvest Cookbook
Gerald Gass

1. To prepare the spice mixture, in a small sauté pan, toast the peppercorns, cumin, coriander, cardamom, and cinnamon over medium-low heat until the cumin seeds begin to darken and the mixture is very fragrant, 4 to 5 minutes. Remove from the heat, let cool, and pour into a mortar. Add the turmeric, paprika, red pepper flakes, and ginger and pound with a pestle to a coarse powder. (Alternatively, grind the spices in an electric spice grinder.) Measure out 1 tablespoon plus 2 teaspoons of the spice mixture to use for the recipe. Store the remainder in a covered jar in a cool, dark place to use another time.

2. To prepare the lamb, in a mortar using a pestle, pound together the garlic, shallot, spice mixture, and olive oil until a rough paste forms. Stir in the yogurt, lemon zest, and lemon juice. Rub the paste onto the lamb chops, coating them on both sides, and allow the meat to rest, covered, at room temperature for at least 1½ hours, or in the refrigerator for up to 24 hours. If refrigerated, bring the meat to room temperature before cooking.

3. Prepare a hot natural-charcoal fire in a grill.

4. To prepare the eggplants, trim off the stem end from each eggplant, then cut in half lengthwise. Use a long knife and cut as straight as possible so that the eggplant halves will lie flat on the grill. Using a sharp paring knife, make a pattern of crosshatch cuts about ¼ inch apart on the cut surface of each eggplant half. The cuts should reach almost to the skin without piercing it. Using your fingers, rub about ¼ teaspoon of the spice mixture into the cuts on each eggplant half. Just before grilling, brush the cut sides with the olive oil and sprinkle with the salt.

5. To grill the lamb chops and eggplants, scrape off the excess marinade from the chops and season them with the salt. Place the eggplants over the fire and grill, turning them several times, until they are dark golden brown on the cut sides and are soft throughout, about 10 minutes in all. Grill the chops at the same time for about 4 minutes on each side for medium-rare, or to the desired degree of doneness.

6. To serve, place 2 lamb chops and 3 eggplant halves on each of 4 warmed dinner plates and serve at once.

The Olive
Harvest Cookbook
Gerald Gass

Celery Salad with Pecorino Cheese

Crisp, moist celery and lettuce, sharp, salty pecorino cheese, and fruity, acidic lemon juice complement one another beautifully in this recipe. As always, choose the freshest, most flavorful ingredients that you can find; they are exposed in this dish and any shortcomings will be readily apparent.

6 TO 8 SERVINGS

VINAIGRETTE

- ½ cup extra virgin olive oil
- 5 tablespoons fresh lemon juice
- 1 shallot, finely diced
- 1 teaspoon grated lemon zest
- ½ teaspoon sea salt or kosher salt
- ¼ teaspoon freshly ground pepper

- 1 small head lettuce, preferably red leaf, leaves separated and torn into bite-sized pieces

Sea salt or kosher salt

Freshly ground pepper

- 12 celery stalks, thinly sliced
- ¼-pound wedge pecorino cheese

1. To prepare the vinaigrette, whisk together all the ingredients. Taste and adjust the seasoning.

2. Place the lettuce in a bowl and season lightly with salt and pepper. Drizzle about half the vinaigrette over the lettuce and toss to coat evenly. Divide the lettuce evenly among chilled salad plates. Place the celery in the bowl that held the lettuce and season lightly with salt and pepper. Drizzle with the remaining vinaigrette and toss to coat evenly. Using a slotted spoon, divide the celery evenly among the plates, placing each portion in a pile in the center of the lettuce. Using a vegetable peeler, shave long strips of pecorino over each salad. Spoon any vinaigrette remaining in the bowl that held the celery over the salads, then top each salad with a grind or two of pepper. Serve immediately.

The Olive
Harvest Cookbook
Gerald Gass

Coriander-Crusted Pork Tenderloin with Roasted New Potatoes

6 TO 8 SERVINGS

- 2 pork tenderloins, 1 pound each
- 1½ teaspoons peppercorns
- 3 tablespoons coriander seeds
- 3 cloves garlic
- 4 tablespoons extra virgin olive oil
- 1½ pounds new potatoes, unpeeled
- 2¼ teaspoons sea salt or kosher salt
- ½ teaspoon freshly ground pepper

1. Trim any silver skin from the pork tenderloins, as it toughens when cooked. In a small sauté pan, toast the peppercorns and coriander seeds over medium-low heat until fragrant, about 5 minutes. Remove from the heat, let cool, then pour into a mortar. Add the garlic and 1 tablespoon of the olive oil and pound with a pestle to form a coarse, moist paste. Put the pork and spice paste in a zippered heavy-duty plastic bag, expel all the air, and seal shut. Massage the bag to coat the pork evenly with the spice paste. Place in the refrigerator and let marinate, turning occasionally, for 1 to 3 days. Remove from the refrigerator 1 hour before you begin cooking.

2. Preheat the oven to 375°F. In a bowl, toss together the potatoes, ¾ teaspoon of the salt, the pepper, and 2 tablespoons of the olive oil until well coated. Pour into a shallow baking pan just large enough to hold the potatoes in a single layer. Place in the oven and roast, stirring occasionally, until tender when pierced with a fork, about 40 minutes.

3. About 20 minutes before the potatoes are ready, preheat a 10-inch cast-iron skillet over high heat. Remove the tenderloins from the bag and sprinkle them with the remaining 1½ teaspoons salt. Add the remaining 1 tablespoon olive oil to the hot pan, reduce the heat to medium, and carefully add the pork. Brown the tenderloins on all sides, being careful not to scorch the crust. Continue to cook, turning often, until an instant-read thermometer inserted into the thickest part of each tenderloin registers 135°F (internal temperature will rise a few degrees as the meat rests), about 10 minutes. It should be a little pink inside and still juicy. Remove the tenderloins to a warmed platter, cover loosely with aluminum foil, and let rest for 5 minutes. Cut the tenderloins on the diagonal into slices ⅜ inch thick. Serve with the potatoes.

Applesauce Spice Cake

MAKES ONE 9-INCH CAKE

1¼ cups plus 1 tablespoon all-purpose flour

 1 tablespoon baking powder

 1 tablespoon cinnamon

½ teaspoon ground ginger

¼ teaspoon ground allspice

¼ teaspoon ground cardamom

⅛ teaspoon ground nutmeg

⅛ teaspoon ground cloves

½ cup golden raisins

 4 large eggs, at room temperature

½ teaspoon salt

 1 cup packed light brown sugar

 1 cup unsweetened applesauce

½ cup extra-virgin olive oil

¼ cup Calvados or other apple brandy

Lightly sweetened whipped cream or crème fraîche, for serving

1. Preheat the oven to 350°. Lightly butter a 9-inch nonstick springform pan. In a small bowl, sift 1¼ cups of the flour with the baking powder, cinnamon, ginger, allspice, cardamom, nutmeg and cloves. In another small bowl, toss the raisins with the remaining 1 tablespoon of flour.

2. In a large bowl, using an electric mixer, beat the eggs with the salt at high speed until broken up. Add the brown sugar and continue to beat for 4 minutes, until the batter is light in color and has doubled in volume. At low speed, beat in the applesauce, olive oil and Calvados and beat for 1 minute. Using a rubber spatula, fold in the dry ingredients in 2 batches, then fold in the raisins.

3. Pour the batter into the prepared pan and bake for 45 minutes, or until the cake is deep golden and a cake tester inserted in the center comes out clean. Transfer to a rack and let cool in the pan for 10 minutes. Remove the side of the pan and let the cake cool on a rack for 30 minutes longer. Serve warm or at room temperature, with whipped cream or crème fraîche.

Editor's Note

Gass uses McEvoy Ranch olive oils in just about everything, even this moist and spicy cake. His favorite way to serve this cake is with homemade buttermilk ice cream or crème fraîche ice cream.

The Olive
Harvest Cookbook
Gerald Gass

Just-picked Italian
vegetables and herbs

Marcella Says...
by Marcella Hazan

Published by HarperCollins, 400 pages, $29.95

"I never cooked in my life until I got married," admits Marcella Hazan, America's leading authority on Italian food for over 40 years. "I knew not one recipe. My husband could put up with many bad things but not a bad meal, and so I tried to reproduce dishes from Italy." *Marcella Says...*, Hazan's sixth book, is based on the famous master classes she taught in Venice for 20 years. With authoritative sections on subjects like matching pasta shapes to sauces as well as wonderful recipes like Baked Squash and Parmesan Cheese Pudding, *Marcella Says...* will rescue those of us who don't know how to cook for our spouses—or ourselves.

Featured Recipes Shrimp Braised with Tomato, Chile Pepper, and Capers; Spicy Beef Meatballs with Bell Peppers; Baked Squash and Parmesan Cheese Pudding

Shrimp Braised with Tomato, Chile Pepper, and Capers

Gamberi in Umido con Pomodoro, Peperoncino, e Capperi

Hazan on the Perfect Sauce

This sauce is ready when the oil separates out and forms a layer on the top. If it doesn't separate, there is still too much water. The sauce is ready when it has the taste of concentrated tomato and has lost some acidity.

As I look over this recipe, I think how typical it is of the Italian way with seafood, how quick and clear, how sparkling fresh its flavors. How many times I have cooked dishes like this is beyond counting, past remembering. I never tire of them. At the end of the recipe are directions for developing the dish into a delicious pasta sauce.

FOR 4 PERSONS

- 3 tablespoons extra virgin olive oil
- ½ cup onion, chopped very fine
- 1 tablespoon chopped garlic
- 2 tablespoons chopped Italian flat-leaf parsley

Chopped chile pepper, ½ tablespoon fresh jalapeño, or 1½ teaspoons dried red chile pepper, adjusting the quantities to taste and to the potency of the chile

- 1 cup tomatoes cut up with their juice, either ripe, firm, fresh plum tomatoes or canned imported San Marzano Italian tomatoes
- 20 large shrimp (or fewer if you decide to make a pasta sauce; see my recommendation at the end of this recipe)

Fine sea salt

- ½ tablespoon capers, drained and rinsed in cold water if packed in vinegar, or if packed in salt, rinsed, soaked in cold water for 10 minutes, then rinsed again

1. Put the oil and chopped onion in a 12-inch skillet, turn on the heat to medium high, and cook the onion, stirring it from time to time, until it becomes colored a pale gold. Add the chopped garlic, stir once or twice, and, when the aroma of the garlic begins to rise, add the parsley and chile pepper. Stir once or twice, then add the tomatoes. Turn all the ingredients over once or twice, turn the heat down to medium, and cook at a steady simmer.

2. While the tomato sauce is cooking, shell and devein the shrimp, rinse them under cold running water, and pat them dry with a dish towel or paper towels.

3. When the oil floats free from the tomato, slip the shrimp into the pan, adding salt and the capers. Turn the shrimp over several times to coat them well. After 2 or 3 minutes, when they have lost their shiny raw color, they are done. Serve at once with all the juices from the pan.

Marcella Says...
Marcella Hazan

 For more recipes by Marcella Hazan go to foodandwine.com/hazan. To access the recipes, log on with this code: **FWBEST05.** Effective through December 31, 2006.

The shrimp are terrific just as they are, with good crusty bread to sop up their juices. At home, I sometimes serve them over polenta or rice cooked pilaf-style, or with boiled Italian rice tossed with a pinch of salt and 1 or 2 tablespoons of olive oil.

UTILIZING THE SHRIMP FOR A PASTA SAUCE SERVING 4 TO 6 PERSONS
If you choose to make a pasta sauce with this recipe, half the shrimp—10 large—will be sufficient. When the shrimp are cooked, retrieve them from the skillet using a slotted spoon. Chop half of them very fine, put them back in the pan, cook for another minute or two, and take the pan off the heat. Cut the remaining shrimp into 3 pieces each and put them in the skillet. When the pasta is nearly done, turn on the heat to medium under the skillet. As soon as the pasta is cooked to al dente, firm to the bite, drain it and toss it in a warm serving bowl with the shrimp sauce.

Marcella Says...
Marcella Hazan

Spicy Beef Meatballs with Bell Peppers

Polpettine di Manzo Piccanti con i Peperoni

The role that tomatoes have always played in the making of Italian meatballs is filled here by red bell peppers. You have, moreover, a say in the direction of that role. If you want the peppers to star—that is, if you would like them to maintain enough of their shape to show on the plate—cook them just until a fork slips easily into them, about 10 minutes. If you think that you may enjoy them more as sauce, and a very tasty sauce it would be, just continue to cook them until they begin to dissolve.

MAKES 30 TO 35 MEATBALLS, SERVING 4 PERSONS

- 4 meaty red bell peppers
- 2 tablespoons chopped Italian flat-leaf parsley
- ½ cup chopped onion

Chopped fresh jalapeño pepper, 2 to 3 tablespoons, or to taste

- ⅔ cup torn fresh bread crumb—the soft, crustless part of a slice of bread
- ⅔ cup whole milk
- 1 pound ground beef chuck
- 1 egg

Fine sea salt

- 1½ cups fine, dry, unflavored bread crumbs, spread on a plate or a sheet of wax paper or aluminum foil
- 4 tablespoons extra virgin olive oil

A warm serving platter

1. Cut the bell peppers lengthwise along the creases, remove the stem, seeds, and pithy core, and skin them with a swivelblade vegetable peeler. Cut the peppers into strips about ½ inch wide.

2. Put the parsley, onion, and jalapeño pepper in a bowl and mix together well. In a small bowl soak the bread crumb in the milk. As soon as the bread is saturated with the milk, squeeze it out gently in your hand and add it to the onion mixture, working it in until combined. Add the ground chuck, egg, and salt, kneading the mixture very gently with your hands.

Marcella Says...
Marcella Hazan

3. Pull off a piece of the meatball mixture about the size of a very small egg and shape it in your hands into a ball, being careful not to squeeze it hard. Roll the meatball in the bread crumbs. Pull off another piece of the meat mixture and repeat the procedure until you have used all of it and the balls have all been rolled in bread crumbs.

4. Pour the oil into a 12-inch skillet and turn the heat on to high. When the oil is hot, slip in the meatballs. Brown them to a dark color on one side, then turn them and do the other side. Do not turn them more than once. If the meatballs do not fit into the pan in a single uncrowded layer, do a batch at a time. When you have browned them all, put all the meatballs into the pan before continuing.

5. Add the peppers with a little bit of salt, turn the contents of the pan over using a wooden spoon and a light touch, lower the heat, and cover the pan. You have a choice of how long to continue cooking. Please refer to the introductory note at the top of the recipe. When the peppers are done to taste, transfer the contents of the pan to a warm platter and serve at once.

MARCELLA SAYS

Jalapeño pepper is not commonly available to cooks in Italy, but it has attributes that make it worth introducing into Italian cooking: its fine fragrance and mellow style of spiciness. I don't see why one should be too dogmatic about authenticity because what matters is whether the taste of an ingredient is compatible with Italian flavors. Not all exotic ingredients pass that test. Cilantro, for example, does not. Jalapeño pepper does. If you prefer to use an ingredient more indigenous to the Italian repertoire, substitute one of the dried small hot chile peppers, the kind Italians call *diavoletti*.

AHEAD-OF-TIME NOTE You can complete the cooking several hours or even 2 or 3 days in advance of serving. In the latter event, refrigerate the meatballs with the peppers in a tightly closed container. Return to room temperature before reheating over medium-low heat.

Hazan on Her Favorite Ingredient
My favorite ingredient is what is available and good. I think, What says eat me? And then I listen!

Marcella Says...
Marcella Hazan

Baked Squash and Parmesan Cheese Pudding

Tortino di Zucca

Test Kitchen Tip

This pudding is a wonderful fall or winter accompaniment to roast lamb, beef or duck. To complete the meal, serve it with a side of greens sautéed in garlic and olive oil.

There are many wonderful Italian dishes with squash, but I had held back from working with them in my classes or for the cookbooks because they usually call for *zucca barucca,* an orange-fleshed pumpkin of exceptional sweetness and silky texture that I have never seen outside of Italy. After looking for but never finding an American equivalent for *zucca barucca,* I resigned myself to keeping my squash recipes in the drawer. When I moved to Florida, my son, who lives here, urged me to try butternut squash. I did and I am glad of it. It may not be quite as flavorful as *zucca barucca,* but it is very similar to an excellent Neapolitan squash that can be exceptionally versatile. This very simple little pudding is one of the tastiest dishes I have made with the squash.

FOR 4 PERSONS

- 1 medium butternut squash, about 1 pound or slightly more
- ½ cup freshly grated Parmigiano-Reggiano cheese
- 1 egg
- 1 teaspoon fine sea salt

Black pepper ground fresh from the mill

- 3 tablespoons butter softened at room temperature plus additional for greasing the ramekins
- ¼ teaspoon freshly grated nutmeg

Four 5-ounce ramekins

- 2 tablespoons fine, dry, unflavored bread crumbs

1. Turn on the oven to 400°.

2. Put the squash in a baking dish, and when the oven reaches the preset temperature, put it in the oven. After 1 hour remove it from the oven, but do not turn off the oven. Split the squash in half lengthwise, and use a spoon to scoop away and discard the seeds and strings. Scoop out the pulp. There should be about 1 cup.

3. Put the pulp, the grated Parmesan, the egg, salt, black pepper, 2 tablespoons of softened butter, and the nutmeg in the large bowl of a food processor. Run the blade just long enough to produce a homogenous but not overly creamy mixture.

Marcella Says...
Marcella Hazan

4. Thickly grease the inside of the ramekins with butter and sprinkle about half of the bread crumbs over the butter.

5. Divide the squash mixture equally among the ramekins. Sprinkle the remaining bread crumbs on top, then dot with the remaining tablespoon of butter, cut into 4 pieces.

6. Bake in the still-hot oven for 20 minutes. Let the ramekins rest for 6 minutes after you remove them from the oven. Turn each ramekin over onto a separate plate and give it a little shake to loosen the pudding, letting it drop onto the plate.

AHEAD-OF-TIME NOTE You can serve this *tortino* while it is still warm, or several hours later at room temperature.

Hazan on Pantry Staples

In my pantry I always have an onion, canned tomatoes and some butter. So if I want a quick meal, I make a good sauce of onion and tomato and serve it over penne. This is one of the Hazan family's favorite recipes.

Marcella Says...
Marcella Hazan

The Bouchon dining
room in Yountville
has a bistro feel.

Bouchon
by Thomas Keller

With Jeffrey Cerciello, published by Artisan, 360 pages, color photos, $50

"I used to joke that I opened Bouchon so I'd have a place to eat after cooking all night at the French Laundry," says Napa-based chef Thomas Keller. "The truth of it is that bistro cooking is my favorite food." In contrast to the brilliant, complex cuisine at French Laundry (and new Per Se in Manhattan), Bouchon serves basic French food. However, Keller produces it with enormous technical mastery, and in this book he explains in meticulous detail how to make humble dishes like french fries and cauliflower gratin. In return for your labor in the kitchen, you'll learn new skills and create wonderfully intense flavors.

Featured Recipes My Favorite Simple Roast Chicken; Herb Gnocchi; Chilled Leeks with Vinaigrette and Eggs Mimosa; Cauliflower Gratin

Best of the Best Exclusive Nutter Butter Cookies

My Favorite Simple Roast Chicken

Mon Poulet Rôti

Bouchon
Thomas Keller

Keller on Trussing

Trussing is not difficult, and if you roast chicken often, it's a good technique to feel comfortable with. When you truss a bird, the wings and legs stay close to the body; the ends of the drumsticks cover the top of the breast and keep it from drying out. Trussing helps the chicken to cook evenly, and it also makes for a more beautiful roasted bird.

2 TO 4 SERVINGS

One 2- to 3-pound farm-raised chicken
Kosher salt and freshly ground black pepper
  2 teaspoons minced thyme (optional)
Unsalted butter
Dijon mustard

Preheat the oven to 450°F. Rinse the chicken, then dry it very well with paper towels, inside and out. The less it steams, the drier the heat, the better. Salt and pepper the cavity, then truss the bird. Now, salt the chicken—I like to rain the salt over the bird so that it has a nice uniform coating that will result in a crisp, salty, flavorful skin (about 1 tablespoon). When it's cooked, you should still be able to make out the salt baked onto the crisp skin. Season to taste with pepper.

Place the chicken in a sauté pan or roasting pan and, when the oven is up to temperature, put the chicken in the oven. I leave it alone—I don't baste it, I don't add butter; you can if you wish, but I feel this creates steam, which I don't want. Roast it until it's done, 50 to 60 minutes. Remove it from the oven and add the thyme, if using, to the pan. Baste the chicken with the juices and thyme and let it rest for 15 minutes on a cutting board.

Remove the twine. Separate the middle wing joint and eat that immediately. Remove the legs and thighs. I like to take off the backbone and eat one of the oysters, the two succulent morsels of meat embedded here, and give the other to the person I'm cooking with. But I take the chicken butt for myself. I could never understand why my brothers always fought over that triangular tip—until one day I got the crispy, juicy fat myself. These are the cook's rewards. Cut the breast down the middle and serve it on the bone, with one wing joint still attached to each. The preparation is not meant to be superelegant. Slather the meat with fresh butter. Serve with mustard on the side and, if you wish, a simple green salad. You'll start using a knife and fork, but finish with your fingers, because it's so good.

 For more recipes by Thomas Keller go to foodandwine.com/keller. To access the recipes, log on with this code: **FWBEST05**. Effective through December 31, 2006.

Herb Gnocchi

Gnocchi à la Parisienne

Parisienne gnocchi are made from *pâte à choux,* a versatile dough made by cooking flour and water together until the flour cooks, after which eggs are stirred in. It can then be piped into various shapes and baked for profiteroles and éclairs for dessert, or savory preparations such as gougères, or gently poached in water as gnocchi.

Parisienne gnocchi are tasty, satisfying morsels that, like Italian gnocchi or any pasta, can be paired with all kinds of ingredients and transformed into countless dishes. They're excellent simply sautéed in butter. They can be additionally flavored with *fines herbes,* mustard, and cheese. At Bouchon, we don't serve much pasta or rice, so we use gnocchi as an interesting base for a number of our vegetarian dishes. They're not a classic bistro food, but the technique is a French one, dating back to before Escoffier.

Once they've been poached, gnocchi can be frozen for a month to six weeks.

MAKES ABOUT 240 GNOCCHI; 8 SERVINGS

1½ cups water

12 tablespoons (6 ounces) unsalted butter

 1 tablespoon plus 1 teaspoon kosher salt

 2 cups all-purpose flour, sifted

 2 tablespoons Dijon mustard

 1 tablespoon chopped chervil

 1 tablespoon chopped chives

 1 tablespoon chopped parsley

 1 tablespoon chopped tarragon

 1 cup loosely packed shredded Comté or Emmentaler cheese

5 to 6 large eggs

Set up a heavy-duty mixer with the paddle attachment. Have all the ingredients ready before you begin cooking.

Combine the water, butter, and the 1 teaspoon salt in a medium saucepan and bring to a simmer over medium-high heat. Reduce the heat to medium, add the flour all at once, and stir rapidly with a stiff heatproof or wooden spoon until the dough pulls away from the sides of the pan and the bottom of the pan is clean, with no dough sticking to it. The dough should be glossy and smooth but still moist.

Bouchon
Thomas Keller

Enough moisture must evaporate from the dough to allow it to absorb more fat when the eggs are added: Continue to stir for about 5 minutes, adjusting the heat as necessary to prevent the dough from coloring. A thin coating will form on the bottom and sides of the pan. When enough moisture has evaporated, steam will rise from the dough and the aroma of cooked flour will be noticeable. Immediately transfer the dough to the mixer bowl. Add the mustard, herbs, and the 1 tablespoon salt. Mix for a few seconds to incorporate the ingredients and release some of the heat, then add the cheese. With the mixer on the lowest speed, add 3 eggs, one at a time, beating until each egg is completely incorporated before adding the next one. Increase the speed to medium and add another 2 eggs, one at a

Test Kitchen Tip

These French-style *pâte à choux* gnocchi are much easier to work with than Italian potato gnocchi. One reason is that they are made from a simple choux pastry that doesn't require kneading. Another difference is that this pastry doesn't contain potatoes, which can vary in starch and moisture content, making it hard to predict how much flour is necessary for the dough.

Bouchon
Thomas Keller

time, mixing well after each one. Turn off the machine. Lift some of the dough on a rubber spatula, then turn the spatula to let it run off: It should move down the spatula very slowly; if it doesn't move at all or is very dry and just falls off in a clump, beat in the additional egg.

Place the dough in a large pastry bag fitted with a ⅝-inch plain tip and let it rest for about 30 minutes at room temperature. (If you have only a small pastry bag, fill it with half the dough two times.)

Bring a large pot of lightly salted water to a simmer. Line a baking sheet with paper towels. Line a second baking sheet with parchment paper.

Because this recipe makes such a large quantity of gnocchi, your arm may get tired: An easy way to pipe the gnocchi is to place a large inverted pot, canister, or other container that is slightly higher than the pot on the right side of the pot (left side if you are left-handed) and set the filled pastry bag on it so that the tip extends over the side and the container serves as a resting place for the bag. Twist the end of the pastry bag to push the dough into the tip. (From time to time, as the bag empties, you will need to twist the end again.) As you squeeze the back of the bag with your right hand, hold a small knife in your left hand and cut off 1-inch lengths of dough, allowing the gnocchi to drop into the pot. Pipe about 24 gnocchi per batch. First, the gnocchi will sink in the pot. Keep the water temperature hot, but do not boil. Once the gnocchi float to the top, poach them for another 1 to 2 minutes, then remove them with a slotted spoon or skimmer and drain on the paper towel–lined baking sheet. Taste one to test the timing; it may still seem slightly undercooked in the center, but it will be cooked again. Repeat with the remaining dough. (See Test Kitchen Tip at left.)

When all the gnocchi have drained, place them in a single layer on the parchment-lined baking sheet, cover with plastic wrap, and refrigerate for at least 30 minutes, or up to a day. Or, for longer storage, place the baking sheet in the freezer. Once the gnocchi have frozen solid, remove them from the baking sheet and place in a freezer bag in the freezer. Before using frozen gnocchi, spread them in a single layer on a baking sheet and defrost in the refrigerator for several hours.

Bouchon
Thomas Keller

Chilled Leeks with Vinaigrette and Eggs Mimosa

Poireaux en Vinaigrette et Oeufs Mimosa

Leeks are a succulent vegetable. When they're cooked correctly, they have a rich, creamy, full texture in the mouth, though in fact they're very lean. I love how they satisfy a craving for richness without fat. They're sweet, but they finish with an acidic effect. Cold leeks served with vinaigrette is a bistro dish I never get tired of eating. The leeks can be boiled or, as at Bouchon, steamed; in either case, they need to be well cooked or they'll be difficult to cut—but not so cooked that they become mushy.

One of the strengths of this recipe is that the cooked leeks are marinated for a day in a vinaigrette that's been diluted by half, so they really absorb that vinaigrette flavor. We serve it with mimosa—a garnish of sieved hard-cooked egg yolks, named after a family of trees and bushes known for its bright yellow flower. The eggs increase the creamy richness of the dish and balance the acidity of the vinaigrette, but if eating eggs is a concern, use fewer than the recipe calls for.

We julienne a special smoked red pepper, a piquillo, from the Basque region of Spain, to top the mimosa. It's got vivid color and a sweet, smoky flavor that's well worth seeking out, but you can substitute roasted red peppers if you wish. Serve with a great baguette to sop up the dressing and egg yolks.

4 SERVINGS

- 8 medium leeks (about 1 inch in diameter)
- Kosher salt and freshly ground black pepper
- 2 cups House Vinaigrette (recipe follows)
- ¼ cup julienned (¼ inch wide) piquillo peppers
- 10 hard-cooked large eggs (see Hard Cooking Eggs on next page)
- 2 tablespoons plus 2 teaspoons minced chives
- Extra virgin olive oil for drizzling

Trim the hairy roots from the leeks, but leave the root end intact. Remove and discard any tough outer leaves. Cut off and discard the dark green tops. To clean the leeks, split each leek lengthwise, beginning about 1 inch up from the root end, and, holding the leek open, rinse under warm water.

Keller on Leftovers

Use the leftover hard-boiled egg whites to make an egg salad. Combine them with lots of mayonnaise, some Dijon mustard, plus some minced celery and onions. Put that on toast and it's *so* good, but if you really want to get decadent, add some caviar on top.

Bouchon

Thomas Keller

Fit a large pot with a steamer insert, add water, and bring to a boil. Tie the tops of the leeks together with kitchen twine to hold them together during steaming. Add the leeks to the steamer, cover, and steam for about 10 minutes, or until tender throughout when pierced with a knife. Remove from the steamer and let cool for about 5 minutes. (Because the leeks will turn "olive drab" after marinating, there is no need to shock them in an ice bath.) Discard the twine and cut through the root ends of the leeks to split them completely in half. Place cut side up in a shallow baking dish and sprinkle lightly with salt and pepper.

Whisk 1 cup of the vinaigrette with 1 cup cold water. Pour over the leeks, cover, and refrigerate for at least 6 hours, or up to 2 days.

TO SERVE

Season the piquillo peppers with salt and pepper. Separate the egg whites and egg yolks. Push the yolks through the large holes of a grater, then finely chop. Reserve the whites for another use, if desired.

Remove the leeks from the marinade; discard the marinade. Trim the root ends, leaving only the tender leek. (If the leeks are longer than your serving plates, trim the greens as necessary to fit.)

Sprinkle the leeks with salt and pepper. Stack the leek halves cut side down in piles of two and crisscross two piles on each plate to form an X. Spoon the remaining vinaigrette over the centers of the salads. Sprinkle the egg yolks over the vinaigrette, then sprinkle the yolks with a pinch of salt and a few grinds of pepper. Garnish the center of each salad with a small mound of peppers, sprinkle each salad with 2 teaspoons minced chives, and drizzle with a little olive oil.

HARD COOKING EGGS Put the eggs in a single layer in a saucepan and cover by about 2 inches with cold water. Bring the water to a boil, then reduce the heat and simmer for 1 minute. Turn off the heat and let the eggs stand in the water for 10 minutes. Meanwhile, prepare an ice bath.

After 10 minutes, remove an egg and crack it open to check the yolk. It should be bright yellow and cooked but still creamy; if it's not, let the eggs stand for 1 to 2 more minutes. Transfer the eggs to the ice bath to chill for several minutes, then drain and peel.

Bouchon
Thomas Keller

House Vinaigrette

This is our basic vinaigrette, three parts oil, one part acid, pared almost to its essentials—no shallots, no salt and pepper—so that it can be used almost like a sauce base. The mustard adds flavor and strengthens the emulsion. Any number of additional ingredients may be added to it, depending on how it's to be used. Most often it's used to dress greens that have been seasoned with salt and tossed with fresh herbs.

MAKES ABOUT 2½ CUPS

¼ cup Dijon mustard

½ cup red wine vinegar

1½ cups canola oil

Combine the mustard and vinegar in a blender and blend at medium speed for about 15 seconds. With the machine running, slowly drizzle in ½ cup of the oil. Don't be tempted to add all the oil to the blender or the vinaigrette will become too thick. It should be very creamy.

Transfer the vinaigrette to a small bowl and, whisking constantly, slowly stream in the remaining 1 cup oil. (The dressing can be refrigerated for up to 2 weeks. Should the vinaigrette separate, use a blender or immersion blender to re-emulsify it.)

Keller on Pizza

One of my guiltiest pleasures is getting a slice of pizza at any corner pizzeria in New York City. How can you not crave that every once in a while?

Bouchon
Thomas Keller

Cauliflower Gratin

Gratin de Chou-fleur

Cauliflower is a great but underused vegetable. One of the things I appreciate, from a cook's standpoint, is that it's almost impossible to overcook it. And I like this recipe in particular because it uses the trimmings of the cauliflower too, in a puree that becomes part of the sauce.

4 SERVINGS

- 1 head (about 1¾ pounds) cauliflower
- Kosher salt
- 1 teaspoon white wine vinegar
- 1 tablespoon unsalted butter
- 2 tablespoons minced shallots
- Freshly ground black pepper
- 1 bay leaf
- 1 thyme sprig
- 1 Italian parsley sprig
- 1 cup heavy cream
- ½ teaspoon prepared horseradish
- Pinch of curry powder
- Freshly grated nutmeg
- ⅓ cup grated Comté or Emmentaler cheese
- 1 tablespoon panko (Japanese bread crumbs) or fine dried bread crumbs

Remove and discard the green leaves from the cauliflower. Cut away the florets, reserving the core. Cut off and reserve the stems. Cut the florets in pieces that measure about 1 inch. (You should have 4 to 5 cups florets.)

With a paring knife, cut away and discard the tough exterior of the core, then cut the core into small pieces and place them in a food processor. Add the reserved stem trimmings and pulse until very finely chopped, just short of a puree. (You should have about 1 cup; if you don't, puree enough of the florets to make 1 cup.)

Meanwhile, bring a large saucepan of water to boil. Season the water with salt and the vinegar. (The acid in the vinegar helps keep the cauliflower white.) Add half the cauliflower florets and blanch for 2 minutes. Remove

Bouchon
Thomas Keller

with a strainer or slotted spoon, drain well, and place in a large bowl. Repeat with the remaining florets: Blanch, drain, and add to the bowl. Set the saucepan aside. Season the florets with salt to taste.

Add the butter and shallots to the saucepan, place over medium heat, and cook gently for 1 to 2 minutes, or until the shallots are translucent. Season with salt and pepper and add the bay leaf, thyme, and parsley. Add the minced cauliflower and ⅔ cup water and cook gently for 5 to 6 minutes, or until most of the moisture has evaporated and the cauliflower is tender. If all the water evaporates before the cauliflower is tender, add more.

Add the cream, bring to a simmer, and simmer for 2 minutes. Remove from the heat and discard the thyme, bay leaf, and parsley. Pour the mixture into a blender and let it cool for 5 minutes.

Add the horseradish to the blender and pulse at the lowest speed to release the heat, then increase the speed and puree until smooth. Add the curry powder and blend at high speed for about 15 seconds. Toss the puree with the cauliflower florets and season with nutmeg, salt, and pepper to taste.

Transfer the cauliflower to an 8-inch round gratin dish or individual gratin dishes. The cream should come about halfway up the florets. Refrigerate for at least 30 minutes, or up to a day to allow the flavors to mature.

Preheat the oven to 450°F.

Sprinkle the gratin(s) with the cheese and bread crumbs. Place in the oven to cook for about 15 minutes, or until it is bubbling and the center is warm. You can test it by inserting a metal skewer into the center of the gratin and touching it to your lower lip: It should feel hot. Remove the gratin(s) from the oven and turn the broiler on. Brown the top of the gratin(s) and serve.

Bouchon
Thomas Keller

Best of the Best Exclusive

Nutter Butter Cookies

MAKES 2½ DOZEN 3-INCH SANDWICH COOKIES

2¼ cups all-purpose flour

2 tablespoons baking soda

1 tablespoon baking powder

½ teaspoon kosher salt

4 sticks (1 pound) unsalted butter, softened

2¼ cups creamy peanut butter

1 cup packed light brown sugar

1 cup granulated sugar

3 eggs

1 tablespoon pure vanilla extract

1½ cups quick-cooking oats

½ cup roasted unsalted peanuts, coarsely chopped

¼ cup confectioners' sugar

1. In a medium bowl, whisk the flour with the baking soda, baking powder and salt. In another medium bowl, beat 3 sticks of the butter with ¾ cup of the peanut butter until smooth. Add the light brown sugar and granulated sugar and beat at medium-high speed until light and fluffy, about 4 minutes. Beat in the eggs, one at a time, then beat in the vanilla. At low speed, beat in the dry ingredients. Add the oats and peanuts and beat until incorporated. Chill the dough for 1 hour.

2. Preheat the oven to 350°. Line 2 large baking sheets with parchment paper. Using a 1-ounce ice cream scoop or tablespoon, scoop the dough onto the prepared baking sheets, 1½ inches apart. Bake for 12 minutes, or until lightly golden. Let the cookies cool on the baking sheets for 5 minutes, then transfer them to wire racks to cool completely. Repeat with the remaining cookie dough.

3. Meanwhile, in a medium bowl, beat the remaining 1 stick of butter with the remaining 1½ cups of peanut butter and the confectioners' sugar until blended. Chill the filling until firm but still spreadable, about 1 hour.

4. Spread 1 tablespoon of the peanut butter filling on the flat side of half of the peanut butter cookies and close the sandwiches. Serve or refrigerate for up to 3 days. If chilled, remove from the refrigerator 30 minutes before serving.

Editor's Note

These buttery peanut butter cookies come from Keller's famed Bouchon Bakery. The crisp, crunchy cookie with the smooth, creamy peanut butter is irresistible.

Bouchon

Thomas Keller

Three kinds of whoopie pie: oatmeal, pumpkin and chocolate, PAGE 116

The King Arthur Flour Cookie Companion

by The King Arthur Flour Company

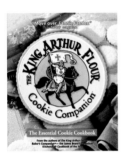

With P. J. Hamel, Susan Reid and the King Arthur test kitchen, published by Countryman, 512 pages, color photos, $29.95

This impressive follow-up to the wide-ranging *King Arthur Flour Baker's Companion* (also from the test kitchen at the 200-year-old New England company King Arthur Flour) focuses on a single subject: cookies. Why just cookies? Explains co-author P. J. Hamel, "Of all the Americans who bake, 95 percent bake cookies." This homage to America's favorite sweet is exhaustive, with over 400 recipes for everything from chewy oatmeal cookies to cakelike whoopie pies. Equipment and techniques are carefully detailed—there's even a thorough section on high-altitude baking—and every single recipe comes with nutrition information.

Featured Recipes Chocolate Whoopie Pies; Classic Apricot Squares; The Essential Chewy Oatmeal Cookie

Best of the Best Exclusive Lemon Zephyr Pancakes

Chocolate Whoopie Pies

Hamel on Whoopie Pies

We almost didn't put the whoopie pies in the book. We kept saying to each other, "Do these really belong in a cookie book? Are they a cookie?" And I finally said, "Well, it's not like a cake that you slice, it's a self-contained thing. You pick it up in your hand and eat it like a cookie, so we're going to call it a cookie!"

If you're not from a particular pocket of America (northern New England, Amish-country Pennsylvania, parts of the Midwest), you may never have heard of whoopie pies—more's the pity! These cakelike cookies, sandwiched around a layer of creamy filling, are ubiquitous at bake sales, where an individually wrapped, overstuffed pie will command a premium price, much more than a cookie or muffin. It's all about supply and demand—the demand usually outstrips the whoopie pie supply, particularly at sporting events, where hungry athletes (and their bored siblings) have been known to strip the whoopie pie section clean in minutes.

YIELD: 7 OR 8 LARGE (4½-INCH) WHOOPIE PIES;
BAKING TEMPERATURE: 350°F; BAKING TIME: 15 MINUTES

COOKIES

- ½ cup (3¼ ounces) vegetable shortening
- 1 cup (8 ounces) brown sugar
- 1 large egg
- ¼ cup plus 2 tablespoons (1⅛ ounces) Dutch process cocoa powder
- 2 cups (8½ ounces) unbleached all-purpose flour
- 1 teaspoon baking powder
- 1 teaspoon baking soda
- 1 teaspoon salt
- 1 teaspoon vanilla extract
- 1 cup (8 ounces) milk (regular or low fat, not nonfat)

FILLING

- 1 cup (6½ ounces) vegetable shortening
- 1 cup (4 ounces) confectioners' sugar
- 1⅓ cups (4 ounces) Marshmallow Fluff or marshmallow creme
- ¼ teaspoon extra-fine salt, or ¼ teaspoon table salt dissolved in 1 tablespoon water
- 1½ teaspoons vanilla extract

The King Arthur Flour Cookie Companion

The King Arthur Flour Company

- Preheat the oven to 350°F. Lightly grease (or line with parchment) two baking sheets.

- TO MAKE THE COOKIES In a large mixing bowl, cream together the shortening, brown sugar, and egg. In a separate bowl, whisk together the cocoa, flour, baking powder, baking soda, and salt. In a small bowl, stir the vanilla into the milk.

- Alternate adding the dry ingredients and the milk mixture to the shortening mixture, beating until smooth. Drop the stiff batter by the ¼-cupful onto the prepared baking sheets, about 2 inches apart.

- Bake the cookies for about 15 minutes, until they're firm to the touch. Remove them from the oven and transfer to a rack to cool completely.

- TO MAKE THE FILLING In a medium-sized bowl, beat all the filling ingredients together.

- TO ASSEMBLE Spread half of the cookies with the filling, using about ¼ cup for each; top with the remaining cookies. For best storage, wrap each pie individually.

MEASURING MARSHMALLOW Sticky, gooey, clinging—supply whatever adjective suits, but we all know that marshmallow creme (or shortening, or peanut butter) is challenging to measure. The best solution, by far, is a Wonder Cup (a measuring cup consisting of a clear, round sleeve with a sliding base set within). Barring that, if your recipe calls for oil, measure that first in your measuring cup, then measure the marshmallow creme. It will slide right out. Or spray your measuring cup with a vegetable oil spray. As a last resort, try rinsing your measuring cup with cold water before adding the marshmallow. The water will help it (somewhat) to slip out of the cup.

Hamel on Storing Whoopie Pies

What's great about whoopie pies is that the fluff kind of keeps the cookies moist—you wrap them individually in plastic and they keep really well.

The King Arthur Flour Cookie Companion

The King Arthur Flour Company

Classic Apricot Squares (opposite), Bakery Date
Squares and Bakery Raspberry Squares

Classic Apricot Squares

YIELD: 24 SQUARES; BAKING TEMPERATURE: 350°F; BAKING TIME: 14 TO 16
MINUTES FOR THE CRUST, 28 TO 32 MINUTES FOR THE SQUARES

FILLING

2 cups (12 ounces) chopped dried apricots

2 tablespoons (1 ounce) brandy (optional)

½ cup (3½ ounces) sugar

1½ cups (12 ounces) water

CRUST AND TOPPING

2¼ cups (9½ ounces) unbleached all-purpose flour

1¼ cups (5 ounces) confectioners' sugar

1 teaspoon salt

1 teaspoon baking powder

1 cup (2 sticks, 8 ounces) unsalted butter

1 cup (4 ounces) chopped pecans or shredded sweetened coconut (optional)

Coarse sugar (optional)

- Preheat the oven to 350°F. Lightly grease a 9 x 13-inch or 11 x 11-inch pan.

- TO MAKE THE FILLING In a medium-sized saucepan, stir together the apricots, brandy, sugar, and water and bring to a boil. Cook the mixture for 8 to 10 minutes, until the fruit is soft and has absorbed most of the water. Cool slightly, then purée it in a food processor or blender, or with an immersion blender.

- TO MAKE THE CRUST AND TOPPING In a medium-sized mixing bowl, whisk together the flour, sugar, salt, and baking powder. Using a pastry blender, your fingers, or a mixer, cut in the butter until the mixture is crumbly but will hold together when squeezed. Transfer about 1¼ cups of the mixture to another bowl, stir in the nuts, and set aside.

- Press the remainder of the crust mixture into the bottom and slightly up the sides of the prepared pan. Bake the crust for 14 to 16 minutes. Remove it from the oven.

- While still warm, spread the crust with the filling. Spread the reserved topping mixture over the filling. Sprinkle with coarse sugar, if desired. Return the pan to the oven and bake for 28 to 32 minutes, until they're golden brown. Remove from the oven and cool on a rack. Cut into squares. These freeze very well.

Hamel on Flavoring Apricot Squares

You can use apricot liqueur instead of brandy in this recipe if you like. If I'm with people who object to the alcohol, I use apple juice. Alcohol is a great flavor carrier, though, so I prefer it.

The King Arthur Flour Cookie Companion
The King Arthur Flour Company

The Essential Chewy Oatmeal Cookie

This flat cookie has a lovely crisp edge, but bends before it breaks—unlike crunchy cookies, which snap cleanly in two. Raisins both enhance the cookie's flavor and add additional moistness, and nuts lend their own distinct, toasty taste.

YIELD: 45 COOKIES; BAKING TEMPERATURE: 375°F; BAKING TIME: 11 MINUTES

- ½ cup (1 stick, 4 ounces) unsalted butter
- ½ cup (3¼ ounces) vegetable shortening
- ½ cup (3½ ounces) granulated sugar
- 1 cup (8 ounces) brown sugar
- 2 teaspoons vanilla extract
- ¼ teaspoon almond extract
- ¾ teaspoon cinnamon
- ⅛ teaspoon ground cloves
- ¼ teaspoon nutmeg
- 1 teaspoon salt
- 1 teaspoon baking soda
- 1 large egg
- 6 tablespoons (4⅛ ounces) light corn syrup
- 2 tablespoons (1 ounce) milk (regular or low fat, not nonfat)
- 3 cups (10½ ounces) quick-cooking oats (or old-fashioned rolled oats pulsed in a food processor, to make smaller, thinner flakes)
- 1½ cups (6¼ ounces) unbleached all-purpose flour
- 1 cup (5¼ ounces) raisins
- 1 cup (4 ounces) chopped pecans or walnuts

- Preheat the oven to 375°F. Lightly grease (or line with parchment) two baking sheets.

- In a large bowl, cream together the butter, shortening, sugars, extracts, spices, salt, and baking soda, beating until fairly smooth. Beat in the egg, scraping the bowl, then beat in the corn syrup and milk. Stir in the oats, flour, raisins, and nuts.

- Drop the dough by the tablespoonful onto the prepared baking sheets. Bake the cookies for 11 minutes, until they're a light golden brown. Remove them from the oven and transfer to a rack to cool.

The King Arthur Flour Cookie Companion

The King Arthur Flour Company

Lemon Zephyr Pancakes

YIELD: SIXTEEN 4-INCH PANCAKES;
COOKING TIME: 30 MINUTES

½   cup quick-cooking oats

1¼ cups buttermilk

1   medium Granny Smith apple,
     peeled and coarsely grated

1   tablespoon finely grated lemon zest

2   tablespoons vegetable shortening,
     at room temperature

1   egg

Pinch of freshly grated nutmeg

1   cup all-purpose flour

1   teaspoon baking powder

½   teaspoon baking soda

½   teaspoon salt

Unsalted butter, for the griddle

Pure maple syrup, for serving

1. In a large bowl, stir the oats with the buttermilk. Add the grated apple, lemon zest, shortening, egg and nutmeg.

2. In a small bowl, stir the flour with the baking powder, baking soda and salt. Stir to combine. Add the dry ingredients to the oat mixture and stir until thoroughly combined.

3. Set a nonstick griddle over moderate heat. Lightly butter the griddle. Spoon 2 tablespoons of the batter onto the griddle for each pancake and use an offset spatula to spread each one into a 4-inch round. Cook the pancakes until the bottoms are golden and the tops are set, 2 to 3 minutes. Flip the pancakes and cook until golden, about 1 minute longer. Transfer the pancakes to plates and serve with maple syrup.

Editor's Note

This recipe comes from co-author Susan Reid. The oats and apples in the batter make sweet, satisfying, hearty pancakes. Reid says the lemony-sweet aroma of these pancakes cooking reminds her of a pleasant, gentle breeze—a zephyr.

The King Arthur Flour Cookie Companion

The King Arthur Flour Company

Gigi's Carrot Cake, PAGE 124

Emeril's Potluck

by Emeril Lagasse

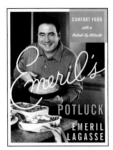

**Published by William Morrow,
336 pages, color photos, $24.95**

In his tenth cookbook, crowd-pleasing TV chef and restaurateur Emeril Lagasse aims to teach you how to entertain potluck-style. As Lagasse writes, his recipes are "straightforward, delicious and meant to be shared. Hey, simple can be kicked up, too!" Many of the dishes, like Penne à la Vodka and Risotto and Wild Mushrooms, have been "potlucked"—revamped as casseroles, making them both portable and easy to serve buffet-style. Lagasse kicks up the portions, too: Most of the recipes, from Curried Chicken Salad to Creole Breakfast Bread Pudding, are designed to serve eight to ten people.

Featured Recipes Gigi's Carrot Cake; Creole Breakfast Bread Pudding; Penne à la Vodka Casserole; Cheesy Chicken Tamales

Best of the Best Exclusive Crabmeat Fettuccine Carbonara

Gigi's Carrot Cake

Gigi's Carrot Cake is legendary among our friends. But, hey, you know how I like to kick things up a bit. For you purists, all of my additions are optional, but why not try them? Oh, and though this cake makes a beautiful presentation when baked in three cake pans as described here, for convenience and transportability, feel free to bake this in one 9 x 13-inch baking pan. Just keep in mind that you will need to adjust the baking time accordingly—40 to 45 minutes should do the trick.

MAKES ONE 9-INCH 3-LAYER CAKE, 10 TO 12 SERVINGS

- ¾ pound (3 sticks) plus 1 tablespoon unsalted butter
- ½ cup dried currants (optional)
- ¼ cup brandy (optional)
- 3 cups grated carrots
- 2 cups all-purpose flour
- 2 cups sugar
- 2 teaspoons baking soda
- 2 teaspoons ground cinnamon
- 1 teaspoon salt
- ⅛ teaspoon freshly grated nutmeg
- 4 large eggs
- 1 teaspoon pure vanilla extract
- 1 cup chopped toasted pecans (optional)
- ¼ cup finely chopped crystallized ginger (optional)

PECAN—CREAM CHEESE ICING

- 12 ounces cream cheese, at room temperature
- 10 tablespoons unsalted butter, at room temperature
- 1½ pounds confectioners' sugar, sifted
- 1½ teaspoons pure vanilla extract
- 1½ cups toasted pecans

1. Preheat the oven to 350°F. Butter three 9-inch cake pans with 1 tablespoon butter. Set aside.

2. In a small saucepan, combine the currants and brandy, if using, and heat until the brandy comes to a boil. Cover, remove from the heat, and allow the currants to "plump" until they've absorbed the brandy, 15 to 20 minutes.

3. Put the grated carrots in a medium bowl. Melt the remaining ¾ pound butter in a small saucepan and pour over the grated carrots. Stir to combine well and set aside.

4. Sift the flour, sugar, baking soda, cinnamon, salt, and nutmeg into a large mixing bowl. Add the eggs, one at a time, beating thoroughly after each addition. Add the vanilla, plumped currants, and the carrot-butter mixture and beat until thoroughly combined. Add the chopped nuts and crystallized ginger, if using, and stir to combine. Divide the batter evenly among the three prepared pans, and bake until a cake tester inserted in the center of each cake layer comes out clean, 22 to 25 minutes. Remove the cakes from the oven and allow to cool in the pans on a wire rack for 5 to 10 minutes before turning out onto a rack to cool. When the cakes have cooled completely, frost as directed below.

5. Meanwhile, make the icing by creaming the cream cheese and butter until smooth and fluffy, 2 to 3 minutes. Add the sugar and vanilla and mix on low speed until combined. Beat on high speed until the icing is smooth and creamy. Fold in the pecans.

6. When the cakes have cooled completely, place 1 layer on a cake plate and top with one-third of the frosting. Smooth the frosting to the edges of the top of the cake layer and then top with another layer. Repeat with another third of the frosting and smooth to the edges as before. Top with the remaining layer and finish frosting the top of the cake with the remaining frosting.

7. Serve immediately or refrigerate, wrapped in plastic wrap, until ready to serve, up to 2 days ahead.

GINGER Ginger is actually the root of a tropical plant found in Africa, the Caribbean, and Southeast Asia. Here, we use ginger in its candied form, meaning it has been preserved in sugar. Candied ginger is a great addition to all sorts of baked items from oatmeal cookies to gingerbread.

Emeril on His Legacy

I would like to be remembered as a caring person, a mentor for people interested in food and a good father. In 2002 I started the Emeril Lagasse Foundation because I wanted to make a difference in the lives of young children. Through the foundation I hope to mentor and inspire kids, especially those in disadvantaged circumstances.

Emeril's Potluck
Emeril Lagasse

Creole Breakfast Bread Pudding

This dish is ideal for any breakfast or brunch menu, and equally good at suppertime when served with a nice green salad and a simple soup to start. Linguiça sausage adds the right savory touch to kick this bread pudding up a notch or two. If you can't find linguiça where you live, substitute any garlicky smoked pork sausage.

8 TO 10 SERVINGS

- ½ pound linguiça sausage, removed from casings and chopped
- ½ cup minced yellow onions
- ¼ cup minced green bell peppers
- ⅓ cup sliced green onions
- ⅓ cup dry white wine
- 8 cups 1-inch cubes day-old French bread
- 2½ cups milk
- ½ cup heavy cream
- ¼ cup melted unsalted butter
- 8 large eggs, beaten
- ½ pound Pepper Jack cheese, grated
- ½ pound Monterey Jack cheese, grated
- ¾ teaspoon salt
- ⅛ teaspoon freshly ground black pepper
- ⅛ teaspoon cayenne pepper
- ¾ cup sour cream
- ½ cup grated Parmesan cheese

1. Preheat the oven to 325°F.

2. Heat a skillet over medium-high heat. Add the sausage and cook until golden brown and the fat is rendered, about 5 minutes. Add the onions and bell peppers, and sauté until soft, 3 minutes. Add the green onions and stir well. Add the white wine and reduce slightly, stirring, about 1 minute over high heat. Remove from the heat.

3. Place the bread in a large mixing bowl. Add the milk and cream and stir well. Let sit for 5 minutes.

4. Pour the melted butter into a 9 x 13-inch casserole dish, and coat the sides and bottom evenly. Pour any extra butter into the bread mixture.

5. Mix the sausage and bread mixtures. Add the eggs, grated Pepper Jack and Monterey Jack cheeses, salt, black pepper, and cayenne, and quickly fold together. Cover with aluminum foil and bake for 1 hour. Uncover and bake for 15 minutes. Remove the casserole from the oven and increase the temperature to 375°F. Spread the sour cream evenly over the top and cover with the Parmesan. Bake uncovered for 10 to 15 minutes, or until the casserole is lightly browned on top. Serve hot.

Lagasse on Creating Creole Flavors

The sausage, bell pepper and cayenne pepper give this bread pudding an unmistakable Creole taste.

Emeril's Potluck
Emeril Lagasse

Penne à la Vodka Casserole

Test Kitchen Tip
If you have trouble finding Emeril's Original Essence for this recipe, you can substitute 1 teaspoon of dried thyme and a pinch of cayenne for a similar effect.

A bit of vodka in pasta sauces gives them a real flavor boost. I like vodka sauce so much that I make one that can be found on the pasta aisle at your local grocery. But you know what? This homemade version is slightly different. Try it the next time you're craving Italian food.

10 TO 12 SERVINGS

4 tablespoons extra virgin olive oil

1 pound sweet Italian sausage, cut crosswise into 1-inch slices

1 pound hot Italian sausage, cut crosswise into 1-inch slices

4 cups thinly sliced onions

1¾ teaspoons salt

¾ teaspoon freshly ground black pepper

¼ cup thinly sliced fresh basil leaves

1 tablespoon minced garlic

½ cup vodka

Two 16-ounce cans whole tomatoes, crushed with their juice

1 teaspoon Emeril's Original Essence

½ cup heavy cream

1 tablespoon olive oil

1 pound penne pasta

15 ounces ricotta cheese

1 cup grated Parmigiano-Reggiano cheese

1½ cups grated mozzarella cheese

Crusty bread, for serving

1. Preheat the oven to 350°F.

2. Heat 2 tablespoons extra virgin olive oil in a large skillet or saucepan over high heat. Add the sausages and cook, stirring, until browned, 4 to 5 minutes. Add the onions, ¾ teaspoon salt, and the black pepper. Cook, stirring occasionally, until the onions are just soft, about 4 minutes. Add the basil and garlic, and cook, stirring, for 2 minutes. Add the vodka and tomatoes, reduce the heat to medium-low, and simmer, uncovered, stirring occasionally, for 40 minutes. Add the Essence and heavy cream, stir to mix, and simmer for 5 minutes. Remove from the heat.

Emeril's Potluck
Emeril Lagasse

3. To cook the pasta, combine 4 quarts water, the olive oil, and the remaining teaspoon salt in a large pot over high heat. Bring to a boil, add the pasta, and cook until al dente, 12 to 14 minutes. Remove from the heat and drain well. Combine half of the ricotta cheese and half of the Parmigiano-Reggiano with the remaining 2 tablespoons extra virgin olive oil in a large mixing bowl. Add the pasta and toss to coat evenly. Add the sausage mixture and mix well. Add the remaining ricotta cheese and the remaining Parmigiano-Reggiano and mix well.

4. Transfer the mixture to a 9 x 13-inch baking dish. Sprinkle with the mozzarella cheese. Bake until bubbly and golden, about 45 minutes. Remove from the oven. Serve warm with crusty bread.

Emeril's Potluck
Emeril Lagasse

Cheesy Chicken Tamales

Lagasse on Roasting Poblanos

I find that roasting poblanos over an open flame on my gas cooktop really gives them a nice flavor. Just be careful not to let them roast too long, since they are thin fleshed and can quickly burn! If your cooktop is electric, the next best method is to rub the peppers with a little oil and blister the skins under the broiler.

When you say *tamale,* most people think of the more common beef- or chili-filled variety—but these Cheesy Chicken Tamales are gonna knock your socks off! They're different, too, in that the outer tamale coating contains grits in addition to the masa harina—and this works well with the cheese, chicken, and poblano filling. Now, this recipe serves 4 to 6, but once you've mastered the art of tamale making, you might want to make a bigger batch for a party, and you'll find that this recipe can be scaled up proportionately with no problem.

MAKES APPROXIMATELY 18 TAMALES, 4 TO 6 SERVINGS

One 8-ounce package dried corn husks

⅔ cup quick-cooking or old-fashioned grits (not instant)

1¼ cups Chicken Stock (recipe follows), plus more for tamale batter if needed

¾ cup masa harina

2 teaspoons ground cumin

1 cup lard or vegetable shortening

1 teaspoon baking powder

½ teaspoon salt

1½ cups shredded cooked chicken meat

½ pound Monterey Jack or mild Cheddar cheese, coarsely grated

4 poblano chiles, roasted, seeded, peeled, and coarsely chopped

1. Combine the corn husks and enough water to cover in a medium saucepan and bring to a boil. Top the husks with a heavy plate or bowl to keep them submerged, and boil for 10 minutes. Remove the pan from the heat and steep until the husks are soft and pliable, 1 to 1½ hours. Drain the husks, remove any corn silk, and pat dry before assembling the tamales.

2. Process the grits in the bowl of a food processor for 1 minute. Bring the Chicken Stock to a low boil in a small saucepan. Transfer the grits to a large bowl and add the hot stock. Let stand, uncovered, for 10 to 12 minutes. Add the masa harina and cumin and mix until evenly combined. Cool to room temperature before proceeding.

Emeril's Potluck
Emeril Lagasse

3. In the bowl of an electric mixer fitted with the paddle attachment, whip the lard until smooth, light, and creamy, about 2 minutes. Stir in half of the masa mixture and whip until well blended. Add the remaining masa mixture, little by little, until the batter resembles thick cake batter, adding additional Chicken Stock if needed. Add the baking powder and salt and whip for 1 to 2 minutes, or until well incorporated and smooth.

4. Lay 1 corn husk on a work surface with the narrow end closest to you. Top with a second corn husk so that the fat ends overlap in the middle and the narrow ends point in opposite directions. Spoon ¼ cup of the masa batter into the center of the husks and, with the back of a spoon, spread it into a 4-inch square. Place about 1 generous tablespoon each of the chicken, grated cheese, and chopped poblanos in the center of the masa square.

5. Fold 1 side of the corn husk over the filling, fold the other side over the filling, and then the top and bottom ends. With a piece of kitchen string or a thin strip of leftover corn husk, tie the tamale together loosely so that it resembles an oblong rectangular package. Repeat with the remaining corn husks and filling.

6. Once the tamales are assembled, line a steamer basket with any remaining corn husks and layer the tamales inside the steamer basket, leaving enough room for the tamales to expand slightly while cooking. Cover the tamales with another corn husk, cover the steamer with a tight-fitting lid, and steam for 1½ hours, or until the tamales are tender and pull away easily from the corn husks. Let sit for 10 to 15 minutes before serving.

TAMALES Traditionally tamales are wrapped in a softened corn husk or banana leaf, but sometimes you will see them wrapped in paper instead. While the paper is a lot easier to use, it lacks that wonderful flavor imparted by husks or leaves.

Emeril's Potluck
Emeril Lagasse

Chicken Stock

If you've never made stock before, I urge you to try it. It is a simple process, the flavor is unequaled, and it beats that store-bought stuff any day of the week.

MAKES 3 QUARTS

- 4 pounds chicken bones
- 2 cups coarsely chopped yellow onions
- 1 cup coarsely chopped carrots
- 1 cup coarsely chopped celery
- 3 garlic cloves, smashed
- 4 bay leaves
- 1 teaspoon black peppercorns
- 2 teaspoons salt
- 1 teaspoon dried thyme
- ½ teaspoon dried rosemary
- ½ teaspoon dried oregano

1. Put all of the ingredients in a heavy 2-gallon stockpot. Add 1 gallon of water, which should cover the ingredients by 1 inch, and bring to a boil over high heat. Reduce the heat to medium-low and simmer, uncovered, for 2 hours, skimming the surface occasionally with a slotted spoon to remove any foam that rises to the surface.

2. Remove the pot from the heat and strain the stock through a fine-mesh sieve into a clean container. Let cool, then cover the stock and refrigerate in an airtight container for up to 3 days or freeze for up to 2 months.

CHICKEN STOCK Be sure to keep all stocks at a simmer as you cook them. This way the impurities will rise to the surface, allowing you to skim them off. If the stock is boiled, the impurities will reemulsify with the stock, resulting in a cloudy broth.

Emeril's Potluck
Emeril Lagasse

Best of the Best Exclusive
Crabmeat Fettuccine Carbonara

6 SERVINGS

1 pound fettuccine

2 tablespoons unsalted butter

1 medium yellow onion, halved lengthwise and thinly sliced

2 garlic cloves, minced

½ cup diced smoked ham, such as Black Forest (2 ounces)

½ cup dry white wine

1 pound jumbo lump crabmeat, picked over

2 large eggs

½ cup heavy cream

½ cup freshly grated Parmesan cheese

1 teaspoon kosher salt

1 teaspoon freshly ground black pepper

⅓ cup coarsely chopped basil

1. In a large pot of boiling salted water, cook the fettuccine until al dente.

2. Meanwhile, in a large skillet, melt the butter. Add the onion and cook over moderate heat until softened, about 4 minutes. Add the garlic and cook until fragrant, about 1 minute. Add the ham and cook for 1 minute longer. Add the white wine and boil until reduced by half, about 1 minute. Remove from the heat and fold in the crabmeat.

3. In a medium bowl, beat the eggs with the cream, Parmesan cheese and salt and pepper. Drain the fettuccine, reserving ⅓ cup of the pasta cooking water. Mix the cooking water into the beaten egg mixture. Return the fettuccine to the pot and toss with the egg sauce. Add the crab mixture and the basil and toss gently, being careful not to break up the lumps of crab. Transfer the pasta to warm bowls and serve.

Editor's Note

This riff on spaghetti carbonara quickly became a favorite at Emeril's New Orleans. If you can't track down sweet lump crabmeat, shrimp or crawfish tails make a nice replacement. But there's no substitute for the ham in this dish; it adds a smoky, complex flavor to the creamy sauce.

Emeril's Potluck
Emeril Lagasse

Ginger and Green Onion Burger
Topped with Thai-Style Slaw, PAGE 136

Lobel's Prime Cuts
by Stanley, Leon, Evan, Mark and David Lobel

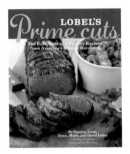

With Mary Goodbody, published by Chronicle Books, 248 pages, color and black-and-white photos, $29.95

Lobel's has been operating in Manhattan since the 1930s, and they are still one of the city's premier butchers. The family's second cookbook includes over 100 tasty recipes plus a wealth of advice on how to get the most out of both expensive and cheap cuts. "The inspiration for this tome," explains Stanley Lobel, "was our customers. They are always asking us questions about how to cook things!" This book provides plenty of good answers: Not only do these wily fifth-generation butchers know the A-to-Z of roasting and braising, they've also got a global culinary perspective.

Featured Recipes Ginger and Green Onion Burgers Topped with Thai-Style Slaw; Sesame-Coated Chicken Thighs with Bacon-Flavored Collard Greens; Spicy Ground Turkey Kabobs with Cucumber-Yogurt Sauce; Beef Stew Topped with Black Pepper Biscuit Crust

Best of the Best Exclusive Chicken with Vinegar Sauce

Ginger and Green Onion Burgers Topped with Thai-Style Slaw

The Lobels on Juicy Burgers

We like to lightly score an X in the top of our burgers before we cook them; it seems to help keep the juices that would normally flow out of the hamburger remain inside. This technique creates a really juicy burger.

We usually suggest this blend of meat to our customers for burgers: equal weights of ground sirloin and ground chuck. The chuck, with its higher fat content, provides moisture; the sirloin adds tenderness. The flavors of both commingle in beef heaven. (Ground chuck is from the forequarter and ground sirloin is from the hindquarter.) Serve these juicy burgers without bread, with an Asian-inspired slaw for a bright-tasting treat.

6 SERVINGS

- 1½ pounds ground sirloin
- 1½ pounds ground chuck
- 8 green onions, including some green parts, finely chopped
- 3 cloves garlic, minced
- ¼ cup soy sauce
- ¼ cup chopped fresh cilantro
- ¼ cup minced fresh ginger
- 1 teaspoon freshly ground pepper
- 1 teaspoon salt
- 1 tablespoon canola oil
- Thai-Style Slaw (recipe follows) for serving
- 1 to 2 teaspoons sesame seeds, lightly toasted (see Note)

1. Preheat the oven to 400°F.

2. In a large bowl, mix the beef with the green onions, garlic, soy sauce, cilantro, ginger, pepper, and salt. Work the ingredients into the beef just until evenly distributed. Do not overmix. Form the beef into 6 patties. Using a small knife, score a large "X" in the top of each patty. This will make the burger juicier.

3. Heat a large ovenproof skillet over medium-high heat. Add the oil and sear the burgers for 2 to 3 minutes on each side. Transfer the skillet to the oven and cook for 2 to 3 minutes, turning once, for medium-rare. (If you prefer, cook the burgers on the stove top, but finishing them in the oven promotes even cooking.)

Lobel's Prime Cuts

Stanley, Leon, Evan, Mark and David Lobel

4. Put a burger on each plate. Top each one with slaw. Garnish with a sprinkling of sesame seeds.

NOTE To toast sesame seeds, spread the seeds in a single layer in a small, dry skillet. Toast over medium heat, stirring constantly, for 20 to 30 seconds, or until fragrant and darkened by a shade. Immediately slide the seeds onto a cool plate to cool.

Thai-Style Slaw

6 SERVINGS

- 5 cups (about 1 pound total) finely shredded green or red cabbage, or a mixture
- 2 large carrots, peeled and julienned
- 2 green onions, cut into 2-inch-long julienne
- ¼ cup chopped fresh cilantro
- 3 tablespoons soy sauce
- 2 tablespoons toasted sesame oil
- 2 tablespoons fresh lime juice

Salt and freshly ground pepper to taste

1. In a large bowl, toss the cabbage, carrots, green onions, and cilantro together.

2. In a small bowl, whisk the soy sauce, oil, and lime juice together. Pour the dressing over the vegetables, toss, and set aside at room temperature for at least 30 minutes but no longer than 1 hour. Add salt and pepper.

Lobel's Prime Cuts

Stanley, Leon, Evan, Mark and David Lobel

Sesame-Coated Chicken Thighs with Bacon-Flavored Collard Greens

In the South, sesame seeds have long been a popular ingredient, although they're likely to be called benne seeds there. These flavorful chicken thighs, coated with honey (use tupelo honey, if you can find it) and sesame seeds, are baked and then served with collard greens cooked quickly in bacon fat. If you prefer, use spinach or mustard greens in place of collards.

6 SERVINGS

6 large or 12 small chicken thighs (about 3 pounds total)
Salt and freshly ground pepper to taste
¼ to ½ cup all-purpose flour
¼ cup canola oil
½ cup tupelo or clover honey
2 tablespoons sesame seeds
Bacon-Flavored Collard Greens (recipe follows) for serving

1. Preheat the oven to 350°F.

2. Sprinkle the chicken with salt and pepper. Dredge the chicken in the flour, shaking off the excess.

3. In a large cast-iron or heavy ovenproof skillet, heat the oil over medium heat. Add the chicken thighs, skin-side down, and sear for 2 to 3 minutes on each side, or until golden brown.

4. With the thighs skin-side up, liberally brush with the honey and sprinkle with the sesame seeds. Transfer the skillet to the oven and bake for 30 to 35 minutes, or until opaque throughout and an instant-read thermometer inserted in a thigh and not touching bone registers 180°F.

5. To serve, spread the collard greens on a warmed platter and arrange the chicken thighs on top.

Lobel's Prime Cuts

Stanley, Leon, Evan, Mark and David Lobel

Bacon-Flavored Collard Greens

6 SERVINGS

- 1 tablespoon canola oil
- 8 ounces thick-sliced bacon or salt pork, cut into ½-inch pieces
- 1 large yellow onion, thinly sliced

Salt and freshly ground pepper to taste

- 3 to 4 cloves garlic, minced
- 3 to 3½ pounds collard greens, large ribs removed, rinsed and coarsely chopped

Pinch of red pepper flakes

1. In a large, heavy skillet, heat the oil over medium heat and sauté the bacon for 5 to 7 minutes, or until crisp. Using a slotted spoon, transfer to paper towels to drain.

2. Add the onion and sauté for 10 to 12 minutes, or until softened and golden brown. Season with salt and pepper and add the garlic. Sauté for 1 to 2 minutes.

3. Add the collard greens and sauté for 8 to 10 minutes, or until the greens have softened. Season to taste with salt and pepper. Add the pepper flakes and bacon. Toss for 1 to 2 minutes to heat through.

Lobel's Prime Cuts

Stanley, Leon, Evan, Mark and David Lobel

Spicy Ground Turkey Kabobs with Cucumber-Yogurt Sauce

We tuck oven-baked turkey patties into pita breads and top them with sliced tomatoes and a light, easy yogurt sauce. Reminiscent of Middle Eastern falafel, these sandwiches are a little fancier than an ordinary burger. The ground turkey is mixed with mashed potatoes to make it moist and keep it from falling apart when threaded on skewers. Make the quick, easy mashed potatoes here, or use leftovers.

6 SERVINGS

   5 ounces red or white potatoes, peeled
   1 tablespoon heavy cream
   2 tablespoons unsalted butter
1¾ pounds ground turkey breast
   1 yellow onion, finely chopped
   2 cloves garlic, minced
   1 tablespoon grated fresh ginger
   1 teaspoon ground cumin
   1 teaspoon cayenne pepper
   1 teaspoon salt
   ½ teaspoon ground coriander
   ½ teaspoon freshly ground pepper
   2 tablespoons minced fresh flat-leaf parsley
   1 tablespoon fresh lemon juice
   1 tablespoon canola oil
   6 pita breads, warmed
   4 plum tomatoes, seeded and diced
Cucumber-Yogurt Sauce (recipe follows) for serving
   ½ cup fresh cilantro leaves

1. In a saucepan of salted boiling water, cook the potatoes for 15 to 20 minutes, or until tender. Drain, mash with a fork, and add the cream and 1 tablespoon butter. Mash well to combine and set aside to cool.

2. Soak twelve 10-inch wooden skewers in water for at least 20 minutes.

3. In a large bowl, mix the ground turkey with the cooled potatoes until blended.

Lobel's Prime Cuts

Stanley, Leon, Evan, Mark and David Lobel

4. In a large skillet, melt the remaining 1 tablespoon butter over medium heat and sauté the onion and garlic for about 1 minute. Add the ginger, cumin, cayenne, salt, coriander, and pepper and sauté for about 1 minute, or until aromatic. Remove from the heat and let cool for about 5 minutes.

5. Add the onion mixture, parsley, and lemon juice to the turkey mixture. Using your hands, mix well. Use now, or cover and refrigerate for up to 12 hours.

6. To make the kabobs, shape about 2 tablespoons of the turkey mixture into an oval about 2 inches long and 1 inch wide. Repeat to make 18 patties. Thread 3 patties lengthwise onto 2 parallel skewers, spacing them evenly. (The parallel skewers hold the kabobs so they won't slip.) Place on a waxed paper–lined tray or roasting pan. Repeat with the remaining skewers and patties. Cover and refrigerate for about 30 minutes.

7. Preheat the oven to 400°F. Line a heavy jelly-roll pan with aluminum foil and brush with the canola oil.

8. Put the foil-lined pan in the oven for 5 minutes. Transfer the skewers to the hot pan and bake for 9 minutes. Turn the skewers and bake about 8 minutes longer, or until opaque throughout.

9. Slide the kabobs from each skewer into a warm pita bread. Top with tomatoes and cucumber sauce and garnish with cilantro.

Lobel's Prime Cuts
Stanley, Leon, Evan, Mark and David Lobel

Cucumber-Yogurt Sauce

MAKES ABOUT 2 CUPS

- 1 cup plain yogurt
- 1 cup diced cucumber
- ½ cup sour cream
- 1 clove garlic, minced
- 2 tablespoons minced fresh mint
- 1 tablespoon finely chopped green onion tops
- ½ teaspoon ground cumin
- ½ teaspoon salt

1. In a medium bowl, combine all the ingredients and stir to blend.

2. Cover and refrigerate for at least 1 hour or up to 24 hours.

Brothers Leon and Stanley flank their sons Evan, David and Mark

Lobel's Prime Cuts

Stanley, Leon, Evan, Mark and David Lobel

Beef Stew Topped with Black Pepper Biscuit Crust

6 SERVINGS

5 to 6 pounds boneless chuck roast or brisket, cut into 1½-inch cubes

Salt and freshly ground pepper to taste

3 tablespoons canola oil

2 yellow onions, coarsely chopped

2 carrots, peeled and cut into 1-inch lengths

3 to 4 stalks celery, coarsely chopped

3 cloves garlic, minced

4 cups Beef Stock (recipe follows)

½ cup dry red wine

Bouquet garni (3 rosemary sprigs, 4 flat-leaf parsley sprigs, 1 bay leaf, 3 to 4 peppercorns)

BISCUIT CRUST

1⅓ cups all-purpose flour

2 tablespoons baking powder

1 tablespoon sugar

1 heaping tablespoon cracked pepper

2 teaspoons salt

4 tablespoons cold unsalted butter, cut into pieces

½ cup whole milk

1 tablespoon unsalted butter, melted

Minced fresh flat-leaf parsley for garnish (optional)

1. Preheat the oven to 350°F.

2. Pat the beef cubes dry with paper towels and sprinkle with salt and pepper.

3. In a large Dutch oven or flameproof casserole, heat 2 tablespoons of the oil over medium-high heat. Sear the beef cubes on all sides until nicely browned. Don't move the meat too much in the pot; let it sear so that it develops a nice browned crust. Transfer the beef cubes to a plate. Pour off the oil from the pot.

4. Return the pot to medium heat and add the remaining 1 tablespoon oil. Add the onions, carrots, and celery and sauté for about 3 minutes, or until the vegetables begin to soften. Add the garlic and sauté for 2 to 3 minutes.

The Lobels' Elegant Variation

We top this stew with a peppery baking powder biscuit crust, which needs to be removed before serving. Yes, this is a little awkward, but the crust tastes so good when allowed to mingle with the gravy, we think it's well worth it—and really, no one will mind. If you prefer a more elegant presentation, make these in individual crocks (as pictured on page 145).

Lobel's Prime Cuts

Stanley, Leon, Evan, Mark and David Lobel

5. Add the stock and wine and stir to scrape up the browned bits from the bottom of the pan. Return the meat and any accumulated juices to the pot.

6. Make a bouquet garni by tying the rosemary and parsley sprigs, bay leaf, and peppercorns in a square of cheesecloth. Put the bouquet garni in the pot.

7. Cover the pot and braise in the oven for 2 hours and 15 minutes, or until tender, stirring the stew several times.

8. Meanwhile, make the biscuit crust: In a medium bowl, whisk the flour, baking powder, sugar, cracked pepper, and salt together. Using your fingertips, a fork, or a pastry cutter, work the butter into the dry ingredients until the mixture resembles coarse crumbs.

9. Add the milk all at once and stir just until the dough comes together in a mass.

10. Turn the dough out onto a lightly floured surface and knead 8 to 10 times, or just until cohesive. Using a rolling pin or your hands, roll or pat the dough into a circle or oval about ¼ inch thick.

11. Remove the stew from the oven, uncover, and lay the dough on top. It will not fit perfectly or seal tightly. This is a rough topping. Brush the dough with the melted butter.

12. Return the stew to the oven and cook, uncovered, for 12 to 15 minutes, or until the crust is golden brown.

13. To serve, remove the crust from the pan and set aside. Serve the stew with the vegetables. Cut the crust into pieces and top the meat with the crust. Ladle sauce from the stew over the crust, meat, and vegetables. Garnish with minced parsley, if desired.

VARIATION

To serve in 6 individual onion soup crocks or similarly sized ovenproof dishes, put the meat into the crocks with the vegetables and sauce from the stew. Increase the oven temperature to 425°F.

Make the biscuit dough and roll it into a round about ½ inch thick. Cut the dough into 6 rounds large enough to overlap the bowls by about ½ inch. Lay the rounds over the crocks and crimp the edges to seal. Brush with melted butter and set the crocks on a baking sheet. Bake for 12 to 14 minutes, or until the crusts are golden brown.

Lobel's Prime Cuts
Stanley, Leon, Evan,
Mark and David Lobel

Individual Beef Stews Topped
with Black Pepper Biscuit Crust

Beef Stock

MAKES ABOUT 8 CUPS

- 1 pound meaty beef bones
- 2 tablespoons canola oil
- 1 yellow onion, coarsely chopped
- 3 carrots, peeled and cut into large chunks
- 3 stalks celery, coarsely chopped
- 1 sprig *each* thyme, marjoram, and tarragon
- 1 tablespoon peppercorns
- 2 bay leaves
- 10 cups water

1. Rinse the beef bones under cold water.

2. In a large stockpot, heat the oil over low heat and cook the onion, carrots, and celery for about 5 minutes, stirring occasionally, or until softened but not colored. Stir in the herb sprigs, peppercorns, and bay leaves.

3. Add the bones and water to the pot. Bring to a boil over medium heat and skim any foam that rises to the surface. Reduce the heat to low and simmer gently, uncovered, for 2 to 3 hours, or until flavorful.

4. Strain the stock through a fine-mesh sieve into a large bowl. Discard the bones and vegetables. Set the bowl in a larger bowl or a sink filled with ice water to cool. When cool, cover and refrigerate until chilled. Remove the layer of congealed fat from the surface. Transfer to covered containers and refrigerate for up to 3 days or freeze for up to 3 months.

Lobel's Prime Cuts

Stanley, Leon, Evan,
Mark and David Lobel

Chicken with Vinegar Sauce

4 SERVINGS

- 2 tablespoons unsalted butter
- 2 tablespoons vegetable oil

One 4-pound chicken, cut into 8 pieces, liver reserved

Kosher salt and freshly ground pepper

- 4 large garlic cloves, minced
- 3 small shallots, finely chopped
- ¾ cup dry white wine
- ¾ cup red wine vinegar
- 1 tablespoon tomato paste
- 1 cup beef stock or low-sodium broth

1. In a large enameled cast-iron casserole, melt the butter in the oil. Season the chicken with salt and pepper, add it to the casserole and cook over moderately high heat, turning once, until browned, about 10 minutes. Transfer the chicken to a plate. Add the chicken liver to the casserole and cook until browned, about 3 minutes. Finely chop the liver and reserve it for the sauce.

2. Pour off all but 4 tablespoons of fat from the casserole. Add the garlic and shallots and cook over low heat, stirring occasionally, until translucent, about 2 minutes. Increase the heat to moderately high. Add the wine and vinegar and simmer until reduced by one-third, scraping up any browned bits from the pan, about 4 minutes. Stir in the tomato paste, stock and ½ teaspoon of salt.

3. Return the legs, thighs and wings to the casserole. Cover partially and simmer for 30 minutes, turning the pieces occasionally. Add the chicken breasts, cover partially and cook until all of the pieces are cooked through, about 15 minutes longer.

4. Preheat the broiler. Transfer the chicken to a foil-lined baking sheet, skin side up. Using a paper towel, pat the chicken skin dry. Broil the chicken 3 inches from the heat for 2 minutes, or until the skin is browned and crisp.

5. Boil the sauce until it has reduced to 1½ cups, about 4 minutes. Add the reserved chicken liver and season with salt and pepper. Transfer the chicken to a platter, spoon the sauce on top and serve at once.

Editor's Note

This chicken recipe is a sneak preview of the forthcoming *Lobel's Meat and Wine Cookbook* (Chronicle, 2006). The sauce gets its richness from chopped chicken liver and its tang from red wine vinegar. The Lobels like to serve this dish with braised and browned pearl onions and thinly sliced fried potatoes. You could also serve it with steamed white rice or crusty bread to soak up the amazing sauce.

Lobel's Prime Cuts

Stanley, Leon, Evan, Mark and David Lobel

Alpine Baked Pasta, PAGE 150

Nightly Specials
by Michael Lomonaco

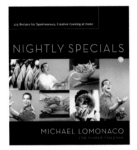

And Andrew Friedman, published by William Morrow, 320 pages, color photos, $34.95

New York City chef Michael Lomonaco was inspired to write his second book, *Nightly Specials,* by his love of spur-of-the-moment cooking: "I want to teach you how to create your own nightly specials—simple, improvised dishes that can be selected at the last minute." Lomonaco wants to train you to think like a chef, encouraging you to weave together fresh foods that you might pick up at the green market with pantry staples. This approach results in recipes that can take as little as 10 minutes. As a bonus, most appear with suggestions for tweaking the dish—substituting fresh basil for sage in the Alpine Baked Pasta, for instance.

Featured Recipes Alpine Baked Pasta; Red Snapper with Littleneck Clams and Tomatoes; Steamed Bass with Lemongrass and Chile-Coconut Broth; Black Currant–Lacquered Duck Breast

Best of the Best Exclusive Fettuccine with Warm Salmon, Tomatoes and Fresh Herbs

149

Alpine Baked Pasta

My first job out of cooking school was working for a team of Swiss chefs. They loved pasta, especially with rich sauces. One recipe they adored featured pasta and potatoes tossed with a cheesy cream sauce. Through our nightly staff, or "family," meals, I became familiar with some of their high-altitude, rustic cooking.

This recipe combines two favorites of my Italian-American upbringing—macaroni and cheese and baked ziti—in the style of my Swiss mentors. It's included here for two reasons: first, it's a delicious, full-flavored dish, a one-pot pasta with a crunchy crust. Second, it demonstrates how you can bring your personal experiences into the kitchen.

6 TO 8 MAIN-COURSE SERVINGS

4 tablespoons (½ stick) unsalted butter, plus more for the dish

Fine sea salt and freshly ground black pepper

2 tablespoons chopped sage

1 tablespoon poppy seeds

1 pound dried penne pasta

1 leek (white part plus 1 inch of green), well washed and thinly sliced crosswise (about 1 cup)

1 bunch spinach, well washed, tough stems removed, coarsely chopped (about 2 cups)

1 cup finely grated fontina

¾ cup finely grated Parmigiano-Reggiano

½ cup heavy cream

1. Preheat the oven to 375°F. Butter a shallow, 12-inch-square baking dish and set it aside.

2. Pour 6 quarts water into a large, heavy-bottomed pot and bring the water to a boil over high heat. Add 2 tablespoons salt.

3. While waiting for the water to boil, melt the 4 tablespoons butter in a pan over medium heat. When the butter becomes a light nut brown, add the sage and poppy seeds, remove the pan from the heat, and set aside.

Nightly Specials
Michael Lomonaco

4. When the water has boiled, add the pasta. When the water returns to a boil, begin to time the pasta carefully; after 8 minutes, add the leek. After the water has again returned to a boil, add the spinach and cook for an additional 2 minutes. Drain the pasta and vegetables in a colander, return them to the hot pot, add the sage butter, 1 teaspoon salt, 1 teaspoon pepper, the fontina, Parmigiano-Reggiano, and cream and toss well to incorporate the ingredients.

5. Turn the pasta out into the greased baking dish. Bake for 12 to 15 minutes, until the cheese has melted and the top edges begin to brown.

6. Serve family style from the center of the table.

YOUR NIGHTLY SPECIALS

• BAKED PASTA PRIMAVERA To create a baked pasta primavera—an excellent side dish to roasted meats and fish—use half as much pasta and a total of 3 to 4 cups blanched, chopped spinach, leeks, broccoli, mushrooms, zucchini, and/or carrots. Use Gruyère cheese to allow the dish to be paired successfully with as many dishes as possible. (Blue and fontina cheeses are too assertive for this recipe and Parmesan alone won't make enough of an impact.)

• ONE OR MORE OF THE FOLLOWING cheeses would be delicious in place of those in the recipe: mozzarella, Taleggio and/or Gruyère.

• OTHER LARGE PASTA SHAPES such as rigatoni, farfalle (bow ties), or orecchiette (ear shaped) also work well.

• FOR A SUBTLE DIFFERENCE, replace the leek and spinach with zucchini, cut into matchsticks and blanched. Finish with some chopped fresh tomato, whose acidity will fill in for the leek's earthy onion flavor.

• USE BLANCHED SWISS CHARD leaves for the spinach or in addition to it to add a richer vegetal flavor.

• FRESH OR DRIED BASIL and parsley are perfect substitutes for the sage and poppy seeds.

Lomonaco on Easy Cleanup

Rather than piling pots high in the kitchen, organize your cooking so that you can use a pot twice. There's nothing wrong with sautéing something in a pan, wiping it out with paper towels, and then sautéing something else for the meal in the same pan.

Nightly Specials
Michael Lomonaco

Red Snapper with Littleneck Clams and Tomatoes

Red snapper is one of the finest eating fish that's commonly available. If it's not available, make this with farm-raised striped bass, which bears little resemblance, in both size (much smaller) and flavor (more subtle), to wild striped bass. But it does have the charm of being regularly available, clean tasting, and versatile.

4 SERVINGS

2	tablespoons olive oil
1	tablespoon unsalted butter
1½	pounds red snapper fillet, cut into 4 pieces

Fine sea salt and freshly ground black pepper

2	garlic cloves, minced
½	pound ripe plum tomatoes, peeled, seeded, and chopped (about 1½ cups)
20	basil leaves, cut into julienne
1	cup dry white wine
12	littleneck clams in their shells, scrubbed under cold running water

1. Heat the olive oil and butter in a heavy-bottomed sauté pan with a lid over medium heat. Season the fish with salt and pepper. Add the fish, skin side down, to the pan and cook over medium heat until browned on both sides, about 3 minutes per side. Transfer the fish to a plate and cover with foil to keep warm.

2. Add the garlic to the pan and sauté for 1 minute. Add the tomatoes and cook for 2 minutes. Add the basil and wine and bring to a boil over high heat, then lower the heat so the liquid is simmering.

3. Return the fish to the pan, resting it on top of the tomatoes. Scatter the clams around the fish, cover the pan with a lid, and steam until the clams open, about 3 minutes. Discard any clams that have not opened.

4. Divide the fish, clams, and broth among 4 rimmed plates or bowls and serve.

TO PEEL TOMATOES Bring a large pot of water to a boil. Fill a large bowl halfway with ice water. Score the ends of the tomatoes, cut out the stem ends, and put them in the boiling water. After 20 seconds, use tongs to remove the tomatoes from the water and transfer them to the ice water. As they cool, the skin will begin to pull away from the flesh. Remove the tomatoes and peel them with a paring knife.

YOUR NIGHTLY SPECIALS

- INSTEAD OF SNAPPER, use sea trout or orange roughy.

- USE MUSSELS instead of clams; cook them for 1 or 2 minutes longer.

- SCATTER A TEASPOON OF CHOPPED FRESH HERBS like oregano and/or parsley over each portion just before serving.

- FINISH EACH SERVING with a drizzle of extra virgin olive oil and/or lemon juice.

- ADD CHILES to the broth.

- ADD A TABLESPOON OF PEELED, MINCED GINGER and a dash of soy sauce to the broth.

Lomonaco on Cleaning Clams

I think the key thing is using lots of cold running water and scrubbing the shells thoroughly—they pick up a lot of sand.

Nightly Specials
Michael Lomonaco

Steamed Bass with Lemongrass and Chile-Coconut Broth

For decades now, steaming has been one of the preferred cooking techniques of the health- and weight-conscious, which might explain why even accomplished home cooks overlook it as an effective way to transmit flavor to vegetables, fish, and poultry. Steaming cooks fish so cleanly, without the use of butter or oil, that even captured in vapor, the flavor of the aromatic ingredients takes to the fish here. And steaming is less aggressive than even poaching would be, though this aromatic broth could be used as a poaching liquid. You will need a bamboo basket steamer.

4 MAIN-COURSE SERVINGS

½ cup bottled clam juice

½ cup dry sherry

2 tablespoons plus 2 teaspoons soy sauce

½ cup unsweetened coconut milk

2 or 3 lemongrass stalks, crushed

2 tablespoons peeled, minced ginger

1 dried chile or ¼ teaspoon crushed red pepper flakes

¼ cup chopped scallions, plus more for serving

12 large shiitake mushrooms, stems removed and discarded

1 small bok choy, halved and sliced lengthwise into wedges

1 tablespoon Thai red curry paste, or to taste (many supermarket brands are available)

Lettuce leaves, for lining the steamer basket

Four 8-ounce boneless sea bass or striped bass fillets, skin on

Fine sea salt and freshly ground black pepper

Coconut-Scented Basmati Rice (recipe follows)

1. Pour the clam juice, sherry, soy sauce, and coconut milk into a heavy-bottomed sauté pan or pot the same diameter as your bamboo steaming basket and bring the mixture to a boil over high heat. Reduce the heat so the liquid is simmering and add the lemongrass, ginger, chile, scallions, mushrooms, bok choy, and curry paste. Continue to simmer gently for 15 minutes to let the flavors mingle.

Lomonaco on Lemongrass

The bulb end of a stalk of lemongrass is where most of the flavorful and aromatic volatile oils are found. Just give the bulb a sharp, crushing rap with the flat side of a knife to release them.

Nightly Specials
Michael Lomonaco

Thai red curry paste can
be very hot. If you aren't
fond of spicy foods, go
light on the paste and
skip the dried chile.

2. Arrange a layer of lettuce leaves in the steamer basket to keep the fish from touching the raw bamboo. Season the fillets with salt and pepper and arrange them on the lettuce in the steamer. Set the steamer over the simmering liquid, cover with the bamboo cover, lower the heat, and steam gently until the fish is cooked through, 8 to 9 minutes.

3. Remove the steamer from the pot. Use tongs to remove the bok choy and mushrooms from the liquid and divide them decoratively among 4 dinner plates or wide, shallow bowls. Arrange the fish fillets on top of the vegetables on each plate. Pass the rice family style from the bowl.

4. Use tongs to fish out and discard the lemongrass and ladle a little of the broth over the fish on each plate. Scatter some scallions over each serving and serve.

YOUR NIGHTLY SPECIALS

• PERCH, TILAPIA, AND FLOUNDER all steam very well and can be used instead of sea bass. You can also make this with shrimp and/or scallops. Cooking times vary, based on the size of the shellfish.

• THE STEAMING TECHNIQUE has almost endless applications. For example, you can take this dish in a Southwestern direction by omitting the coconut milk, lemongrass, and ginger, adding some cider vinegar, crumbling a dried chipotle pepper into the broth, and adding 1 teaspoon ground cumin. Serve the fish as it is here, passing flour tortillas alongside.

Nightly Specials
Michael Lomonaco

Coconut-Scented Basmati Rice

4 TO 6 SIDE-DISH SERVINGS

- 2 tablespoons olive oil
- 1 small onion, minced (about ½ cup)
- 2 cups basmati rice, or other similar long-grained rice, picked over for stones and rinsed of excess starch
- 1 bay leaf

Fine sea salt

- 3 cups homemade chicken stock, low-sodium, store-brought chicken broth, vegetable broth, or water, simmering in a pot set over medium heat

Freshly ground white pepper

- 5 tablespoons unsalted butter
- ½ cup unsweetened coconut milk
- ¼ cup chopped cilantro

1. Heat the oil in a large, heavy-bottomed pot over medium heat. Add the onion and sauté until softened but not browned, about 4 minutes. Add the rice and stir to coat well with the oil, then add the bay leaf, 1 teaspoon salt, and hot broth. Season lightly with pepper. Bring to a boil over high heat, cover the pot with a tight-fitting lid, reduce the heat, and let simmer, removing the lid occasionally to stir with a fork to prevent scorching, until the grains are fully cooked but not clumped together, 18 to 20 minutes.

2. Use tongs to remove and discard the bay leaf. Use a fork to gently stir and separate the grains and stir in the butter, coconut milk, and cilantro.

3. Transfer the rice to a serving dish, or spoon it alongside other components, and serve at once.

YOUR NIGHTLY SPECIALS
- ADD TOASTED COCONUT, raisins plumped in hot water, and/or crushed almonds or walnuts during the last few minutes of cooking.
- ADD ⅛ TEASPOON CAYENNE pepper while the rice is cooking.
- ADD A PEELED, JULIENNED LARGE CARROT while the rice is cooking.
- FOR SAFFRON RICE, add a pinch of saffron threads to the broth.

Nightly Specials
Michael Lomonaco

Black Currant–Lacquered Duck Breast

This dish is much simpler than it reads or looks. The duck is pan-roasted on the stovetop and the lacquer comes together quickly in the same pan. The combination takes its cue from the hoisin sauce that's traditionally served with Peking duck to balance the rich, crisp-skinned bird with sweet relief.

4 SERVINGS

Four 6- to 8-ounce whole duck breasts, or two 1-pound
  magret duck breasts (from a Moulard duck)
Fine sea salt and freshly ground black pepper
  3 **tablespoons chopped shallots**
  1 **tablespoon grated ginger**
  2 **tablespoons honey**
  ½ **cup black currant jam**
  ¼ **cup cider vinegar**

1. Preheat the oven to 375°F.

2. With the point of a knife, score the skin side of the duck breasts in a crosshatch pattern, being careful not to pierce the flesh. This helps release and render the layer of fat under the skin and makes the finished duck look stunning.

3. Heat a sauté pan over medium heat for 2 minutes. Season the duck breasts with salt and pepper. Put the breasts in the pan, skin side down, and cook over medium to low heat to render the fat and brown the skin, 6 to 8 minutes. Carefully drain off and discard any accumulated fat from the pan and return the pan to the stove.

4. Carefully turn the breasts over and brown the flesh side for 3 to 4 minutes, or several more minutes for magret breasts. Remove the breasts to a plate and cover to keep warm.

5. Add the shallots to the pan and return the pan to the heat. Sauté the shallots until softened but not browned, 2 minutes, then add the ginger, honey, jam, and vinegar and stir. Bring to a simmer and let simmer for 2 or 3 minutes to reduce and thicken to a lacquer-like glaze.

Nightly Specials
Michael Lomonaco

6. Put the breasts, skin side up, on a nonstick cookie sheet, brush some lacquer on the upward-facing side of each breast, and reheat in the oven for 3 minutes.

7. To serve, slice the breasts lengthwise or crosswise and arrange the slices of 1 breast on each of 4 plates. Quickly reheat the sauce, if necessary, and drizzle some around the duck breasts.

YOUR NIGHTLY SPECIALS

• SEMI-BONELESS QUAIL can be cooked following the same recipe and cooking times.

• IN THE SUMMER, grill chicken breasts with the skin on, basting with the lacquer as they cook.

Nightly Specials
Michael Lomonaco

Fettuccine with Warm Salmon, Tomatoes and Fresh Herbs

4 SERVINGS

¾ pound skinless salmon fillet, sliced crosswise ¼ inch thick

¼ cup plus 2 tablespoons extra-virgin olive oil

3 tablespoons unsalted butter, cut into cubes, at room temperature

1 pound ripe plum tomatoes—halved, seeded and cut into ½-inch dice

¼ cup coarsely chopped dill

¼ cup coarsely chopped flat-leaf parsley

Kosher salt and freshly ground pepper

1 pound fettuccine

1. Cut the salmon into ½-inch-wide strips. In a large serving bowl, combine the salmon with the olive oil, butter, tomatoes, dill and parsley. Season with salt and pepper.

2. In a large pot of boiling salted water, cook the fettuccine until al dente. Drain the pasta, reserving ¼ cup of the cooking water. Transfer the pasta to the bowl with the salmon and toss until the butter melts and the salmon is warmed through, adding the pasta water 1 tablespoon at a time until a sauce forms. Season the fettuccine with salt and pepper and serve.

Editor's Note

Lomonaco points out that this recipe is a great example of "save-a-step cooking": The fresh salmon is sliced so thinly that it actually cooks when stirred together with the steaming hot pasta. Adding a splash of the pasta cooking water creates a simple, light sauce. And because the ingredients are just barely cooked, each retains its fresh flavor and texture. This recipe will be featured in a forthcoming book from Lomonaco.

Nightly Specials
Michael Lomonaco

Tuscan Bean and
Spelt Soup, PAGE 164

The Spiaggia Cookbook

by Tony Mantuano

And Cathy Mantuano, published by Chronicle Books, 192 pages, color photos, $40

"I don't see why the majority of Italian restaurants only have to be about mama's home cooking and not high style," says Tony Mantuano, the chef and partner at Chicago's famed Spiaggia. "My food is all about luxury." In his first-ever cookbook, Mantuano emphasizes Italian dishes centered on decadent ingredients, with recipes like Kobe Beef Tartare with Truffle, Celery and Parmigiano-Reggiano. As a counterpoint, he also provides a few simple and delicious dishes like Tuscan Bean and Spelt Soup. Ideal for ambitious cooks ready to leave red sauce behind and explore a new world of haute Italian cuisine.

Featured Recipes Tuscan Bean and Spelt Soup; Boneless Pork Chop with White Corn Polenta and Broccoli Rabe; Crescenza Ravioli with Parmigiano-Reggiano and Truffle Butter Sauce

Best of the Best Exclusive Lemon Panna Cotta

Tuscan Bean and Spelt Soup

Zuppa Gran Faro

This soup, a traditional Tuscan dish made with spelt, is a specialty of the area around Lucca. Trattoria La Mora in Ponte a Moriano, just outside of Lucca, is a busy restaurant on the road to Abetone, a popular ski town. The Brunicardi family, the owners of the trattoria, warm up many skiers with this incredible hot and hearty fare. Spelt is an ancient cereal grain with a nutty flavor that has a higher protein content than wheat. It can be found in natural foods stores and well-stocked supermarkets.

MAKES 8 CUPS

- ¼ cup olive oil
- 1 ounce prosciutto, diced
- 1 ounce pancetta, diced
- 1 slice bacon, diced
- ⅓ cup chopped celery
- ⅓ cup peeled and diced carrot
- ⅓ cup diced yellow onion
- 2 cloves garlic, chopped
- 1¾ cups dried white beans such as cannellini or Great Northern, picked over, rinsed, and soaked in cold water to cover overnight
- 8 cups Chicken Stock (recipe follows) or prepared broth
- One 16-ounce can Italian plum tomatoes, preferably San Marzano, with their juices, or 16 ounces Italian tomato purée
- 2 large sprigs fresh rosemary
- 1 cup spelt (see recipe introduction)
- Extra-virgin olive oil for drizzling
- Parmigiano-Reggiano or Parmesan cheese shavings for garnish
- 12 sprigs chervil for garnish

In a large stockpot over medium-low heat, heat the olive oil. Add the prosciutto, pancetta, and bacon and sauté until crisp, 7 to 10 minutes. Add the celery, carrot, onion, and garlic and continue to sauté until slightly caramelized, about 8 minutes. Drain the beans and add to the pot with the stock. Pass the tomatoes through a food mill and add to the pot with the rosemary. Raise the heat to medium-high, bring to a simmer, and then reduce the heat to low and cook until the beans are tender, about 40 minutes. Discard the rosemary.

Meanwhile, put the spelt in a medium saucepan of lightly salted water and bring to a boil over high heat. Reduce the heat to medium-low and cook until al dente (tender but firm to the bite), about 25 minutes. Drain and set aside.

Purée the soup in small batches in a blender or food processor until smooth and transfer to a heavy saucepan. (The soup should be on the thick side, but can be thinned with more stock or water to the desired consistency.) Reheat gently.

Divide the spelt among warmed individual bowls. Ladle the soup over the spelt and drizzle each serving with extra-virgin olive oil. Garnish with Parmigiano-Reggiano and chervil. Serve immediately.

Chicken Stock, *Brodo di Pollo*

This is our recipe for what we call "liquid gold." Use chicken backs and necks whenever possible; some butchers keep them on hand, others will save them for you if you call ahead. Chicken wings and drumsticks also make good stock.

MAKES ABOUT 2 QUARTS

- 4 **pounds chicken parts**
- 1 **small yellow onion, coarsely chopped**
- 3 **small carrots, cut into chunks**
- 3 **large stalks celery, cut into chunks**
- 2 **bay leaves**
- 1 **teaspoon peppercorns, lightly crushed**

Place the chicken in a large stockpot and add cold water to cover by 3 inches. Bring to a simmer over medium-high heat, skimming the stock of any fat or foam that rises to the surface. Add the onion, carrots, celery, bay leaves, and peppercorns. Reduce the heat to low and simmer, uncovered, for 2 to 3 hours. Strain through a fine-mesh sieve and let cool. Refrigerate overnight. With a large spoon, lift off and discard any solidified fat.

NOTE The stock can be frozen for up to 1 month. Freezing it in ice-cube trays makes it easy to use for small-portion recipes.

Mantuano on His Co-author
The most humbling thing about writing this book was having my wife as co-author. It would be 3:30 A.M. and I'd be trying to fall asleep and the questions would just keep on coming!

The Spiaggia Cookbook
Tony Mantuano

Boneless Pork Chop with White Corn Polenta and Broccoli Rabe

Costoletta di Maiale Senz'osso con Polenta Bianca e Rapini

Some pork producers are once again raising pork that isn't too lean; the resulting flavor reminds us of how good old-fashioned naturally raised pork can be. Be careful not to overcook the chops.

We love broccoli rabe and find it the perfect accompaniment to pork. Also known as *rapini,* it looks like broccoli but with longer stems and leaves and a slightly bitter taste. Broccoli rabe is best sautéed with garlic, with a sprinkling of red pepper flakes on top, if you like heat. When we shop on Harlem Avenue in the old Italian section of Chicago, we have to compete with the venerable Italian women even to get near the mountain of broccoli rabe at the main grocery store. In the produce section of our downtown grocer, there is plenty of room to pick out *rapini,* but it's not nearly as much fun.

4 SERVINGS

- 4 cups water
- ¼ cup sugar
- ¼ cup salt
- 4 boneless pork loin chops, 5 ounces each
- 1 bunch broccoli rabe, about 1 pound (see Note)
- 4 tablespoons extra-virgin olive oil, plus extra for drizzling

Freshly ground pepper

- 2 cups Chicken Stock (page 165) or prepared broth
- 1 large sprig fresh rosemary
- 2 tablespoons unsalted butter

Sea salt

- 1 clove garlic, thinly sliced

White Corn Polenta (recipe follows) for serving

In a large saucepan over medium heat, combine the water, sugar, and the ¼ cup salt. Heat the brine, stirring, until the sugar and salt dissolve. Let cool. Arrange the chops in a baking pan in a single layer and pour the cool brine over. Cover and refrigerate for 24 hours.

Preheat the oven to 425 degrees F.

Test Kitchen Tip

Brining is a simple, effective way to keep lean meats like pork loin moist and juicy. Try the same technique with chicken breasts. Add fresh herbs or whole spices to the brine to impart a different flavor.

The Spiaggia Cookbook

Tony Mantuano

Trim the broccoli rabe just below the leaves and discard the bottom inch of the stems. Have ready a bowl of ice water. Bring a saucepan of lightly salted water to a boil over high heat. Add the broccoli rabe and blanch for 1 minute.

Drain and plunge into the ice water to stop the cooking. Drain and chop into 1-inch pieces. Set aside.

Remove the chops from the brine and pat dry. In a large, ovenproof, nonstick sauté pan, heat 2 tablespoons of the olive oil over medium heat. Season the chops with pepper. When the pan and oil are hot, add the chops and cook for 5 minutes on one side. Turn them over, transfer to the oven, and bake until an instant-read thermometer registers 160 degrees F when inserted into the thickest part, 10 to 15 minutes. Transfer the chops to a platter, tent with aluminum foil, and keep warm.

Pour off any excess fat from the pan and place over medium-high heat. Add the stock and scrape any browned bits off the bottom of the pan. Add the rosemary, bring to a simmer, and cook until reduced by half, about 8 minutes. Remove from the heat, discard the rosemary, and whisk in the butter. Season to taste with sea salt and pepper. Set the sauce aside and keep warm.

In a sauté pan over medium-high heat, heat the remaining 2 tablespoons olive oil. Add the garlic and sauté until lightly browned. Add the blanched broccoli rabe and cook until crisp-tender, about 2 minutes. Season to taste with sea salt and pepper.

To serve, place ½ cup of the polenta in the center of each of 4 warmed plates. Slice a chop on the diagonal and arrange over the polenta. Arrange one-fourth of the broccoli rabe around the plate and drizzle with olive oil. Drizzle sauce around the polenta and on the plate in front of the meat. Repeat to make the remaining 3 servings. Serve immediately.

NOTE You can blanch and chop the broccoli rabe a day ahead and refrigerate it until needed.

White Corn Polenta, *Polenta Bianca*

At Spiaggia, we serve polenta that has a creamy consistency, usually white corn polenta because it is the lightest and most elegant variety. When you make white corn polenta, the finished texture should be that of runny mashed potatoes or very creamy risotto. You should be able to pour the polenta; it should actually relax onto the plate and then spread out slightly, but not too far. If the polenta stands up like whipped cream, you need to add more water or stock to achieve the desired consistency. Always taste and adjust the seasoning after adding more liquid.

MAKES 2 CUPS

- 2 cups water
- Sea salt
- ½ cup white polenta
- 1 tablespoon unsalted butter
- 6 tablespoons heavy cream
- 3 tablespoons grated Parmigiano-Reggiano or Parmesan cheese
- Freshly ground white pepper

In a large saucepan over medium heat, bring the water to a boil. Add a pinch of salt and slowly pour in the polenta, stirring constantly to avoid lumps. (Crush any lumps that form by pressing them against the side of the pot with a spoon.) Stir vigorously as the polenta thickens. Continue to cook the polenta, stirring often, until it loses its grainy texture and becomes smooth, about 30 minutes. Add the butter, cream, and Parmigiano-Reggiano and stir until well incorporated. Season to taste with salt and white pepper. Serve immediately.

The Spiaggia Cookbook

Tony Mantuano

Crescenza Ravioli with Parmigiano-Reggiano and Truffle Butter Sauce

Ravioletti di Crescenza con Salsa di Parmigiano-Reggiano e Burro al Tartufo

Elegant and rich, this pasta dish is all about top-quality ingredients. Crescenza cheese is a soft, fresh creamy cheese that is ideal for these pasta pillows.

12 SERVINGS

Basic Pasta Dough (recipe follows)
½ stick cold butter, plus 1½ cups unsalted butter
1 pound Crescenza cheese
⅓ cup truffle oil
1½ cups grated Parmigiano-Reggiano or Parmesan cheese
12 cloves garlic, thinly sliced, crisped in olive oil
12 small sprigs fresh rosemary
1 cup edible flower petals (optional)

Preheat the oven to 375 degrees F.

Roll out the pasta dough into thin sheets as directed on page 172. Using a chef's knife or pastry wheel, cut the pasta sheets into twenty-four 5-by-5-inch squares. Place the squares on a lightly floured board or cloth until ready to cook. Cut out 24 rectangles of parchment paper, each 7 by 7½ inches. Grease each piece using the cold stick of butter, leaving a 1½-inch border unbuttered.

Have ready a bowl of ice water. Bring a large pot of lightly salted water to a boil. Add the pasta squares to the boiling water and cook until al dente (tender but firm to the bite), 1 to 2 minutes. Remove the pasta squares with a slotted spoon, shaking to remove excess moisture, and transfer carefully to the ice water to stop the cooking. Working quickly, remove the pasta squares from the ice water one at a time, and lay flat on a cloth to dry. Do not overlap, or the squares will stick together.

Cut the Crescenza cheese into 24 pieces, each about 2 inches wide, 2 inches long, and ¼ inch thick. Place a piece of the cheese in the middle of each pasta square and fold the bottom and top flap of pasta over the middle, wrapping it around the cheese. Then fold the sides into the middle, burrito style. Place the *ravioletto,* seam side down, in the middle of a buttered parchment piece and fold the parchment around the pasta, repeating the technique used to wrap the pasta around the cheese. Place the parchment

The Spiaggia
Cookbook
Tony Mantuano

packet, seam side down, on a baking sheet. Repeat with the remaining pasta, cheese, and parchment. Bake until the edges of the parchment paper are barely golden brown, 10 to 12 minutes.

Meanwhile, in a saucepan over medium heat, melt the 1½ cups butter. Cook to a nutty brown color, 4 to 6 minutes. Stir in the truffle oil.

To serve, place 1 tablespoon of the Parmigiano-Reggiano in the center of each of 12 warmed plates. Carefully remove the parchment around a *ravioletto* and place it on the grated cheese. Arrange a second *ravioletto* next to the first. Spoon 2 tablespoons of the truffle butter over the *ravioletti*. Sprinkle with another 1 tablespoon Parmigiano-Reggiano. Garnish with the garlic crisps, rosemary, and flower petals, if using. Repeat to make the remaining 11 servings. Serve immediately.

NOTE Wrapped in the parchment and placed in an airtight container, the *ravioletti* freeze well for up to 1 month. Bake right from the freezer for 25 minutes, and continue as directed.

The Spiaggia
Cookbook
Tony Mantuano

Test Kitchen Tip
The pasta dough in this recipe may seem a little crumbly and dry at first. Keep passing it through your pasta machine and it will slowly come together, resulting in a wonderful smooth dough.

Basic Pasta Dough, *La Pasta*

We have tried many pasta dough recipes and have found this to be the best, yielding a firm dough with a texture that's easy to handle. Use this dough for all shapes and sizes of pasta.

MAKES ABOUT 1 POUND OF PASTA DOUGH, OR TWELVE 6-BY-12-INCH SHEETS

2 cups type 00 semolina flour

1 teaspoon salt

8 egg yolks, lightly beaten

⅓ cup water

Mound the flour on a pastry board or other wood or plastic work surface. Make a well in the center and add the salt and egg yolks. Using a fork, gradually fold the flour into the eggs, adding the water little by little until you have a soft dough. Knead a few times until smooth, then form the dough into a ball, wrap in plastic, and refrigerate for 1 hour.

To roll and cut pasta, cut the dough into 6 pieces. Working with one piece at a time (cover the remaining dough with a moist cloth until ready to use), dust the dough with flour and place between the rollers of a manual or motorized pasta machine at the widest setting. Pass the dough through. Fold the dough in half, sprinkle with flour, and roll again. Dust again with flour if the dough becomes sticky. Continue this process, reducing the space between the rollers one setting at a time, until the dough is a thin, smooth sheet. Generally, you can roll the dough 6 times on the first setting before tightening the rollers; then reduce the times you roll by one with each new setting until you reach the last setting (No. 6), when rolling once will be enough.

The finished pasta sheets should be about 6 inches wide and 12 inches long. Let the pasta sheets dry on a lightly floured board or parchment paper for 5 minutes before cutting.

NOTE The basic pasta dough can be refrigerated, wrapped in plastic, for up to 2 days.

Lemon Panna Cotta

Panna Cotta al Limone

8 SERVINGS

- 4 lemons
- 2½ cups heavy cream
- 1½ cups milk
- ½ vanilla bean, split lengthwise, seeds scraped
- 2½ cups sugar
- 1 tablespoon unflavored gelatin
- ¾ cup water
- ½ cup lemon-flavored vodka, such as Charbay Meyer Lemon

1. Using a vegetable peeler, remove the zest from the lemons; reserve the zest. Using a sharp knife, peel off all of the bitter white pith from the lemons. Working over a bowl, cut in between the membranes to release the lemon sections.

2. In a medium saucepan, combine the lemon zest with the heavy cream, milk, vanilla beans and seeds and ½ cup of the sugar. Simmer over moderate heat just until the sugar dissolves, about 5 minutes. Remove from the heat and let stand for at least 1 hour, or refrigerate overnight.

3. Transfer ¼ cup of the cooled lemon cream to a small bowl. Sprinkle the gelatin over the cream and let stand for 5 minutes.

4. Bring the remaining lemon cream to a gentle simmer over moderately high heat. Remove from the heat and whisk in the gelatin mixture until it dissolves. Strain the lemon cream into a large glass measuring cup, then pour it into eight ½-cup ramekins. Refrigerate until set, at least 3 hours.

5. Meanwhile, in a medium saucepan, combine the remaining 2 cups of sugar with the water and vodka. Cook over moderately high heat, stirring occasionally, until the sugar dissolves, about 5 minutes. Remove from the heat. Add the lemon sections and refrigerate for at least 1 hour.

6. Serve the panna cotta in the ramekins, topped with a few lemon sections and a drizzle of the lemon-vodka syrup.

MAKE AHEAD The recipe can be made and refrigerated 2 days in advance.

Editor's Note

This panna cotta from the menu at Spiaggia is creamy but light. Mantuano likes to make this dessert year-round, substituting any citrus fruit for the lemon here; try tangerine or lime.

The Spiaggia Cookbook

Tony Mantuano

Olives growing in a sunny Sicilian grove.

Olive Trees and Honey
by Gil Marks

Published by Wiley, 464 pages, $29.95

"Don't get me wrong—I like a nicely cooked prime rib," says cookbook author, food historian and rabbi Gil Marks. "But I really *love* vegetarian cooking—it's much more exciting than meat." Part cookbook, part social history, Marks's fourth cookbook offers a detailed exploration of Jewish vegetarian cuisine around the world. In his search for authentic, delicious recipes, Marks has unearthed dishes as diverse as Italian Eggplant Relish, Syrian Spinach Soup and Romanian Stuffed Mushrooms. In addition to 300 recipes, *Olive Trees and Honey* includes a list of appropriate foods and menus for Jewish holidays and other special occasions.

Featured Recipes Italian Eggplant Relish; Syrian Spinach Soup; Romanian Stuffed Mushrooms

Best of the Best Exclusive Indian Mixed Vegetable Curry

Italian Eggplant Relish

Caponata alla Giudea

Marks on Toasting Pine Nuts

Though they can be eaten raw, pine nuts are frequently toasted to enhance their buttery flavor. To toast them, spread the pine nuts on a dry baking sheet and place in a preheated 375°F oven, stirring several times, until golden, 5 to 10 minutes.

Or stir them in a dry, heavy skillet over medium heat until golden. Be careful, as pine nuts burn easily.

Packed with the heady flavors of the Mediterranean—sweet tomatoes, meaty eggplant chunks, salty capers, and aromatic olive oil—this sweet-and-sour relish is highly addictive. For the best flavor, buy high quality olives and pit them yourself. Adjust the amount of vinegar and sugar to personal preference. Caponata is served with bread as an appetizer, alone as a side dish, or as a pasta sauce, but it also makes a delicious filling for phyllo and other pastries. One of my favorite ways to use caponata is to spoon it onto crostini (garlic-rubbed toasted bread) or toasted pita triangles.

ABOUT 3 CUPS, OR 5 TO 6 SERVINGS

- 2 medium eggplants (about 1 pound each), peeled and cut into ¾-inch cubes
- 2 tablespoons kosher salt plus 1 teaspoon, or 1 tablespoon table salt plus ½ teaspoon
- ¾ cup olive oil
- 2 large onions, coarsely chopped
- 3 to 4 inner stalks celery, coarsely chopped
- 2 to 3 cloves garlic, minced
- 1¼ pounds plum tomatoes, peeled, seeded, and chopped (about 3 cups)
- ¾ cup green olives, pitted and coarsely chopped
- ¼ cup chopped fresh parsley
- 4 to 6 tablespoons red wine vinegar
- 2 to 3 tablespoons sugar
- About ¼ teaspoon ground black pepper
- ¼ cup capers, drained
- ¼ cup (1½ ounces) pine nuts, toasted (optional)

1. Put the diced eggplant in a colander, sprinkle with the 2 tablespoons kosher salt or 1 tablespoon table salt, and let stand for 1 hour. Rinse with water and press between several layers of paper towels until dry.

2. In a large saucepan, heat ½ cup of the oil over medium heat. Add the eggplant and sauté until golden brown and tender but still firm, about 10 minutes. Transfer the eggplant to a plate and drain off any oil.

Olive Trees and Honey

Gil Marks

3. In the same pan, heat the remaining ¼ cup oil. Add the onions, celery, and garlic and sauté until softened, about 10 minutes. Add the tomatoes, olives, parsley, vinegar, sugar, the remaining salt, and the pepper. Cover and simmer over low heat, stirring occasionally, until the tomatoes break down into a thick sauce, about 15 minutes.

4. Add the eggplant and capers and cook, stirring occasionally, until all the vegetables are tender, about 10 minutes. Taste and adjust the seasoning. If using, stir in the pine nuts. Caponata keeps well in the refrigerator for up to 4 days; the flavors will meld as it stands.

TO PEEL TOMATOES Very ripe tomatoes can be peeled without blanching. Run the blade of a dull knife (such as a butter knife) over the entire surface, cut out the stem end, then pull off the skin. To peel younger tomatoes, cut an "X" at the bottom of the fruit and drop in boiling water for 15 to 30 seconds, then immediately plunge into a bowl of ice water to stop the cooking. The skin will easily peel off.

TO SEED TOMATOES Cut them in half horizontally, hold upside down, and gently squeeze to remove the seeds and juice, while leaving the pulp.

Marks on Cooking with Leftovers

If you have any leftover relish, reheat it and serve it over pasta the next day. Or team it with eggs for breakfast—it's delicious.

Olive Trees and Honey

Gil Marks

Syrian Spinach Soup

Shoorbah Sabanekh

Test Kitchen Tip

We pureed half the soup and then combined it with the remaining unpureed soup, resulting in a thick and creamy yet chunky texture. This technique works especially well if you decide to omit the yogurt to make this a nondairy soup.

Spinach soup is a light spring and early summer treat in many parts of the Middle East and Mediterranean. This Syrian version is accented with mint, but a little ground ginger or nutmeg is a tasty alternative. The soup is sometimes called *labaneya,* from the Arabic word for "yogurt." It is always made without meat or chicken stock so that it can be served with plenty of yogurt, but for a nondairy soup use pomegranate concentrate or lemon juice for a touch of tartness. Some cooks stir the yogurt into the soup, while others spoon a large dollop over each serving for the individual diners to stir in. Spinach soup is commonly served with pita bread.

6 TO 8 SERVINGS

- ¼ cup vegetable oil or unsalted butter
- 2 onions, chopped
- 3 to 4 cloves garlic, minced
- 2 pounds fresh spinach or Swiss chard, washed, stemmed, and coarsely chopped, or 20 ounces thawed frozen spinach, squeezed dry
- 7 cups Vegetable Stock (recipe follows) or water
- ¾ cup basmati or other long-grain white rice
- 2 teaspoons dried mint, crushed, or ½ cup chopped fresh mint
- About 1 teaspoon table salt or 2 teaspoons kosher salt
- Ground black pepper to taste
- 2 to 4 cups plain yogurt or 2 tablespoons pomegranate concentrate (see facing page) or 2 to 4 tablespoons fresh lemon juice

1. In a large pot, heat the oil over medium heat. Add the onions and garlic and sauté until soft and translucent, 5 to 10 minutes. Gradually add the spinach, stirring until wilted, about 5 minutes.

2. Add the stock, rice, dried mint, if using, salt, and pepper. Bring to a boil, cover, reduce the heat to medium-low, and simmer until the rice is tender, about 20 minutes. If using fresh mint, add it after cooking for 15 minutes, then simmer another 5 minutes.

3. Leave the soup with a chunky texture or process in a blender or food processor until nearly smooth. If too thick, add a little more stock. Top each portion with several dollops of yogurt or stir it into the soup. If reheating after adding the yogurt, be careful not to boil. Serve hot or chilled.

Olive Trees and Honey
Gil Marks

FRENCH SPINACH AND PEA SOUP (*Potage aux Épinards et Petits Pois*): Omit the rice, reduce the spinach to 1 pound, and add 20 ounces fresh or frozen green peas.

GREEK SPINACH SOUP (*Spanakosoupa*): Substitute ⅓ cup chopped fresh dill for the mint and 1 cup orzo (rice-shaped pasta) for the rice, cooked in boiling water until al dente, adding the dill, pasta, and 2 to 4 tablespoons fresh lemon juice about 5 minutes before serving.

PERSIAN SPINACH SOUP (*Pshal Dueah*): Substitute 2 tablespoons chopped fresh dill for the mint, and add 1 teaspoon ground turmeric when the rice is tender.

INDIAN SPINACH SOUP (*Palak Shorva*): Omit the mint. In Step 1, before adding the spinach, stir in 1 teaspoon ground cumin, ½ teaspoon ground turmeric, and ⅛ teaspoon ground cinnamon or 1 teaspoon ground fenugreek. Add 1 tablespoon fresh lemon juice with the spinach. If desired, substitute 2 cups canned coconut milk for the yogurt and garnish with toasted unsweetened shredded coconut.

POMEGRANATE CONCENTRATE To preserve the tart flavor of pomegranate juice for year-round use, Middle Eastern cooks learned to boil the juice down to a thick syrup the consistency of molasses. Pomegranate juice is widely used in Iran, Iraq, Turkey, and Georgia to give a tart flavor to stews and savory fillings. Add a little to vinaigrettes, marinades, relishes, stuffed vegetables, and even vodka martinis. To make, boil down 2 cups unsweetened pomegranate juice until reduced to ½ cup, about 1 hour. Let cool, then pour into a sterilized jar. It will keep at room temperature for at least a year, and almost indefinitely in the refrigerator. The concentrate, sometimes called pomegranate molasses, is also available in Middle Eastern stores.

Olive Trees
and Honey
Gil Marks

Vegetable Stock

Vegetable stock has a delicate flavor, which will vary slightly from batch to batch even if you always use the same vegetables. You can add other vegetables than those listed, but do not overdo strongly flavored ones, particularly members of the cabbage family, such as broccoli, Brussels sprouts, cauliflower, kale, and kohlrabi. Avoid adding bell peppers, which impart an off flavor. For a more delicate taste, do not sauté or roast the vegetables. If you don't have time to make stock, use vegetable bouillon cubes, but beware of the extra sodium and MSG in some brands. Use vegetable stock as a base for other soups, or serve it by itself with noodles, matza balls, or rice.

ABOUT 2½ QUARTS

- 3 tablespoons vegetable oil
- 3 onions, coarsely chopped (for a darker stock, do not skin)
- 3 carrots, scrubbed and coarsely chopped
- 3 stalks celery with leaves, coarsely chopped
- 2 leeks (white and light green parts only), washed and coarsely chopped
- 3 quarts water
- 1 to 2 parsnips or turnips, peeled and coarsely chopped
- 1 cup peelings from well-scrubbed potatoes, or ¼ cup brown lentils, or 2 sweet potatoes, peeled and quartered (optional)
- 5 to 6 cloves garlic
- 10 to 12 sprigs fresh parsley
- 2 sprigs fresh thyme or ½ teaspoon dried thyme
- 2 bay leaves
- About 2 teaspoons table salt or 1 tablespoon kosher salt (optional)
- 6 to 8 whole black peppercorns

1. In a large pot, heat the oil over medium-high heat. Add the onions, carrots, celery, and leeks and sauté until lightly browned, about 15 minutes. Or, combine those ingredients in a roasting pan and bake, uncovered, in a preheated 450°F oven for 1 hour, then transfer to a large pot.

Olive Trees and Honey

Gil Marks

2. Add all the remaining ingredients. Bring to a boil, partially cover, reduce the heat to low, and simmer for 1 hour. Remove from the heat and let stand for 30 minutes.

3. Strain the stock through a colander, pressing out any liquid, then discard the solids. Store in the refrigerator for up to 4 days or freeze for up to 3 months.

NOTES For extra richness, save the water after cooking vegetables and use it as part or all of your vegetable stock's cooking liquid. You can also save vegetable scraps and trimmings (onion skins, carrot tops and peels, potato skins, celery leaves, and so on) in the freezer and add them to enhance your stock. In fact, some restaurants use only scraps to make stock, about 2 cups for every 4 cups of water—but at a loss of flavor.

A general rule of thumb when seasoning stock is, for every 4 cups of water, use 2 tablespoons fresh herbs or 2 teaspoons dried herbs, and ¼ to ½ teaspoon table salt (½ to 1 teaspoon kosher salt), 1 tablespoon soy sauce, or 3 tablespoons miso (fermented soy paste). Stock reduces as it simmers, intensifying its flavors, so it is best not to add too much salt at the beginning of cooking. If you use stock as the base for a soup, be careful about adding additional salt called for in the soup recipe. If the soup tastes too salty, try adding a peeled raw potato and cook until enough excess salt is absorbed, then discard the potato.

Olive Trees
and Honey
Gil Marks

Romanian Stuffed Mushrooms

Ciuperci Umplute

Every culture has its idiosyncrasies. Among those of Romanian cookery is garlic and typically plenty of it. To me, it is sometimes overdone. Then again, seasoning is always a subjective matter. Mushroom caps are a popular and versatile base for hors d'oeuvres; the Romanian version, of course, contains garlic. Romanians serve these hot or at room temperature as part of a *meze* (appetizer assortment) or as a side dish.

ABOUT 24 HORS D'OEUVRES

- 1 pound (about 24) large button mushrooms, rinsed
- ¼ cup vegetable oil
- 8 to 10 scallions (white and light green parts only), thinly sliced, or 1 large onion, finely chopped
- 1 to 3 cloves garlic, minced
- ¼ cup fresh bread crumbs or matza meal
- 2 tablespoons chopped fresh parsley
- 1 tablespoon chopped fresh dill
- About 2 teaspoons table salt or 1 tablespoon kosher salt
- About 1 teaspoon ground black pepper
- ¼ cup unsalted butter, melted, or vegetable oil
- ¾ cup grated aged kashkaval, kefalotyri, or Parmesan cheese (optional)
- ⅓ cup dry white wine

1. Remove the stems from the mushroom caps and finely chop them.

2. In a large skillet, heat the oil over medium heat. Add the scallions and garlic and sauté until soft, about 5 minutes. Add the chopped stems and sauté until the mushrooms release their liquid and it evaporates, about 5 minutes. Stir in the bread crumbs, parsley, dill, salt, and pepper. Let cool. Store in the refrigerator for up to 3 days.

3. Preheat the oven to 350°F. Grease a large shallow casserole or baking sheet.

4. Place the mushroom caps in the prepared baking dish and drizzle the butter over top. Bake, uncovered, for 10 minutes.

5. Fill the mushrooms with the stuffing and, if using, sprinkle with the cheese. Bake until browned, about 20 minutes. Drizzle with the wine. Serve warm.

Olive Trees
and Honey
Gil Marks

Best of the Best Exclusive
Indian Mixed Vegetable Curry

6 SIDE-DISH SERVINGS

3 tablespoons vegetable oil

1½ teaspoons cumin seeds

2 garlic cloves, minced

1 jalapeño, seeded and minced

1 tablespoon plus 1 teaspoon minced fresh ginger

1 teaspoon turmeric

1 teaspoon ground coriander

3 medium carrots, sliced ¼ inch thick

1 small cauliflower (1½ pounds), cut into 1-inch florets

1 large green bell pepper, cut into ½-inch dice

Kosher salt

2 tablespoons water

3 plum tomatoes, diced

One 15-ounce can chickpeas, drained and rinsed

¼ cup chopped cilantro

Steamed rice or Indian flat bread, for serving

1. In a very large skillet, heat the oil. Add the cumin seeds and cook over moderate heat until they begin to crackle and are toasted, about 1 minute. Add the garlic, jalapeño and ginger and cook for 1 minute. Stir in the turmeric and coriander. Add the carrots, cauliflower, bell pepper and a large pinch of salt and cook, stirring frequently, until the vegetables are thoroughly coated with the spices, about 3 minutes. Add the water, cover and cook, stirring occasionally, until the vegetables are tender, about 10 minutes.

2. Add the tomatoes, chickpeas and a pinch of salt, cover and cook over low heat until the tomatoes have softened, about 3 minutes. Sprinkle with the cilantro, transfer to a bowl and serve with steamed rice or Indian flat bread.

Editor's Note
This fresh, spicy curry was inspired by those served in the kosher Indian restaurants in New York City's "Curry Hill." For a nonvegetarian version, you can add diced chicken.

Olive Trees and Honey
Gil Marks

Tagine of Chicken, Apricots and Mint, PAGE 190

Nick Nairn's Top 100 Chicken Recipes

by Nick Nairn

Published by BBC Books, 144 pages, color photos, $16.95

"Chicken is sort of a blank canvas for chefs, so when I was writing this cookbook, there were literally thousands of recipes to choose from," explains Nick Nairn, Scottish chef, TV personality and cookbook author. Nairn uses chicken's flexibility to explore a global set of dishes touching on Moroccan, Chinese, Spanish and Thai cooking techniques. And he makes good use of all parts of the bird, not just the ever-popular white meat; so expect to be cooking with thighs and drumsticks and making chicken stock, too.

Featured Recipes Spicy Barbecued Chicken Wings; Chicken Burgers with Garlic, Rosemary and Rocket; Tagine of Chicken, Apricots and Mint

Best of the Best Exclusive Herb Blinis with Smoked Salmon and Horseradish Crème Fraîche

185

Spicy Barbecued Chicken Wings

Nairn on Honey

When I make this dish, I like using runny honey. There's no point using the finest honey for this recipe because it gets charred. The run-of-the-mill stuff works just fine.

I like to rub a spice mix into blanched and cooled chicken wings and leave them to marinate for a while before finishing them off on the barbecue and glazing them. This means the chicken is cooked through completely, without the glaze burning. The thing is to keep them moving, so that they cook evenly and build up a good glaze. Make sure you have plenty of napkins to hand—these are definitely a cutlery-free eating experience!

PREPARATION TIME: 35 MINUTES
4 SERVINGS

- 16 chicken wings, wing tips removed
- 1 teaspoon ground cumin
- 2 teaspoons ground coriander
- Juice and finely grated rind of 1 lemon
- Freshly ground sea salt and freshly ground black pepper
- 4 tablespoons roughly chopped fresh parsley or coriander (cilantro)
- Guacamole (recipe follows) and sour cream, to serve

FOR THE BARBECUE GLAZE

- 4 tablespoons tomato ketchup
- 2 tablespoons maple syrup or honey
- 1 tablespoon Worcestershire sauce
- 1 garlic clove, crushed
- 2 tablespoons lime juice
- A good dash of Tabasco sauce (I like the jalapeño one)

1. Soak 16 bamboo skewers, if using, in cold water for 20 to 25 minutes. Meanwhile, bring a large pan of water to the boil and add the chicken wings. Simmer for 3 minutes, then drain and cool.

2. Mix the spices with the lemon juice and rind and salt and pepper. Rub the chicken wings with the spice mix and leave to marinate for 20 minutes.

3. Preheat the barbecue—allow about 40 minutes for the coals to reach the right temperature. Mix all the glaze ingredients together in a small pan, bring to the boil and simmer for 2 minutes.

Nick Nairn's Top 100 Chicken Recipes
Nick Nairn

4. Thread the marinated wings two at a time onto double bamboo or metal skewers. Barbecue over a medium heat for 2 to 3 minutes, watching that the spices don't burn.

5. Now brush the wings liberally with the glaze and continue to barbecue over a medium heat for another 6 to 10 minutes, turning them often so they don't catch and burn. Baste occasionally with more sauce until they are well browned, sticky and crisp. (Alternatively, grill the wings under a medium-hot grill or bake them in the oven at 400°F for 20 minutes.) When done, pile onto a serving dish and sprinkle with the parsley or coriander before serving. Serve with guacamole and sour cream.

Guacamole

  2 ripe avocados, halved, stoned and peeled
Juice of 1 or 2 limes (depending on juiciness)
  ½ onion, grated, or 1 garlic clove creamed with a little salt
  1 fresh green chile, seeded and very finely chopped
  2 tablespoons chopped fresh coriander (cilantro), plus extra to serve
Freshly ground sea salt and freshly ground black pepper

Put all the ingredients into a bowl and roughly mash with a fork.

Nick Nairn's Top
100 Chicken Recipes
Nick Nairn

Chicken Burgers with Garlic, Rosemary and Rocket

I have to say that the thought of a chicken burger usually fills me with dread, but when I came up with this punchy one full of Italian or Mediterranean flavors, I soon changed my mind! Not only does it taste fantastic, but it contains less fat than a conventional burger. Making the burgers with chicken thighs really improves both texture and flavor.

PREPARATION TIME: 45 MINUTES, PLUS CHILLING TIME
4 SERVINGS

- 4 fat garlic cloves, unpeeled
- ½ ounce dried porcini mushrooms
- 1 tablespoon olive oil, plus extra for brushing
- 1 red onion, very finely diced
- 1 tablespoon chopped fresh rosemary
- 12 ounces chicken thigh meat, coarsely minced
- 4 ounces lardons (*cubetti di pancetta*) or smoked dry-cure streaky bacon, finely minced

A splash of balsamic vinegar

Freshly ground sea salt and freshly ground black pepper

TO SERVE

- 4 ciabatta rolls

Mustard mayonnaise (dijonnaise)

- 4 ounces rocket (arugula)

1. Put the garlic cloves and mushrooms in a small pan of cold water and bring slowly to the boil. Simmer for 20 minutes, then drain and cool. Squeeze the mushrooms dry and chop them finely. Squeeze the garlic flesh out of the skins and chop roughly.

2. Heat the olive oil in a frying pan over a medium heat and add the onion, chopped cooked garlic and the mushrooms. Cook for 5 minutes, until the onion is very soft and the garlic is beginning to brown. Add the rosemary. Tip out of the pan into a bowl to cool.

3. Mix the minced chicken and lardons or bacon with a splash of balsamic vinegar. Work in the onion and mushroom mixture and then season well with salt and pepper. Divide into four and, wetting your hands, shape into burgers. Put on a tray, cover and chill.

4. When ready to cook, remove the burgers from the fridge and allow to come to room temperature. Brush with olive oil and grill, griddle or barbecue for about 5 minutes per side, or until completely cooked through with no pinkness in the center when cut open.

5. Meanwhile, warm the ciabatta rolls in the oven. Then, halve them, spread the base of each with a little mustard mayonnaise, top with a burger and add a handful of rocket. Slam on the lid and tuck in!

Test Kitchen Tip

Using thigh meat in this recipe makes the burgers very moist and tender. Don't be tempted to use finely ground chicken meat from the supermarket; it can be too lean, resulting in dense, dry burgers. If you're pressed for time, have your butcher coarsely grind the chicken thighs for you.

Nick Nairn's Top
100 Chicken Recipes
Nick Nairn

Tagine of Chicken, Apricots and Mint

Nairn on Making Stock

I think that stock tastes better when you make it in big batches. Cook the stock so that it is just trembling in the pot, not boiling—cooking it at a lower temperature naturally clarifies it. I cook mine for up to 3 hours and just keep tasting it. When it's not getting any better, it's done.

A tagine is a Moroccan stew named after the closed dish in which it is cooked. It simmers for hours, concentrating the flavors and thickening the sauce. The whole dish, usually made out of terra-cotta, sits over glowing charcoal as it cooks. I've devised a tagine using chicken thighs—free-range or organic ones will stand up to the long, slow cooking, as the flesh is firmer than that of ordinary chickens. The ground almonds thicken the sauce and give it a really good flavor.

PREPARATION TIME: 1 HOUR 5 MINUTES
4 SERVINGS

- 2 ounces butter
- 6 (5- to 6-ounce) free-range or organic chicken thighs
- 1 onion, finely chopped
- ¼ teaspoon ground cumin
- ¼ teaspoon ground ginger
- ¼ teaspoon ground cinnamon
- 2 teaspoons sweet paprika

Freshly ground sea salt and freshly ground black pepper

- 4 ounces ground almonds

Juice and finely grated rind of 1 orange

- 1 pint Light Chicken Stock (recipe follows)
- 6 ounces no-need-to-soak dried apricots
- 3 tablespoons chopped fresh mint, plus extra to garnish

Couscous, to serve

1. Preheat the oven to 325°F. Melt the butter in the bottom of a large, heavy casserole. Brown the chicken thighs all over, three at a time, removing them to a plate as you go.

2. Stir the onion and spices into the juices at the bottom of the dish and cook for about 5 minutes to release the aroma and soften the onion a little. Season with salt and a good grinding of pepper. Stir in the ground almonds.

3. Return the chicken to the casserole with the orange juice and rind and cover with the stock. Bring to the boil and then turn the heat to very low. Cover the surface of the stew with a sheet of crumpled greaseproof paper (a "cartouche") and then the lid—this will prevent too much steam from escaping during the cooking. Bake in the oven for 30 minutes.

Nick Nairn's Top 100 Chicken Recipes
Nick Nairn

4. Add the apricots and mint, stir them into the liquid, and bake, uncovered, for a further 15 minutes. By this time the chicken should be falling off the bone and the apricots should be plump and the sauce thickened (if not, boil to reduce). Taste and adjust the seasoning, sprinkle with more mint and serve at the table with a big bowl of couscous.

Light Chicken Stock

Making stock can be a lengthy process, so it's best to tackle it when you have some spare time. I usually make the biggest possible batch by multiplying the ingredients to fill my largest stockpot. Then I put the stock into clearly labelled 1-pint tubs and freeze it for future use. Not only is it easier to make it in big batches, but the stock will have a better flavor. In summer it's best to freeze stock immediately, but in winter it will keep for up to 48 hours in the fridge. A good, rich chicken stock should have a slightly jellied consistency when cold.

  If you need a poached chicken, replace the three carcasses in this recipe with one medium chicken and follow the method below. Cutting the head of garlic across its "equator" gives just the sweet garlic flavors and not the harsh garlic oil.

PREPARATION TIME: 4 HOURS
MAKES 2¼ PINTS

- 3 chicken carcasses, skin and fat removed
- 1 large carrot, quartered
- 1 leek, washed and quartered
- 2 celery sticks, halved lengthwise
- 1 onion with skin left on, quartered
- 1 small head of garlic, halved across its equator
- 6 black peppercorns
- 1 bay leaf
- A sprig of fresh thyme
- A few fresh parsley or tarragon stalks

Nick Nairn's Top
100 Chicken Recipes
Nick Nairn

1. Place the carcasses in a pan large enough for the bones to fill it only halfway. Just cover them with about 4½ pints cold water (too much water will dilute the flavor of the stock) and bring to the boil. Once boiling, reduce the heat immediately to a simmer and then, using a large spoon or ladle, skim off the fat and any scum from the surface. Add the rest of the ingredients, all of which should lie on top of the carcasses. Adjust the heat to a very slow simmer and skim once more.

2. The simmering stock will now rise and fall through the vegetables, which act as a filter, absorbing all of the gunk from the liquid and leaving it crystal-clear. Leave it to simmer like this for 2 to 3 hours, tasting regularly. You should eventually notice the point at which the flavor stops improving. This means it's ready.

3. Remove the pan from the heat and empty the stock into a colander set over a bowl. Now pass the stock through a fine sieve into a tall container or 4½-pint jug. Cover it and allow it to cool by placing it in a sink of cold water.

4. When it's cool, place it in the fridge overnight. Skim off any fat that settles on top and spoon out the jellied stock into tubs. Freeze until ready to use.

Nick Nairn's Top
100 Chicken Recipes
Nick Nairn

Herb Blinis with Smoked Salmon and Horseradish Crème Fraîche

PREPARATION TIME: 1 HOUR 20 MINUTES
4 SERVINGS

¾ cup instant oatmeal

¾ cup all-purpose flour

Kosher salt

¾ cup milk, warmed

1 tablespoon sugar

1 envelope (¼ ounce) active dry yeast

2 large egg whites, at room temperature

2 tablespoons chopped dill

1 tablespoon chopped flat-leaf parsley

2 tablespoons chopped chives

2 teaspoons extra-virgin olive oil

¼ cup crème fraîche

2 tablespoons prepared horseradish

Freshly ground pepper

½ pound sliced smoked salmon

1. In a food processor, pulse the oatmeal just to break it down a little. In a medium bowl, combine the ground oats with the flour and ½ teaspoon of salt. In a small bowl, mix the warm milk with the sugar and yeast. Add the milk mixture to the oatmeal mixture and stir well. Cover the bowl with plastic wrap and let stand in a warm place until the batter has doubled in volume, about 45 minutes.

2. In a bowl, using an electric mixer, beat the egg whites at medium speed until soft peaks form. Fold one-third of the egg whites into the oatmeal batter, then fold in the remaining whites along with the dill, parsley and 1 tablespoon of the chives.

3. In a large nonstick skillet, heat 1 teaspoon of the olive oil. Ladle 2 tablespoons of batter into the skillet for each blini, gently spreading them to 3½-inch rounds. Cook over moderate heat until golden on both sides, about 6 minutes. Transfer the cooked blinis to a warmed platter and repeat with the remaining oil and batter.

4. In a bowl, mix the crème fraîche with the horseradish; season with salt and pepper. Spoon some horseradish crème fraîche on each blini, top with smoked salmon and sprinkle with the remaining chives and some pepper. Serve immediately.

Editor's Note

This recipe comes from Nairn's Cook School in Stirling, Scotland. Because Nairn is a passionate advocate of Scottish produce, he's reinvented the blinis here to include oatmeal, a traditional Scottish ingredient that provides a hearty flavor and texture.

Nick Nairn's Top
100 Chicken Recipes
Nick Nairn

Frisée fine du Nord

Perle du Nord

Frisée fine du Nord

Perle du Nord

Jamie Oliver goes in search of good greens.

Jamie's Dinners
by Jamie Oliver

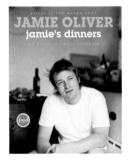

Published by Hyperion, 336 pages, color photos, $34.95

"I think a lot of people just don't understand the importance of where their food comes from or what might have been done to it before they buy it," declares British celebrity chef Jamie Oliver. Passionate, chatty and accessible, *Jamie's Dinners* is full of simple, flavor-packed recipes—some of which take as little as five minutes to make—plus suggestions for fun, healthy kids' lunch boxes and flexible family meals. Cheerfully named dishes like Good Old French Bean Salad and Tasty Fish Bake deliver results without demanding hours in the kitchen.

Featured Recipes Working Girl's Pasta; Good Old French Bean Salad; Tender and Crisp Chicken Legs with Sweet Tomatoes; Tasty Fish Bake

Best of the Best Exclusive Chicken Noodle Stir-Fry

195

Working Girl's Pasta

This is a pasta dish that Gennaro Contaldo used to make for our staff dinners when we worked at the Neal Street Restaurant in Covent Garden in London. In Italian this is called "pasta puttanesca," which basically translates as "whore's pasta"! I wanted to know why, as I'd never heard of this before. Maybe it's because the dish was cooked very quickly, with no effort involved, or maybe it's something the local prostitutes used to eat at home—who knows?!

But this is the way my darling Gennaro taught me to make it. He comes from the Amalfi coast, where fresh tuna would have been available. If you can get hold of some, it will make the dish much more luxurious and an event to eat. But if you can't, then canned will do.

4 SERVINGS

A handful of fresh basil

Sea salt and freshly ground black pepper

Zest and juice of 1 lemon

Extra virgin olive oil

Two 8-ounce tuna steaks, chopped into bite-size chunks, or 2 cans of good-quality tuna, packed in oil, drained

14 ounces penne or spaghetti

8 anchovy fillets

2 cloves of garlic, peeled and finely chopped

2 handfuls of soaked capers

A handful of black olives, pitted and roughly chopped

1 to 3 small dried chiles, crumbled to your taste, or 1 fresh red chile, deseeded and finely sliced

2 handfuls of really ripe tomatoes, finely chopped

Optional: a swig of white wine

A handful of fresh flat-leaf parsley, finely chopped

Smash the basil to a pulp with a pinch of salt and pepper. Add the lemon zest and juice and 2 good lugs of extra virgin olive oil. Mix this up and either rub over your chopped-up fresh tuna or mix with your broken-up canned tuna and allow to marinate.

Get a large pan of salted boiling water on and cook the pasta according to the package instructions. As soon as you put the pasta on, put 3 or 4 good lugs of

For more recipes by Jamie Oliver go to foodandwine.com/oliver. To access the recipes, log on with this code: **FWBEST05**. Effective through December 31, 2006.

extra virgin olive oil into a large frying pan and put on the heat. As the pan starts to get warm, add your anchovy fillets and allow them to fry and melt. At this point add your garlic, capers, olives and chile and stir around for a couple of minutes. If you have used fresh tuna, add it to the pan now with all of the marinating juices and sear it on both sides. When done, add the tomatoes and a little swig of white wine if you have some. If you have used canned tuna, add it to the pan at the same time as the tomatoes. Bring to the boil, then simmer for around 5 minutes, stirring regularly with a spoon, breaking the tuna up into smaller pieces. What you don't want to do is overcook the tuna so it goes tough. You want it to be soft and silky. Correct the seasoning carefully with salt and pepper.

The pasta should now be ready, so drain it in a colander, reserving some of the cooking liquid. Toss the hot pasta with the hot tuna sauce, add the parsley and mix well. You may need a few more lugs of olive oil and a spoonful of cooking water to make the sauce nice and loose.

Oliver on Anchovies

I use anchovies packed in salt for this dish, as they are the meatiest, tastiest, largest anchovies in the market. They are tinned very quickly, and this is reflected in their fresh flavor.

Jamie's Dinners
Jamie Oliver

Good Old French Bean Salad

I had this salad a while ago in a bistro in France and it was fantastic. You know, twangy and mustardy and so nice to eat as a starter before the main course arrived. It reminded me that sometimes cooking rules should be broken. We're told that beans should only be cooked until they're al dente, but I think we should cook them for a bit longer. I'd rather run my nails down a blackboard than eat a squeaky al dente green bean! So here's a recipe for properly cooked beans! Keep your eyes open for different colored beans— green, yellow or black—as a mixture will make it even more interesting. And when preparing them, leave the wispy ends on as they look so nice.

4 SERVINGS

- 4 handfuls of French beans (haricots verts), stalk ends removed
- 2 to 3 heaping teaspoons good French mustard, to taste
- 2 tablespoons good-quality white wine vinegar
- 7 tablespoons extra virgin olive oil

Sea salt and freshly ground black pepper

- 1 medium shallot, peeled and finely chopped

Optional: 1 tablespoon capers

- ½ clove of garlic, finely grated

Optional: a small handful of fresh chervil

Bring a pan of water to a fast boil, add your beans, put a lid on the pan and cook for at least 4 to 5 minutes. Boiling the beans fast like this helps them to retain all their nutrients. Meanwhile, put the mustard and vinegar into a jam jar or bowl and, while stirring, add the olive oil to make a good hot French dressing. Season carefully with sea salt and freshly ground black pepper, then add the finely chopped shallot, the capers if you're using them and the garlic.

Remove one of the beans from the pan to check if it's cooked. If it holds its shape but is also soft to the bite, it's perfect. Drain in a colander. Now, while the beans are steaming hot, this is the perfect moment to dress them—a hot bean will take on more of the wonderful dressing than a cold one. It is best to serve the beans warm, not cold, and certainly not at fridge temperature because the flavors will be muted and boring. Serve the beans in a bowl, sprinkled with chervil if you like—it's a delicate, crunchy herb that goes well with beans. Serve as a salad in its own right, or as an accompaniment to a main meal.

Jamie's Dinners
Jamie Oliver

Tender and Crisp Chicken Legs with Sweet Tomatoes

This recipe takes literally minutes to put together but then requires slow, gentle cooking. However, in return for your patience, what happens in the pan from just a couple of ingredients is an absolute joy and never fails, so it's a good one to serve if you have guests. Basically the skin of the chicken goes beautifully crisp and the meat becomes sticky and tender and falls away from the bone, while the tomatoes are slow-roasting and creating the most fabulous broth. The finished dish can be flaked into warm salads, tossed with some cooked and drained pappardelle or simply eaten as it is. A great recipe.

4 SERVINGS

- 4 chicken legs, jointed
- Sea salt and freshly ground black pepper
- A big bunch of fresh basil, leaves picked, stalks finely chopped
- 2 big handfuls of red and yellow cherry tomatoes, halved, and ripe plum tomatoes, quartered
- 1 whole bulb of garlic, broken up into cloves
- 1 fresh red chile, finely chopped
- Olive oil
- Optional: One 14-ounce can of cannellini beans, drained
- Optional: 2 handfuls of new potatoes, scrubbed

Preheat your oven to 350°F. Season your chicken pieces all over and put them into a snug-fitting pan in one layer. Throw in all the basil leaves and stalks, then chuck in your tomatoes. Scatter the garlic cloves into the pan with the chopped chile and drizzle over some olive oil. Mix around a bit, pushing the tomatoes underneath. Place in the oven for 1½ hours, turning the tomatoes halfway through, until the chicken skin is crisp and the meat falls off the bone. If you fancy, you can add some drained cannellini beans or some sliced new potatoes to the pan and cook them with the chicken. Or you can serve the chicken with some simple mashed potato. Squeeze the garlic out of the skins before serving. You could even make this dish part of a pasta meal—remove the chicken meat from the bone and shred it, then toss into a bowl of linguine, pappardelle or spaghetti and serve at once.

Tasty Fish Bake

Test Kitchen Tip
Roughly chopping the anchovies really helps them melt into this dish, dispersing their flavor evenly throughout the sauce.

Although I've eaten dishes similar to this in the past, this particular fish bake was brought to my attention recently by one of my students. It's essentially some slow-cooked "jammified" sweet onions and fennel, layered with lovely, flaky fish, crunchy potatoes and bread crumbs with a little cream and cheese, and baked in the oven. When you eat it, make sure to get a bit of every layer on your fork! The dish makes wonderful use of trout (as I've used here), sardines, salmon or mackerel—any fish, really, but oily ones are great to use, especially for kids. Try to get hold of the freshest fish you can, and ask your fishmonger to prepare it and get rid of the bones for you.

4 SERVINGS

- 14 ounces potatoes, scrubbed and finely sliced
- 4 tablespoons olive oil
- 1 clove of garlic, peeled and chopped
- 1 onion, peeled and sliced
- 1 bulb of fennel, trimmed and sliced
- 1 teaspoon fennel seeds
- 4 medium or 8 small fillets of trout, pinboned
- 1¼ cups light cream
- 2 handfuls of freshly grated Parmesan cheese, plus extra for sprinkling
- 2 anchovy fillets
- Sea salt and freshly ground black pepper
- 2 handfuls of fresh bread crumbs
- 2 lemons, halved

Preheat the oven to 400°F. First of all, parboil the sliced potatoes in salted boiling water for a few minutes until softened and then drain in a colander. Place an 8-inch casserole-type pan on a low heat, and add the oil, garlic, onion, fennel and fennel seeds. Cook slowly for 10 minutes with the lid on, stirring every so often.

Take the pan off the heat. Lay your trout fillets skin-side up over the onion and fennel. Mix together your cream, Parmesan and anchovies, season with salt and freshly ground black pepper, and pour over the fish. Toss the potato slices in a little olive oil, salt and pepper and layer these over the top. Place in the oven for 20 minutes, sprinkling with the bread crumbs and a little grated Parmesan 5 minutes before the end. Serve with lemon halves, a green salad and cold beers!

Jamie's Dinners
Jamie Oliver

Chicken Noodle Stir-Fry

4 SERVINGS

¾ pound egg fettuccine

3 tablespoons vegetable oil

½ cup roasted, unsalted cashews

1½ pounds skinless, boneless chicken thighs,
   cut into ¼-inch strips

Kosher salt and freshly ground pepper

3 large garlic cloves, finely chopped

1½ tablespoons finely chopped fresh ginger

8 scallions, sliced

3 long red chiles, seeded and thinly sliced

2 cups bean sprouts

¾ cup coarsely chopped cilantro leaves,
   plus 8 cilantro sprigs for garnish

¼ cup plus 2 tablespoons soy sauce

3 tablespoons fish sauce

1½ tablespoons fresh lime juice,
   plus 4 lime wedges for serving

1½ teaspoons sugar

1. In a large pot of boiling salted water, cook the fettuccine until al dente. Drain and transfer to a large bowl. Toss with 1 tablespoon of the oil.

2. In a small skillet, toast the cashews over moderate heat, stirring constantly, until fragrant and golden, about 4 minutes. Coarsely chop the cashews.

3. Season the chicken with salt and pepper. In a very large skillet or wok, heat the remaining 2 tablespoons of oil. When it is very hot, add the chicken and stir-fry over moderately high heat until just cooked through, about 3 minutes. Add the garlic and ginger and stir-fry for 1 minute. Add the scallions, chiles and bean sprouts and stir-fry for 30 seconds. Add the fettuccine and chopped cilantro and toss for 1 minute. Add the soy sauce, fish sauce, lime juice and sugar and toss again. Transfer to a bowl, garnish with the cilantro sprigs and chopped cashews and serve with lime wedges.

Editor's Note
Oliver likes to make this dish with egg fettuccine, which adds a delicious richness to the dish. You can also try buckwheat or rice noodles.

Jamie's Dinners
Jamie Oliver

Hoisin sauce for Chinatown Barbecued Pork Tenderloins, PAGE 206

Raichlen's Indoor! Grilling

by Steven Raichlen

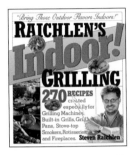

Published by Workman,
432 pages, color photos, $18.95

"The reason I wanted to write this book is that people have been grilling indoors for thousands of years. There's a deep story here that's important to tell," says Steven Raichlen, one of America's grill masters and author of over 25 cookbooks. His latest book sets out to help people create the smoky, satisfying flavors of outdoor grills—indoors. Quite a goal, but one Raichlen achieves with a wide array of equipment, from a George Foreman machine to a countertop rotisserie to a grill set in a fireplace. Raichlen also covers many cuisines, among them Chinese (Chinatown Barbecued Pork Tenderloins) and Argentinean (Lamb Steaks with Mint Chimichurri), with meticulous instructions.

Featured Recipes Chinatown Barbecued Pork Tenderloins; Lamb Steaks with Mint Chimichurri; Chicken Paillards with "Virgin" Sauce

Best of the Best Exclusive Buffa-Que Shrimp

205

Chinatown Barbecued Pork Tenderloins

Test Kitchen Tip
If you don't have a rotisserie, you can still make this delicious recipe by roasting the pork in the oven at 375° for about 20 minutes, basting the meat halfway through.

You've seen them hanging in the kitchen windows of Chinese restaurants—pork tenderloins roasted until they're dark and crusty, glistening with honey and hoisin sauce, and perfumed with garlic and five-spice powder, a mix of spices including star anise, fennel seeds, cinnamon, cloves, and pepper. This is Chinese "barbecue" at its best and it's easy to make at home. The combination of garlic and sugar with pork, widespread in Asia, may sound a bit odd, until you pause to think of the many sweet American barbecue sauces that contain garlic. Traditionally, Chinese pork is roasted suspended in a special oven. However, the rotisserie turns out a spectacular tenderloin that's succulent, and candy sweet.

4 SERVINGS

2 teaspoons Chinese five-spice powder

1 teaspoon sugar

1 teaspoon coarse salt (kosher or sea)

1 teaspoon freshly ground black pepper

1½ pounds pork tenderloin (2 to 3 tenderloins)

4 cloves garlic, thinly sliced

1 piece (2 inches) fresh ginger, peeled and thinly sliced

3 tablespoons *char siu* sauce (see Note) or hoisin sauce

3 tablespoons rice wine or dry sherry

3 tablespoons honey

2 tablespoons soy sauce

1. Place the five-spice powder, sugar, salt, and pepper in a small bowl and stir to mix. Sprinkle this rub over the tenderloins on all sides, patting it onto the meat with your fingertips.

2. Remove the silver skins (the sinewlike covering) from the tenderloins by trimming them off with a knife. Place the pork in a nonreactive baking dish or resealable plastic bag and add the garlic and ginger. Place the *char siu* sauce, rice wine, honey, and soy sauce in a small nonreactive bowl and whisk to mix. Pour this mixture over the pork and turn it to coat on all sides. Let the pork marinate in the refrigerator, covered, for at least 6 hours or as long as overnight.

Raichlen's
Indoor! Grilling
Steven Raichlen

3. When ready to cook, drain the pork in a strainer over a nonreactive saucepan and set the marinade aside. Place the drip pan in the bottom of the rotisserie (see Raichlen on Using a Countertop Rotisserie at right). Skewer the tenderloins onto the rotisserie spit (ideally, they should be positioned so that they will be perpendicular to the spit). Attach the spit to the rotisserie and turn on the motor. If your rotisserie has a temperature control, set it to 400°F. Cook the pork until golden brown and cooked through, 40 minutes to 1 hour. Use an instant-read meat thermometer to test for doneness; don't let the thermometer touch the spit. When done the internal temperature of the meat should be about 160°F.

4. Meanwhile, as the pork cooks, bring the reserved marinade to a boil over high heat and let boil until thick and syrupy, 2 to 4 minutes. Baste the pork tenderloins with the boiled marinade after they have cooked for 30 minutes and again once or twice more before removing them from the rotisserie.

5. Transfer the pork tenderloins to a platter or cutting board and let rest for 3 minutes, then thinly slice them crosswise. Pour any remaining marinade over the pork and serve at once.

NOTE *Char siu* (sometimes spelled *chu hou*) sauce is a dark red Chinese barbecue sauce sold in jars in Asian markets and many specialty food stores.

Raichlen on Using a Countertop Rotisserie

Line the drip pan with aluminum foil to facilitate cleanup.

Skewer food on the spit so that the weight will be as evenly distributed as possible.

When carrying the spit, hold it so that the removable gear wheel is slightly elevated, to keep the gear wheel from falling off.

Raichlen's Indoor! Grilling
Steven Raichlen

Lamb Steaks with Mint Chimichurri

Raichlen on Lamb Steaks

Your chief challenge in this recipe will be finding lamb steaks. Some supermarkets sell them; if not, try a butcher or Greek market. If you can't find lamb steaks, substitute rib or loin lamb chops. Rib chops that are ½ inch thick will be cooked to medium-rare after 3 to 5 minutes per side; 1-inch-thick loin chops will be medium-rare after 4 to 6 minutes.

4 SERVINGS

1 to 2 bunches fresh mint, rinsed and shaken dry (for about 1 cup loosely packed leaves)

3 cloves garlic, coarsely chopped

1 teaspoon coarse salt (kosher or sea), or more to taste

½ teaspoon freshly ground black pepper, or more to taste

⅓ cup extra-virgin olive oil (preferably Spanish)

2 tablespoons red wine vinegar

4 lamb steaks (each about ½ inch thick and 6 to 8 ounces)

1. Set aside 4 mint sprigs for garnish, then remove the stems from the remaining mint. Place the mint leaves, garlic, salt, and pepper in a food processor and finely chop them, running the machine in short bursts. Add the olive oil and wine vinegar in a thin stream, again running the machine in short bursts. Add 2 to 4 tablespoons of water, enough to thin the mixture to a pourable sauce. Taste for seasoning, adding more salt and/or pepper as necessary; the *chimichurri* should be highly seasoned.

2. Spoon about ¼ cup of the *chimichurri* into the bottom of a nonreactive baking dish that is just large enough to hold the lamb steaks in a single layer. Arrange the lamb steaks on top and spoon about a third of the remaining *chimichurri* over them, spreading it over the lamb with the back of the spoon. Let the lamb marinate, covered, in the refrigerator for at least 30 minutes or as long as 4 hours; the longer the lamb marinates, the richer the flavor will be. Refrigerate the remaining *chimichurri*, covered; you'll use this as a sauce (let it return to room temperature before serving).

3. When ready to cook, drain the lamb well, scraping off the excess marinade with a rubber spatula. Discard the marinade.

4. To cook the lamb on a **contact grill**, preheat to high, lightly oil, and cook the steaks 3 to 4 minutes for medium-rare, 5 to 6 minutes for medium. To cook on a **grill pan**, preheat to medium-high, lightly oil, and cook the steaks 3 to 4 minutes per side for medium-rare, 5 to 6 minutes per side for medium. To cook on a **built-in grill**, preheat to high and cook the steaks 3 to 4 minutes per side for medium-rare, 5 to 6 minutes per side for medium. If desired, rotate each steak a quarter turn after 1½ minutes to create a handsome crosshatch of grill marks.

5. Transfer the lamb steaks to a platter or plates. Garnish each with a sprig of mint and serve the remaining *chimichurri* on the side.

Raichlen's Indoor! Grilling
Steven Raichlen

Chicken Paillards with "Virgin" Sauce

Starting with a classic Mediterranean leitmotif, tomato, garlic, basil, and olive oil, this recipe builds to a crescendo of flavor. It does this using the most plebeian cut of poultry, the skinless, boneless chicken breast. To lend it interest, the chicken breast is pounded into a thin sheet known as a paillard. The "Virgin" Sauce—a mixture of fresh tomatoes, basil, garlic, and olive oil—may be uncomplicated, but the flavors are as bright as the midday sun.

4 SERVINGS

- 2 whole skinless, boneless chicken breasts (each 12 to 16 ounces), or 4 half breasts (each half 6 to 8 ounces)
- 1 clove garlic, minced
- 3 fresh basil leaves, minced, plus 4 basil sprigs for garnish
- Coarse salt (kosher or sea) and freshly ground black pepper
- 2 tablespoons extra-virgin olive oil
- "Virgin" Sauce (recipe follows)

1. If using whole chicken breasts, divide them in half. Trim any sinews or excess fat off the chicken breasts and discard. Remove the tenders from the breasts and set aside for kebabs or satés. Rinse the breasts under cold running water, then drain (don't blot them dry with paper towels; the breasts should be damp). Place a breast half between 2 pieces of plastic wrap and gently pound it to a thickness of between ¼ and ⅛ inch using a meat pounder, the side of a heavy cleaver, a rolling pin, or the bottom of a heavy saucepan. Repeat with the remaining breast halves.

2. Place the garlic and minced basil, ½ teaspoon of salt, and ½ teaspoon of pepper in a bowl and mash to a paste with the back of a spoon. Stir in the olive oil. Brush each paillard on both sides with the garlic and basil mixture and season lightly with salt and pepper.

3. To cook the paillards, preheat a **grill pan** to medium-high, lightly oil, and cook for 1 to 2 minutes per side. Alternatively, heat a **built-in grill** to high and cook for 1 to 2 minutes per side. Check for doneness; the chicken should feel firm when pressed. You may need to work in more than one batch; cover the grilled paillards with aluminum foil to keep warm until ready to serve.

Raichlen's
Indoor! Grilling
Steven Raichlen

To seed a tomato, cut it
in half crosswise. Hold
the tomato cut side
down over a bowl and
squeeze it between your
fingers to wring out the
seeds. If necessary, use
the tip of a butter knife
to help scrape them out.

4. Transfer the paillards to a platter or plates and spoon "Virgin" Sauce over them. Garnish each with a sprig of basil and serve at once.

NOTE The only even remotely tricky part of this recipe is pounding the chicken breasts into paillards. You can use small boneless whole breasts or large breast halves; whole breasts are easier to work with as they are thinner to begin with.

"Virgin" Sauce *Fresh Tomato Sauce*

The French call this redolent garlic, basil, and tomato condiment *sauce vierge* (literally virgin sauce), perhaps because it's not cooked. It lives or dies by the quality of the ingredients: verdant basil leaves (fresh, of course); tomatoes so luscious and ripe they go splat if you drop them; and olive oil of a noticeably green color and with a fragrance and flavor you can only describe as fruity. The olives in the sauce are not strictly traditional, but they add a nice touch.

MAKES ABOUT 1 CUP

- 1 clove garlic, minced
- ½ teaspoon salt, or more to taste
- 1 large ripe red tomato (6 to 8 ounces), seeded (see Raichlen on Seeding Tomatoes at left) and cut into ¼-inch dice
- 12 niçoise olives, or 6 black olives, pitted and cut into ¼-inch dice
- 8 fresh basil leaves, thinly slivered
- ¼ cup extra-virgin olive oil
- 1 tablespoon red wine vinegar, or more to taste
- Freshly ground black pepper

Place the garlic and salt in a nonreactive bowl and mash to a paste with the back of a spoon. Add the tomato, olives, basil, olive oil, and vinegar and stir to mix. Taste for seasoning, adding more salt and/or vinegar as necessary and pepper to taste; the sauce should be highly seasoned.

Best of the Best Exclusive
Buffa-Que Shrimp

6 SERVINGS

2 pounds jumbo shrimp

½ cup hot sauce, such as Tabasco

¼ cup plus 2 teaspoons fresh lemon juice

3 tablespoons extra-virgin olive oil

1 tablespoon Worcestershire sauce

3 garlic cloves, minced

Kosher salt and freshly ground pepper

3 ounces Maytag blue cheese, crumbled (½ cup)

¾ cup mayonnaise

⅓ cup sour cream

2 tablespoons minced onion

4 tablespoons unsalted butter

6 medium celery ribs, cut into 3-inch sticks

1. Light a grill or preheat a grill pan over moderately high heat. Using kitchen scissors, cut through the back of each shrimp shell and remove the vein. In a shallow baking dish, toss the shrimp with ¼ cup of the hot sauce, ¼ cup of the lemon juice, the olive oil, Worcestershire sauce, garlic, 1 teaspoon of salt and ½ teaspoon of pepper. Refrigerate for up to 1 hour.

2. Meanwhile, place a strainer over a small bowl and press the blue cheese through the strainer. Stir in the mayonnaise, sour cream, onion and the remaining 2 teaspoons of lemon juice; season with salt and pepper.

3. In a small pot, combine the butter with the remaining ¼ cup of hot sauce and simmer over moderately low heat for 3 minutes. Remove from the heat.

4. Grill the shrimp for 6 minutes, turning once, until the shells are pink and lightly charred. Transfer the shrimp to a serving bowl. Pour the sauce on top and toss. Serve the shrimp with celery sticks and the blue cheese dressing.

Editor's Note

The idea for this dish is rooted in two classic American bar foods: peel-and-eat shrimp and spicy Buffalo wings. Grilling the shrimp in their shells helps them stay juicy and flavorful. Half the fun of these shrimp is how messy they are to eat. Provide your guests with lots of napkins when you serve them.

Raichlen's
Indoor! Grilling
Steven Raichlen

211

Blue-Ribbon Chili, PAGE 214

Celebrations 101
by Rick Rodgers

Published by Broadway Books, 304 pages, color photos, $29.95

In *Celebrations 101,* Rick Rodgers— ex-caterer, cooking teacher and author of over 20 cookbooks—tackles the subject of cooking for parties. "I wrote this cookbook because most of the entertaining books I've seen are about how to walk on water while making crêpes," he explains. "I just felt that a more realistic approach was needed." So Rodgers conceived his book to make entertaining simple and stress-free, with cooking timetables and shopping lists to provide clear guidance for all kinds of events, from a Super Bowl bash centered around excellent Blue-Ribbon Chili to a small Thanksgiving dinner of Herbed Turkey Breasts with Cranberry-Merlot Sauce.

Featured Recipes Blue-Ribbon Chili; Hickory-Smoked Baby Back Ribs with Vidalia Onion BBQ Sauce; Caesar Coleslaw

Best of the Best Exclusive Riesling-Glazed Chicken with Root Vegetables

Blue-Ribbon Chili

Cooks can get into very heated arguments over how to make chili—tomatoes or no tomatoes; beans or not; stew meat over ground meat—and so on. The bottom line is that there are no set rules, so I make my bowl of red with everything. There are no shortcuts to great chili, but at least you have a heap of it when you're finished. Because this chili is so flavorful, I resist the temptation to offer the traditional toppings of sour cream, shredded Cheddar cheese, pickled jalapeño rings, chopped onions, and the like, but you can do so if you wish. It's your party.

10 TO 12 SERVINGS

- 6 bacon slices, coarsely chopped
- 5 pounds boneless beef chuck, cut into 1-inch cubes
- 2 tablespoons vegetable oil
- 3 medium onions, chopped
- 1 green bell pepper, seeds and ribs discarded, chopped
- 1 red bell pepper, seeds and ribs discarded, chopped
- 2 jalapeños, seeds and ribs discarded, minced
- 6 garlic cloves, minced
- ⅓ cup plus 1 tablespoon chili powder, preferably Gebhardt's, or use pure ground mild chile, such as ancho
- 2 tablespoons smoky Spanish paprika, such as pimentón de la Vera, or sweet Hungarian paprika
- 1 tablespoon ground cumin
- 1 tablespoon dried oregano
- 1 tablespoon salt, plus more to taste
- ½ teaspoon freshly ground black pepper

One 14½-ounce can diced tomatoes with juice

One 14½-ounce can beef broth, preferably reduced-sodium

One 12-ounce bottle lager beer

One 28-ounce can pinto beans, drained and rinsed

One 28-ounce can hominy, drained and rinsed

1. Cook the bacon in a large Dutch oven or flameproof casserole over medium heat, stirring occasionally, until crisp, about 8 minutes. Using a slotted spoon, transfer the bacon to paper towels to drain.

2. Increase the heat to medium-high. In batches without crowding, cook the beef cubes, turning occasionally, until browned on all sides, about 5 minutes. Using a slotted spoon, transfer the beef to a platter. The beef should give off enough fat and juices to brown, but if needed, add some of the vegetable oil to the pot.

3. Add the oil to the pot and heat. Stir in the onions, green and red bell peppers, jalapeños, and garlic, and return the heat to medium. Cover and cook, stirring occasionally, until the vegetables soften, about 10 minutes.

4. Return the meat and any juices on the platter to the pot. Sprinkle with the chili powder, paprika, cumin, oregano, salt, and pepper, and mix well. Stir in the tomatoes with their juices, the beef broth, and beer. Bring to a boil over high heat. Reduce the heat to medium-low. Cover and simmer until the beef is tender, about 1¾ hours. During the last 20 minutes, stir in the reserved bacon, beans, and hominy.

5. Remove the chili from the heat and let stand 10 minutes. Skim off any fat that rises to surface. If you like thick chili, return the chili to medium heat and bring to a simmer. Mash some of the beans and hominy into the sauce with a slotted spoon to thicken the juices. Adjust the seasoning with additional salt. Serve hot.

MAKE AHEAD The chili can be made up to 2 days ahead, cooled, covered, and refrigerated, or frozen for up to 3 months.

Rodgers on Buying Chili Powder

When making chili, the quality of the spices is very important because you are using a fairly large quantity. Chili powder is a blend of mild ground chiles mixed with other spices such as cumin, oregano and garlic powder. Watch out for the "hot" varieties, as they can make your chili too incendiary for everyone in the party to enjoy. You can also use pure ground chile, which is processed into a powder without any additional seasonings, but use a mild kind, such as ancho, New Mexican Hatch or California. Spanish smoked paprika has recently hit the market, and it's great for adding a smoky flavor to food.

Celebrations 101
Rick Rodgers

Hickory-Smoked Baby Back Ribs with Vidalia Onion BBQ Sauce

Test Kitchen Tip

This recipe calls for baking the ribs and then cooking them over hickory chips in an outdoor grill for an extra hit of smokiness. If you don't feel like grilling outside, you can still make this recipe—just finish the ribs on a hot preheated grill pan or under the broiler. Cook for 5 minutes on each side, basting regularly, until deep brown.

There are many ways to grill ribs, but whenever I teach this method in my cooking classes, I gain a whole new group of converts. The trick is to wrap the ribs in aluminum foil, then bake the ribs in the foil so they have a chance to cook in their own juices. (The ribs can even be prepared a few hours ahead at this point.) The ribs are then unwrapped and grilled with lots of hickory smoke, and brushed with a sweet-tangy sauce to give them a glaze. I think you'll like the results.

8 SERVINGS

- ¼ cup chili powder
- 1 tablespoon salt
- 7 pounds baby back ribs, cut into slabs
- 2 cups hickory chips, soaked in water for at least 30 minutes

Vidalia Onion BBQ Sauce (recipe follows)

1. Mix the chili powder and salt in a small bowl. Sprinkle the ribs with the spice mixture. Wrap each slab of ribs in aluminum foil. Let the ribs stand at room temperature for 1 hour. (The wrapped ribs can be refrigerated up to 1 day ahead; remove from the refrigerator 1 hour before baking.)

2. Position racks in the center and top third of the oven and preheat to 350°F.

3. Place the foil-wrapped ribs on baking sheets (they can overlap). Bake until the ribs are just tender (open a foil packet to check), about 1½ hours. (The ribs can be prepared up to 1 day ahead, cooled, and refrigerated.)

4. Meanwhile, build a charcoal fire in an outdoor grill and let burn until the coals are covered with white ash. Sprinkle the drained chips over the grill—they will begin to smoke almost immediately. For a gas grill, place the drained chips on a piece of aluminum foil. Place the foil directly on the source of heat. Preheat the grill on High, allowing about 30 minutes for the chips to smolder and give off smoke (be patient, as some grills take longer than others). Reduce the heat to Medium.

Celebrations 101
Rick Rodgers

5. Unwrap the ribs, discarding the juices and rendered fat, and place on the grill. Cover and grill until the ribs are browned, about 5 minutes. Turn, cover, and brown the other side, about 5 minutes more. Brush the top of the ribs with some of the sauce and turn. Grill, covered, until the underside is glazed, about 3 minutes. Brush again with sauce, turn, cover, and grill to glaze the other side, about 3 minutes. Transfer the ribs to a cutting board and let stand for a few minutes.

6. Cut the slabs into individual ribs and transfer to a serving platter. Serve hot, with the remaining sauce passed on the side.

MAKE AHEAD The spice-rubbed ribs can be refrigerated 1 day ahead. The cooked ribs can be made up to 4 hours ahead, and glazed just before serving.

NOTE Master grillers argue over the benefits of hardwood charcoal versus charcoal briquettes (gas grill fans are left out of this discussion). Hardwood charcoal does have superior flavor, but it burns very quickly and very hot and you have ashes before you know what happened.

Celebrations 101
Rick Rodgers

Vidalia Onion BBQ Sauce

Some kind of sweet onion (such as Maui, Walla Walla, or Texas Sweets) is available at any time of the year, but late spring is the time for Georgia's Vidalia onions. While their inherent sweetness is a fine accent to smoky ribs, keep this sauce in mind for chicken, too. If you have leftover sauce after cooking the ribs, serve it on the side as a dip, or refrigerate it for another meal. It keeps very well.

MAKES ABOUT 6 CUPS

- 2 tablespoons unsalted butter
- 3 medium sweet onions, such as Vidalia, finely chopped
- 6 garlic cloves, finely chopped
- Two 10-ounce jars sugarless peach fruit spread made with fruit juice
- Two 12-ounce bottles American-style chili sauce
- ⅔ cup spicy brown mustard
- ½ cup light (unsulfured) molasses
- ⅔ cup cider vinegar
- 3 tablespoons Worcestershire sauce

Melt the butter in a heavy-bottomed, medium saucepan over medium-low heat. Add the onions and cover. Cook, stirring often, until the onions are golden brown, about 15 minutes. Add the garlic and cook, uncovered, until it gives off its fragrance, about 2 minutes. Stir in the peach fruit spread, chili sauce, mustard, molasses, vinegar, and Worcestershire sauce. Bring to a simmer, stirring often. Reduce the heat to low and simmer, stirring often to avoid scorching, until lightly thickened, about 30 minutes.

MAKE AHEAD The sauce can be made up to 2 weeks ahead, cooled, covered, and refrigerated.

Rodgers on Adding Spice to the Sauce

If you want to spice up this recipe, I would add a little minced habanero to the sauce; it goes nicely with the peaches. There's nothing wrong with adding a little jalapeño, either.

Celebrations 101
Rick Rodgers

Caesar Coleslaw

Anchovies used to be very unpopular little fishes. Now, thanks to Caesar salad and rustic cooking, the little guys are making a comeback. This bold coleslaw goes well with many grilled foods. To shred the cabbage, use the slicing blade (not the shredding blade) of a food processor or a V-slicer.

8 SERVINGS

1¼ cups mayonnaise

⅓ cup lemon juice

2 teaspoons anchovy paste

2 garlic cloves, crushed through a press

1 medium head Savoy or green cabbage (2¼ pounds), cored and thinly shredded

6 scallions, white and green parts, thinly sliced

½ cup freshly grated Parmesan cheese

Salt and freshly ground black pepper, to taste

1. In a large bowl, whisk the mayonnaise, lemon juice, anchovy paste, and garlic until smooth. Add the cabbage and scallions and mix well. Cover tightly and refrigerate until chilled, at least 1 hour.

2. Just before serving, mix in the cheese. Season with the salt and pepper. Serve chilled.

MAKE AHEAD The slaw can be made up to 1 day ahead, covered, and refrigerated. Add the Parmesan cheese just before serving.

Celebrations 101
Rick Rodgers

Riesling-Glazed Chicken with Root Vegetables

4 SERVINGS

4 whole chicken legs (about 2 pounds)

Kosher salt and freshly ground pepper

2 teaspoons chopped thyme

2 teaspoons chopped rosemary

¼ cup extra-virgin olive oil

2 pounds celery root, peeled and cut into ¾-inch dice

½ pound parsnips, peeled and cut into ¾-inch dice

½ pound carrots, peeled and cut into ¾-inch dice

4 large shallots, peeled

½ cup Riesling

½ cup chicken stock or low-sodium broth

1. Preheat the oven to 400°. Season the chicken legs with salt, pepper, 1 teaspoon of thyme and 1 teaspoon of rosemary. In a very large ovenproof skillet, heat 2 tablespoons of the olive oil. Add the chicken, skin side down, and cook over moderately high heat until the skin is golden brown and crisp, about 6 minutes. Transfer the chicken to a plate.

2. Discard the fat from the skillet. Return the skillet to moderately high heat and add the remaining 2 tablespoons of olive oil. Add the celery root, parsnips, carrots, shallots and the remaining 1 teaspoon each of thyme and rosemary; season with salt and pepper. Cook the vegetables, stirring occasionally, until golden brown, about 5 minutes. Add the wine and stock and bring to a simmer over moderate heat, scraping up the browned bits from the bottom of the skillet.

3. Set the chicken legs skin side up on top of the vegetables. Roast uncovered for 45 minutes, or until the chicken skin is crisp and the vegetables are tender. Transfer the chicken to a platter and serve with the glazed vegetables.

Editor's Note

Rick Rodgers has had enough of boneless, skinless chicken breasts. He prefers to cook dark-meat chicken, which is less likely to dry out, as in the one-pot dish here. Rodgers sometimes experiments by replacing the chicken with duck.

Celebrations 101
Rick Rodgers

Roast Monkfish with Crushed Potatoes, Olive Oil, and Watercress, PAGE 224

Rick Stein's Complete Seafood

by Rick Stein

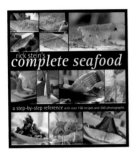

Published by Ten Speed Press, 264 pages, color photos, $40

British TV food personality Rick Stein, owner of the highly regarded Seafood Restaurant and Padstow Seafood School in Cornwall, England, offers a truly comprehensive guide to cooking fish, a subject he calls his "greatest love." Inside this hefty book, Stein's first in the States, you'll find step-by-step photographs showing how to skin, bone, fillet and cook myriad types of seafood as well as an illustrated A-to-Z of fish varieties to help you shop before you cook—whether you're making homey Fish Pie or elegant Roast Monkfish with Crushed Potatoes, Olive Oil, and Watercress.

Featured Recipes Roast Monkfish with Crushed Potatoes, Olive Oil, and Watercress; Braised Ling with Lettuce, Peas, and Crisp Smoked Pancetta; Thai Fish Cakes with Green Beans

Best of the Best Exclusive Hake with Sauce Verte and Butter Beans

223

Roast Monkfish with Crushed Potatoes, Olive Oil, and Watercress

4 SERVINGS

  2 (12-ounce) pieces of prepared thick monkfish fillet (see facing page)

1½ pounds new potatoes, scraped clean

  2 tablespoons olive oil

⅓ cup extra virgin olive oil, plus extra for serving

½ cup watercress sprigs, very roughly chopped

Balsamic vinegar, Maldon sea salt flakes, and
    coarsely crushed black pepper, for serving

1. Preheat the oven to 400°F. Season the monkfish with some salt, then set it aside for 15 minutes.

2. Cook the potatoes in well-salted boiling water until tender. While the potatoes are cooking, heat the 2 tablespoons of olive oil in a large frying pan that can be transferred to the oven. Pat the monkfish dry on paper towels, add to the pan, and sear for 3 to 4 minutes, turning it three or four times, until nicely browned on all sides. Transfer the pan to the oven and roast for 10 to 12 minutes, until the fish is cooked through but still moist and juicy in the center. Remove from the oven, cover with foil, and set aside for 5 minutes.

3. When the potatoes are done, drain them well and return them to the pot, then add the extra virgin olive oil. Gently crush each potato against the side of the pan with the back of a fork until it just bursts open.

4. Season the potatoes and add any juices from the fish. Add the watercress and turn over gently until the watercress is well mixed in.

5. To serve, cut the monkfish across into thick slices. Spoon the crushed potatoes onto four warmed plates and put the monkfish on top. Put your thumb over the top of the bottle of extra virgin olive oil and drizzle a little of it around the outside edge of each plate. Do the same with the balsamic vinegar, then sprinkle around a few sea salt flakes and coarsely crushed black pepper.

*Rick Stein's
Complete Seafood*
Rick Stein

Preparing Monkfish

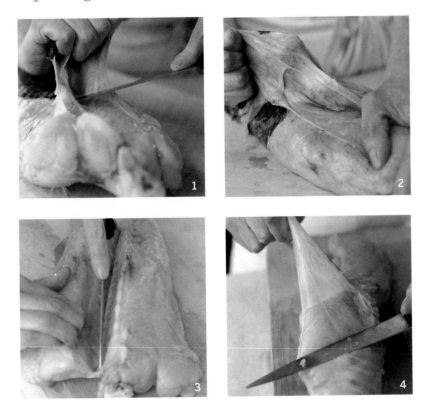

Stein on Preparing Monkfish

Removing the membrane from the monkfish is tricky, but it's not the end of the world if you don't do it. The membrane changes the look of the fillet when it cooks (it curls up) but won't change the flavor. Ask your fishmonger to remove it if you don't want to do it yourself.

1. First, remove the skin from the monkfish tail: Put the monkfish tail belly-side down on a board. Release some of the skin at the wider end of the tail and pull back so that you can get a sharp, flexible-bladed knife underneath to cut through the fine dorsal spines.

2. Grab hold of the wider end of the tail in one hand and the skin in the other, and briskly pull the skin away, down over the tail.

3. Remove the two fillets by cutting along either side of the thick backbone using a sharp, thin-bladed, flexible knife, keeping the blade as close to the bone as you can.

4. Pull off the thin membrane that encases the fillets, releasing it with the knife where necessary.

Rick Stein's
Complete Seafood
Rick Stein

Braised Ling with Lettuce, Peas, and Crisp Smoked Pancetta

Stein on Fish

For some reason people try to do too much with fish, as if they have to make up for the fact it isn't meat. That's a mistake. Often there's just too much happening on the plate, and people overcook the fish—that's when you really miss the point.

4 SERVINGS

- 4 (6- to 8-ounce) pieces of thick ling or cod fillet, skinned
- 7 tablespoons chicken stock
- ½ cup butter
- 12 large green onions, trimmed and cut into 1-inch pieces
- 4 small romaine hearts, cut into quarters
- 2⅓ cups freshly shelled or frozen green peas
- 8 very thin slices smoked pancetta or bacon
- 1 tablespoon chopped chervil or flat-leaf parsley

Salt and freshly ground white pepper

1. Season the pieces of ling with some salt. Bring the chicken stock to a boil in a small pan and keep hot.

2. Melt half the butter in a wide, shallow casserole that can be used for serving. Add the onions, and cook gently for 2 to 3 minutes, until tender but not browned. Add the quartered lettuce hearts and turn them over once or twice in the butter. Add the peas, hot chicken stock, and some salt and pepper, and simmer rapidly for 3 to 4 minutes, turning the lettuce hearts now and then, until the vegetables have started to soften and about three-fourths of the liquid has evaporated. Put the pieces of ling on top of the vegetables, then cover and simmer for 7 to 8 minutes, until the fish is cooked.

3. Shortly before the fish is done, heat a ridged cast-iron grill pan over a high heat. Pan-grill the pancetta or bacon for about 1 minute on each side, until crisp and golden. Keep warm.

4. Uncover the casserole, dot the remaining butter around the pan, and sprinkle the chopped chervil or parsley over the vegetables. Shake the pan over the heat until the butter has melted and amalgamated with the cooking juices to make a sauce. Garnish the fish with the pan-grilled pancetta, take the casserole to the table, and serve with some small new potatoes.

Rick Stein's
Complete Seafood

Rick Stein

Thai Fish Cakes with Green Beans

Tod Man Pla

Stein on Thai Fish Cakes

These fish cakes are great food for drinks parties. The dipping sauce is traditional, but you can use a sweet Thai chile sauce, too, and just add a pinch of five-spice powder to it; that works nicely.

4 SERVINGS

SWEET-AND-SOUR CUCUMBER SAUCE

¼ cup white wine vinegar

½ cup sugar

1½ tablespoons water

2 teaspoons Thai fish sauce *(nam pla)*

⅓ cup very finely diced hothouse cucumber

2 tablespoons very finely diced carrot

2 tablespoons minced onion

2 red bird chile peppers, thinly sliced

1 pound pollock fillets, skinned and cut into chunks

1 tablespoon Thai fish sauce *(nam pla)*

1 tablespoon Thai Red Curry Paste (recipe follows)

1 kaffir lime leaf or 1 strip of lime zest, very finely shredded

1 tablespoon chopped cilantro

1 egg

1 teaspoon palm sugar or raw brown sugar

½ teaspoon salt

⅓ cup green beans, thinly sliced into rounds

⅔ cup peanut or canola oil

1. For the sauce, gently heat the vinegar, sugar, and water in a small pan until the sugar has dissolved. Bring to a boil and boil for 1 minute, then remove from the heat and let cool. Stir in the fish sauce, cucumber, carrot, onion, and chiles. Pour into four small dipping saucers or ramekins and set aside.

2. For the fish cakes, put the fish in a food processor with the fish sauce, curry paste, kaffir lime leaf or lime zest, chopped cilantro, egg, sugar, and salt. Process until smooth, then stir in the sliced green beans.

3. Divide the mixture into 16 pieces. Roll each one into a ball, then flatten into a 2½-inch patty. Heat the oil in a large frying pan and fry the fish cakes, in batches, for 1 minute on each side, until golden brown. Lift out and drain briefly on paper towels, then serve with the sweet-and-sour cucumber sauce.

Rick Stein's Complete Seafood

Rick Stein

Thai Red Curry Paste

4 SERVINGS

- 5 large, medium-hot red chile peppers, stems removed, then roughly chopped
- 1-inch piece of fresh ginger, chopped
- 2 lemongrass stalks, outer leaves removed and core roughly chopped
- 6 garlic cloves
- 3 shallots, roughly chopped
- 1 teaspoon ground coriander
- 1 teaspoon ground cumin
- ¼ teaspoon *blachan* (Thai shrimp paste)
- 2 teaspoons paprika
- ½ teaspoon turmeric powder
- 1 teaspoon salt
- 1 tablespoon sunflower oil

Put everything into a food processor and blend to a smooth paste.

Editor's Note

This recipe makes a spicy and intensely flavored curry paste. If you don't have time to make your own, you can buy it in a jar. It's available at most supermarkets and will keep in the refrigerator for up to a year.

Rick Stein's Complete Seafood

Rick Stein

Hake with Sauce Verte and Butter Beans

Editor's Note
This recipe will be published in the forthcoming book *Rick Stein's Food Heroes* (BBC). It calls for hake, which becomes tender when cooked. If it is unavailable, Stein suggests using cod or orange roughy. He loves pairing warm fish with cold sauce, particularly a mayonnaise-based sauce like this delicate *sauce verte*.

4 SERVINGS

- 4 cups water
- 6 black peppercorns
- 2 bay leaves
- 1 small onion, sliced

Kosher salt

- 1 lemon, halved, plus 2 teaspoons fresh lemon juice

Four 7-ounce skinless hake or cod fillets

- 1½ cups baby spinach leaves
- 1½ cups watercress leaves
- 1 cup chervil leaves
- 1 cup tarragon leaves
- ¾ cup coarsely chopped chives
- 1 cup flat-leaf parsley leaves, plus 1 tablespoon chopped
- 2 egg yolks
- 1 teaspoon Dijon mustard
- 1 small garlic clove, crushed
- ⅔ cup extra-virgin olive oil
- ⅔ cup vegetable oil
- 1 tablespoon unsalted butter

Two 15-ounce cans butter beans, drained and rinsed

- 2 tomatoes—halved, seeded and diced
- 1 long red chile, seeded and minced

Freshly ground white pepper

1. In a large, deep skillet combine the water, peppercorns, bay leaves, onion and 2 teaspoons of salt. Squeeze the lemon halves over the skillet, drop them in and bring to a simmer. Cover and cook over moderately low heat for 20 minutes. Add the fish, skin side up, cover the skillet and simmer until just cooked through, about 6 minutes.

Rick Stein's
Complete Seafood
Rick Stein

2. Meanwhile, bring a medium pot of water to a boil. Add the spinach, watercress, chervil, tarragon, chives and the 1 cup of parsley leaves and cook just until bright green, about 5 seconds. Drain the greens and rinse under cold water until cool. Squeeze the greens dry and coarsely chop.

3. In a food processor, combine the greens with the 2 teaspoons of lemon juice, egg yolks, mustard, garlic and 1 teaspoon of salt. With the machine on, slowly drizzle in the olive oil and vegetable oil until emulsified.

4. In a small saucepan, melt the butter. Add the butter beans, tomatoes, chile and the chopped parsley and cook over moderate heat until warmed through, about 3 minutes. Season with salt and pepper. Transfer the beans to a platter and top with the fish. Spoon some of the *sauce verte* alongside and serve with the remaining sauce on the side.

MAKE AHEAD The *sauce verte* can be refrigerated for up to 1 day.

Stein on Mayo

I'm an absolute slug [addict] for homemade mayonnaise. I just have to keep it away from me. Some people have chocolate problems, I have mayo problems! Shrimp, which is what you Americans call prawns, dunked in mayo—I can't resist.

Rick Stein's Complete Seafood
Rick Stein

Short Ribs Braised in Porter Ale
with Maple-Rosemary Glaze, PAGE 245

All About Braising

by Molly Stevens

Published by Norton, 496 pages, color photos, $35

In a world of 30-minute meals, this book extols the benefits of a slow cooking technique that Molly Stevens describes as "tucking a few ingredients into a heavy pot with a bit of liquid, covering the pot tightly and letting everything simmer peacefully until tender and intensely flavored." Braising is famed for tenderizing even the toughest and cheapest cuts of meat (such as pork shoulder), but Stevens artfully modifies it to give delicate fish (like scallops) a flavor boost, too. Not a book for the novice, this is a good choice for those who enjoy the challenge of more complex recipes.

Featured Recipes Escarole Braised with Cannellini Beans; Braised Whole Chicken with Bread Stuffing and Bacon; Short Ribs Braised in Porter Ale with Maple-Rosemary Glaze

Best of the Best Exclusive Roasted Halibut with Potatoes, Lemons and Thyme

Escarole Braised with Cannellini Beans

Stevens on Beans

My tip for this recipe is to be picky when you choose your beans. Even though the recipe calls for dried beans, there are fresh dried beans and stale dried beans. I encourage you to buy your beans at bulk bins and places with high turnover. Dusty plastic bags of beans you find in the supermarket are not going to be the best quality. Even dried beans have a shelf life, so buy them in small quantities.

I have a deep fondness for the casual family-run southern Italian restaurants scattered throughout the cities of the Northeast. Just a step up from pizza places, the best of these eateries offer honest food heavily laced with garlic and olive oil, serve pasta only as a first course or side dish, and almost always have escarole and white beans somewhere on the menu. The silky bitterness of escarole braised with tender, meaty cannellini beans tempts me every time.

Serve this in pasta bowls as a first course, either on or accompanied by toasted Italian bread rubbed with garlic. The escarole also makes a fine side dish to meats and poultry.

For a shortcut version, use canned cannellini beans. You sacrifice some depth of flavor, but get a wonderfully quick weeknight dish in return. (See A Note on Canned Beans on page 237.)

BRAISING TIME: ABOUT 20 MINUTES, PLUS 1¼ HOURS BEAN COOKING TIME
6 SERVINGS

THE BEANS

- 1 cup (8 ounces) dried cannellini beans, picked over and rinsed
- 1 cup chicken stock, homemade (recipe follows) or store-bought

Water as needed

- 1 small onion (about 4 ounces), peeled and quartered
- 1 small carrot, peeled and quartered
- 2 garlic cloves, peeled and bruised
- 1 bay leaf
- 1 tablespoon extra-virgin olive oil

Coarse salt

THE BRAISE

- 1 medium head escarole (about 1 pound)
- ¼ cup extra-virgin olive oil
- 3 garlic cloves, thinly sliced

Pinch of crushed red pepper flakes

Coarse salt and freshly ground black pepper

- ½ lemon

Best-quality extra-virgin olive oil for drizzling

All About Braising
Molly Stevens

The cannellini beans require a bit of advance planning (Step 1). First they need to soak for 8 to 12 hours. Then they simmer for 1 to 1½ hours. Once the beans are tender, you need to let them cool in the cooking water—a step that helps them absorb more flavor. At this point, the beans can be refrigerated for 1 to 2 days, as suits your schedule.

1. SOAKING THE BEANS—8 TO 10 HOURS IN ADVANCE Place the beans in a medium bowl, cover with cool water, and leave to soak for 8 to 12 hours at room temperature. Drain and rinse.

2. COOKING THE BEANS Place the soaked beans in a medium heavy-based saucepan (2½- to 3-quart). Add the stock and enough water to cover by 1½ inches, then add the onion, carrot, garlic, bay leaf, and oil. Bring to a simmer over medium heat. Once the liquid simmers, partially cover the pot, lower the heat to a gentle simmer, and cook until the beans are tender, 1 to 1½ hours. (The cooking time will vary according to the dryness of the beans.) If at any time the level of the liquid threatens to drop below the level of the beans, add just enough water to cover. Ideally, when the beans are tender, they should have absorbed enough of the cooking liquid so that the pot is moist but not soupy. Season with salt to taste, and set aside to cool in the cooking liquid. (*The beans may be made 1 to 2 days ahead. If they will be sitting for more than 2 hours, transfer the beans and the cooking liquid to a bowl and keep them covered and refrigerated.*)

3. WASHING AND TRIMMING THE ESCAROLE Tear the escarole leaves from the head and soak them in a large bowl of cold water for 10 to 15 minutes to loosen any dirt. Rinse and drain, paying special attention to the hollows at the base of the outer leaves, the place where dirt usually collects. You may need to rub any stubborn dirt away with your thumb. Rinse again and drain briefly in a colander. Slice the escarole leaves into 1½-inch-wide strips and return the strips to the colander to drain.

4. THE AROMATICS Combine the oil, garlic, and crushed red pepper in a large lidded skillet (12- to 13-inch) over medium heat. Warm just until the garlic becomes fragrant and golden around the edges, about 2 minutes. Don't allow the garlic to become dark brown or you'll have to start over.

All About Braising
Molly Stevens

5. WILTING THE ESCAROLE Add the escarole a handful at a time, stirring and allowing it to wilt some before adding the next handful. (It's fine if the escarole still has water clinging to it; this will help it begin to braise.) Season with salt and pepper.

6. THE BRAISE Pull the carrot and onion pieces and the bay leaf from the pot of beans and discard. But don't be too fussy and try to get every last bit of onion, as some may have disintegrated right into the beans, along with the garlic. When all the escarole has wilted, spoon the beans and cooking liquid into the skillet, season with salt and pepper, and gently stir to incorporate the beans. Bring to a gentle simmer. Cover, adjust the heat to maintain a low simmer, and braise until the greens are very tender and the cooking liquid has thickened some from the starch released from the beans, about 20 minutes.

7. THE FINISH I prefer this dish soupy, so I serve as is. If you would like it less soupy, remove the lid and boil to reduce the liquid for about 5 minutes. Season the braise with a generous squeeze of fresh lemon juice and salt and pepper. Serve warm or at room temperature, with a thread of best-quality olive oil drizzled over the top.

A NOTE ON CANNED BEANS Many cooks suggest that canned beans can stand for home-cooked beans. I don't always agree. Canned beans don't deliver the same earthy flavor and creamy texture. They taste bland and often become mushy and broken—especially when cooked a second time. When you cook dried beans from scratch, you also end up with a tasty bean broth to add to braises and soups. Although simmering dried beans takes a few hours, they cook largely unattended and can be made a day or two ahead.

If you choose to use canned beans for convenience sake, the brands with the truest bean flavor and nicest texture are Goya and Bush's. Before using, drain and rinse beans thoroughly—the liquid they come packed in can be unpleasantly viscous and salty. If using canned beans for the Escarole Braised with Cannellini Beans, you'll need about 2½ cups (a little less than two 15-ounce cans). Omit Steps 1 and 2 in the recipe, and add the beans as directed in Step 6, along with 1 cup of chicken stock. Without the starchy bean broth, the liquid won't have much body.

WINE NOTES Vibrant white with citrus and herbal flavors from Italy, such as Pinot Grigio, Soave, or Vernaccia di San Gimignano.

Test Kitchen Tip
A good way to finish this dish is with a sprinkling of sharp, salty grated Romano cheese.

All About Braising
Molly Stevens

Chicken Stock

If you are going to make only one type of stock, let it be chicken stock. Indeed, I know more than a few chefs who cook with nothing else. I lightly roast the chicken bones before making stock to render off some of the excess fat. Plus, the pan drippings created by roasting the bones gives the stock a more appealing caramel color and richer chicken flavor. If you want a darker, meatier-tasting stock, roast the bones until they are deeply browned, about 15 minutes longer than directed in Step 2. If you want a more delicate, pale chicken stock, simply skip the roasting step altogether. Darker chicken stocks are best for braising dark meats, such as beef and lamb. When braising vegetables and other delicate foods, use a lighter stock. For braising chicken, any type will do.

MAKES ABOUT 2 QUARTS

About 4 pounds chicken backs and necks, or a mix
    of legs and thighs, skin removed

1 medium yellow onion (about 6 ounces), coarsely chopped

1 medium carrot, coarsely chopped

1 celery stalk, coarsely chopped

Five 3- to 4-inch leafy fresh thyme sprigs

Five 6- to 8-inch leafy flat-leaf parsley sprigs

1 bay leaf

6 black peppercorns

10½ cups cold water, or as needed

1. Heat the oven to 400 degrees.

2. Rinse the chicken under cool water and drain. Trim off any large bits of fat, such as the plump triangular section at the base of the tail. Dry the chicken thoroughly with paper towels. Arrange the chicken parts in a loose single layer in a large roasting pan. If they don't all fit, use two pans (a rimmed baking sheet will also work). Roast, turning with tongs halfway through, until golden brown, about 35 minutes. With the tongs, transfer the chicken pieces to a deep stockpot (8- to 10-quart). Pour off the excess fat from the roasting pan and discard.

3. Set the roasting pan over two burners on medium heat. Add enough cold water to generously cover the bottom of the pan, about ½ cup, and bring to a boil, stirring and scraping with a wooden spoon or heatproof spatula until you have dissolved the drippings in the bottom of the pan. Pour this seasoned water into the stockpot. Add the onion, carrot, and celery.

4. Tie the herbs together with a piece of kitchen twine so they are in a little bundle (this is known as a bouquet garni and prevents the herbs from getting in the way when you skim). Add the herb bundle to the pot, along with the peppercorns. Fill the pot with the cold water, adding enough to cover the bones by about 1 inch. Gently bring to a simmer over medium heat. Adjust the heat to maintain a gentle simmer, and simmer until the stock is fragrant and takes on the sweet taste of chicken, about 3 hours. Check the pot often and skim the surface of any large rafts of foam or scum and add more water any time the bones emerge above the surface. Never let the stock boil, or it will turn greasy and cloudy.

5. Strain the stock and discard the solids. (I find it's easiest to strain first though a colander to remove the large pieces, and then through a fine-mesh sieve to remove the finer particles.) Taste the stock. It should have a mild, sweet, chickeny flavor. If you prefer a more concentrated flavor, return the strained stock to the cleaned stockpot and simmer to reduce by one-third.

6. Let the stock cool to room temperature, then chill until the fat solidifies on the surface. Scrape the fat from the surface of the chilled stock before using. Refrigerate for up to 3 days, or freeze for up to 6 months.

All About Braising
Molly Stevens

Braised Whole Chicken with Bread Stuffing and Bacon

Stevens on Braising

I wrote this book because I love braising. I feel it's never been given its due in a cookbook and it's such a great way to cook—it's so forgiving.

Braising a plump roasting chicken makes a comforting family dinner. It's also just the dish to serve to guests when you want them to feel like family. What I love about braising a chicken is that there's none of that fuss over turning the bird to roast evenly or worry about getting the timing just right. The moist, gentle heat cooks the bird through to tender doneness in about 2 hours, and it doesn't threaten to dry out if you happen to braise it a few minutes too long. Plus, you end up with a perfectly balanced sauce that you quickly whir in the blender to make smooth and creamy. The bread stuffing accented with sliced ham, pine nuts, and raisins tastes so good that I make extra to bake alongside the chicken, just to be sure there's plenty to go around.

The only challenge in braising such a large bird is getting the outside browned. Its size and the stuffing make it too unwieldy to brown on top of the stove. I solve this by briefly roasting the chicken *after* braising. This way, the strips of bacon draped over the top of the chicken, which basted the meat as it braised, become all crisp and brown. Splendid.

BRAISING TIME: ABOUT 2 HOURS
6 SERVINGS

THE STUFFING

4 tablespoons rendered chicken fat or unsalted butter

1½ cups finely chopped yellow onion (1 large)

⅔ cup finely chopped inner celery stalks with leaves (4 small stalks)

⅔ cup finely chopped good-quality baked ham (4 thin slices), such as Black Forest or Westphalian

⅓ cup pine nuts, lightly toasted

⅓ cup currants, soaked in warm water for 20 minutes and drained

½ cup coarsely chopped flat-leaf parsley

5 cups ¾-inch bread pieces with crust—torn from a slightly stale rustic white loaf, preferably not sourdough (about 8 ounces)

Coarse salt and freshly ground black pepper

THE BRAISE

One 6- to 7-pound roasting chicken, neck, heart, and gizzard reserved

Coarse salt and freshly ground black pepper

2 to 2¼ cups chicken stock, homemade (page 238) or store-bought

1 tablespoon unsalted butter or rendered chicken fat

1 tablespoon extra-virgin olive oil

1 large or 2 small carrots, coarsely chopped

2 celery stalks, coarsely chopped

1 large yellow onion (about 8 ounces), coarsely chopped

1 teaspoon chopped fresh rosemary

1 teaspoon chopped fresh thyme

2 bay leaves

3 strips lemon zest, removed with a vegetable peeler (each about 2½ inches by ¾ inch)

½ cup dry white wine or dry white vermouth

5 strips lean bacon

¼ cup heavy cream (optional)

1. THE STUFFING Melt the fat or butter in a medium skillet (8-inch) over medium-low heat. Add the onion and celery and sauté, stirring once or twice, until translucent and soft, about 7 minutes. Transfer to a medium bowl. Add the ham, pine nuts, drained currants, parsley, and bread to the onion-celery mix and toss with a large spoon to distribute the ingredients evenly. Season with salt and pepper and toss again.

2. HEAT THE OVEN TO 325 DEGREES.

3. STUFFING THE CHICKEN Rinse the chicken inside and out under cool running water. Drain and then dry inside and out with paper towels. Pull any lumps of chicken fat from the opening of the cavity and discard. Chop off the last 2 joints of the wings with a cleaver or large kitchen knife, and reserve them with the neck, heart, and gizzard. Season the chicken inside and out with salt and pepper, and scoop enough stuffing into the cavity to fill it generously without jamming it full; the stuffing needs some room to expand as the chicken braises. Butter a small baking dish large enough to hold the remaining stuffing. Fill the dish with the leftover stuffing, and pour over ½ to ¾ cup of the stock, enough to barely moisten the stuffing. Cover with foil and set aside.

4. TRUSSING THE CHICKEN Using a length of kitchen string about 30 inches long, truss the chicken: Loop the middle of the string around the ends of the two drumsticks to pull them together. Now bring the ends of the string back

All About Braising
Molly Stevens

along the sides of the chicken, running the string between the leg and the breast on both sides, then turn the chicken over and snag the string over the base of the neck so that it won't slide down the chicken's back. Knot the string securely and trim off close to the knot.

5. THE AROMATICS AND BRAISING LIQUID Heat the butter and oil in a large Dutch oven (a 9½-quart oval works well) or deep flameproof roasting pan (3- to 4-inch sides) over medium-high heat. When the butter stops foaming, add the carrots, celery, onion, wing tips, neck, heart, and gizzard (discard the liver or save it for another use). Stir with a large wooden spoon to coat the vegetables in fat, and sauté until the vegetables begin to brown in spots, about 10 minutes. Add the rosemary, thyme, bay leaves, lemon zest, and salt and pepper to taste. Sauté for another minute. Pour in the wine and bring to a rapid simmer.

6. THE BRAISE Set the chicken on top of the vegetables. Lay 4 strips of bacon lengthwise from head to tail over the chicken to cover the entire breast. Cut the remaining strip of bacon in half and drape one half over each leg. Gently pour the remaining 1½ cups stock over the bacon. Once the stock begins to boil, lay a sheet of parchment paper over the chicken and tuck the edges around the chicken. Cover the pan tightly with the lid or with a sheet of heavy-duty foil. Slide the pan onto a rack in the lower part of the oven. Braise at a gentle simmer, basting every 30 to 40 minutes by spooning some of the braising liquid over the breast and legs. When you lift the lid or foil to baste, check to see that the liquid is at a slow simmer; if it appears to be simmering ferociously, reduce the oven heat by 10 or 15 degrees. Continue braising until the juices run clear when you prick the center of a thigh with a thin blade and an instant-read thermometer inserted between the thigh and the breast registers about 170 degrees, 1¾ to 2¼ hours. (You do not need to turn the chicken during braising. Since the dark meat, which takes longer than white meat to cook, sits in the liquid at the bottom of the pot, it will cook more quickly than the white meat above it. In the end, both white and dark meat are done at the same time. Another benefit of braising.)

7. MEANWHILE, HEAT THE REMAINING STUFFING When the chicken is almost done (1½ to 2 hours into braising), put the dish of stuffing into the oven alongside the chicken or on a rack above it to heat through, about 25 minutes.

All About Braising
Molly Stevens

Transfer the chicken to a sturdy baking sheet or half sheet pan and loosely cover it with foil so it doesn't cool too much. Increase the oven temperature to 475 degrees. If the dish of stuffing is heated through, remove it and set aside in a warm place. If it needs more time, leave it in the oven for a little while. Don't forget about the stuffing, however, as it will burn if left too long at 475 degrees.

8. THE SAUCE While the oven is heating, tilt the braising pan so that all the juices pool in one end, and skim off as much of the surface fat as you can with a wide metal spoon. Retrieve the bay leaves, lemon zest, wing tips, neck, heart, and gizzard with tongs and discard. Transfer the vegetables and cooking juices to a blender. With the blender lid ajar, puree until smooth. Pour the sauce into a medium saucepan and bring to a simmer over medium-high heat. Stir in the cream, if using. (The cream will round out the flavor of the sauce and impart a silky luxurious texture.)

9. WHILE THE SAUCE IS SIMMERING, BROWN THE CHICKEN Slide the chicken onto a rack in the middle of the oven to roast until the bacon begins to brown, 10 to 12 minutes. At the same time, remove the foil from the dish of stuffing, and return to the oven to roast until the top becomes browned and crusty, about 10 minutes. If there's room on the oven rack for the stuffing next to the chicken, slide it onto the same rack; otherwise, put the stuffing beneath the chicken.

10. FINISH THE SAUCE Taste the simmering sauce and assess its consistency. With or without the cream, it should be saucy but not too thick. If you want it a bit thicker, increase the heat and simmer vigorously to reduce. Otherwise, turn the heat to low to keep the sauce warm. Season to taste with salt and pepper.

11. SERVING Transfer the chicken to a carving platter. Remove the trussing string and carve into serving pieces, making sure to give everyone a few bits of crisp bacon. Scoop some stuffing onto each plate, and ladle the sauce over the top. Pass the remaining sauce at the table.

WINE NOTES Medium-bodied red with youthful fruit, a touch of earthiness, and bright acidity—Pinot Noir from California, Oregon, or New Zealand; lighter-style red Burgundy; Cru Beaujolais; or Italian Barbera.

All About Braising
Molly Stevens

Short Ribs Braised in Porter Ale with Maple-Rosemary Glaze

Ale-braised short ribs are thoroughly satisfying on their own, but finishing them with a rosemary-infused maple glaze makes them special enough for even your best company. To make things easy, they can be made ahead and briefly reheated and glazed under the broiler just before serving. Their flavor actually improves as they sit for a day or two in the refrigerator.

For the braise, I use a local porter ale from Otter Creek Brewery in Middlebury, Vermont, because it's robust and smooth but not too strong or too bitter. Select an ale with some body and a smoky taste—all the better if you can find one that's brewed locally. Stout will be too strong. The bit of horseradish in the maple glaze adds piquancy to balance the other elements in the dish.

Roasted beets would be a good choice with these ribs. If you can find golden beets, they look especially stunning next to the glistening ribs.

BRAISING TIME: 2½ TO 3 HOURS
6 SERVINGS

3½ to 4 pounds meaty bone-in short ribs

Coarse salt

Freshly ground black pepper

2 tablespoons extra-virgin olive oil

2 large yellow onions (about 1 pound total), sliced about ½ inch thick

1 carrot, chopped into ½-inch pieces

1½ cups porter ale, or more if needed

¾ cup beef, veal, or chicken stock, homemade (page 238) or store-bought, or water

One 3- to 4-inch leafy fresh rosemary sprig

1 large or 2 small bay leaves

THE GLAZE

3 tablespoons pure maple syrup

Two 3- to 4-inch leafy fresh rosemary sprigs

1 tablespoon prepared horseradish

WORKING AHEAD

If you have the time and forethought, beef short ribs benefit greatly from advance salting (see Step 2). This mini-cure will tighten the meat a bit,

Test Kitchen Tip

Add some new potatoes, mushrooms and a few extra carrots to the braising liquid about half an hour before the short ribs are finished cooking to make this a tasty one-pot dinner.

All About Braising
Molly Stevens

improving its texture, help it to brown more readily in the first step of the braise, and deepen its hearty taste. If there's no time for advance salting, simply skip Step 2 below, seasoning with a bit of salt along with the black pepper as directed.

If you braise the short ribs ahead of time (from a few hours to a full two days) and then glaze them just before serving, the dish will taste even better. The flavors meld and develop as the ribs sit. Simply complete the recipe through Step 9 up to 2 days before you plan to serve them. Pour the strained and reduced braising liquid over the ribs, let cool, cover, and refrigerate. To serve, reheat, covered with foil, in a 350-degree oven until just heated through, about 25 minutes. Remove from the oven, and heat the broiler. Brush on the glaze and proceed as directed in Step 10.

1. TRIMMING THE RIBS Trim any excess fat from the short ribs, but don't take off any of the silverskin or tough-looking bits that hold the ribs together.

2. SALTING THE RIBS—1 OR 2 DAYS BEFORE BRAISING (OPTIONAL) Arrange the short ribs in a loose layer on a tray or in a nonreactive dish. Sprinkle them all over with 1½ to 2 teaspoons salt (there's no need to rub the salt into the meat) and cover loosely with waxed paper or plastic wrap. Refrigerate for 1 to 2 days.

3. HEAT THE OVEN TO 300 DEGREES Pat the ribs dry with a paper towel, but don't try to rub off the salt. Season with pepper. (If you didn't salt the ribs in advance, season them with both salt and pepper.)

4. BROWNING THE RIBS Pour the oil into a Dutch oven or other heavy braising pot (4- to 6-quart) wide enough to accommodate the short ribs in a crowded single layer and heat over medium heat. Add only as many ribs as will fit without touching, and brown them, turning with tongs, until chestnut-brown on all sides, about 4 minutes per side. Transfer the seared ribs to a platter, without stacking, and continue until all the ribs are browned. (*Alternatively, you may want to brown the ribs under the broiler to avoid some of the spatter, although this will mean dirtying another pan. See directions on page 248.*)

5. THE AROMATICS Pour off and discard all but about a tablespoon of fat from the pot. If there are any charred bits in the pot, wipe them out with a damp paper towel, being careful not to remove the precious caramelized drippings. Return the pot to medium-high heat and add the onions and carrot. Season with salt and pepper and sauté, stirring a few times, until the vegetables start to brown and soften, about 5 minutes.

6. THE BRAISING LIQUID Add the ale and bring to a full boil. Boil for 2 minutes, scraping the bottom of the pot with a wooden spoon to dislodge and dissolve any tasty bits cooked onto it. Pour in the stock, bring again to a boil, and reduce the heat to a simmer. Return the ribs to the pot, along with any juices released as they sat. Tuck the rosemary sprig and bay leaves in between the ribs. The ribs should be partially submerged in the liquid. If necessary, add a bit more ale or water.

7. THE BRAISE Cover with a sheet of parchment paper, pressing down so that it nearly touches the ribs and hangs over the edges of the pot by about an inch. Set the lid securely in place. Slide the pot into the oven and braise at a gentle simmer, turning the ribs with tongs so as not to tear up the meat, every 40 to 45 minutes, until fork-tender, about 2½ hours. Check under the lid after the first 10 minutes to see that the liquid isn't simmering too aggressively; if it is, lower the oven temperature 10 or 15 degrees.

8. MEANWHILE, PREPARE THE GLAZE While the ribs are braising, combine the maple syrup with the rosemary sprigs in a small saucepan. Heat to a gentle boil over medium heat. Turn off the heat, cover, and set aside to infuse for 1 hour. (*The glaze can be made up to a few days ahead and refrigerated.*)

9. REMOVING THE RIBS FROM THE BRAISING LIQUID When the ribs are tender and the meat is pulling away from the bones, use tongs or a slotted spoon to carefully transfer them to a flameproof gratin dish or shallow baking dish that is large enough to accommodate them in a single layer. Try your best to keep the ribs on the bones and intact, but don't worry if some bones slip out. (Discard these clean bones, or save them for the dog.) Scoop out the vegetables with a slotted spoon and arrange them around the ribs. Cover loosely with foil to keep warm.

10. FINISHING THE BRAISING LIQUID Tilt the braising pot to collect the juices in one end and skim off as much surface fat as you can with a large spoon. If there is more fat than you care to skim off a spoonful at a time, transfer the braising liquid to a gravy separator and then pour the liquid into a medium saucepan, leaving the fat behind. If the braising liquid exceeds ½ cup, bring it to a vigorous simmer over medium-high heat and cook it down to close to ½ cup, 10 to 15 minutes; it should have a syrupy consistency. Taste and season with salt and pepper. Keep warm.

Stevens on Leftovers

The short ribs make great leftovers. I often turn them into a pasta sauce, like a ragù. They also make the best sandwiches. Just split a crusty baguette, put some of the warm meat inside and spoon the juices over.

All About Braising
Molly Stevens

11. **GLAZING THE SHORT RIBS** Heat the broiler on high. If the glaze has been refrigerated, warm it slightly so that it's pourable. Remove the rosemary sprigs, lightly running your fingers down the length of the sprigs so you save every drop of glaze. Put the horseradish in a small strainer (a tea strainer works great) or in the palm of your hand and press or squeeze over the sink to eliminate as much liquid as possible, then stir the horseradish into the glaze. Brush the glaze on the tops of the short ribs. Pour the reduced braising liquid around the ribs—*don't pour it over the ribs, or you'll wash off the glaze*. Slide the ribs under the broiler and broil until the surface of the ribs develops a shiny, almost caramelized glaze and you can hear them sizzle, about 4 minutes.

12. **SERVING** Transfer the ribs to serving plates—the number per serving depends on the size of the ribs. Spoon the braising liquid around, not over, the ribs, and serve immediately.

BROWNING THE SHORT RIBS UNDER A BROILER You can also sear the ribs under the broiler, not in the braising pan on top of the stove. In place of Step 4, preheat the broiler on high and adjust the oven rack so that it sits about 6 inches from the flames or heating element. Arrange the ribs 1 to 2 inches apart on a rimmed baking sheet (a half sheet pan) or broiler pan, and slide them under the broiler. Broil, turning with tongs as each side browns, until sizzling and chestnut-brown on all sides, about 5 minutes per side. Transfer the ribs to a platter, without stacking. Pour off and discard the grease remaining in the pan, and deglaze to capture any precious caramelized beef drippings: Set the pan over medium-high heat, add a small amount of ale, stock, or water, and bring to a boil, stirring with a wooden spoon to scrape up and dissolve the drippings. Reserve this liquid.

Heat 1 tablespoon oil (you will only need 1 tablespoon in all if using this method) in a medium Dutch oven or other heavy braising pot (4-quart) over medium-high heat. Add the onion and carrot to the pot and continue with Step 5 as directed. In Step 6, add the deglazing liquid from the broiler pan, along with any meat juices, when you add the short ribs.

BEER AND WINE NOTES Rich dark beer, such as Anchor Steam Porter or Guiness Stout; or try an intensely flavored red wine, such as an old-vine Zinfandel from Sonoma County or a concentrated Australian Shiraz.

All About Braising
Molly Stevens

Roasted Halibut with Potatoes, Lemons and Thyme

ROASTING TIME: 55 MINUTES
4 SERVINGS

1½ pounds small red potatoes, halved

  2 small lemons, 1 thinly sliced, 1 halved

  1 tablespoon chopped thyme

½ teaspoon crushed red pepper

¼ cup extra-virgin olive oil

Kosher salt and freshly ground pepper

Two 1-pound skinless halibut fillets

1. Preheat the oven to 400°. In a large baking dish, toss the potatoes with the lemon slices, thyme, crushed red pepper and 3 tablespoons of the olive oil; season with salt and pepper. Spread the potatoes in an even layer and bake for 40 minutes, stirring halfway through, until the potatoes are tender and beginning to brown.

2. Season the halibut with salt and pepper. Stir the potatoes, place the fillets on top and drizzle with the remaining 1 tablespoon of olive oil. Squeeze the juice of the halved lemon over the fish and potatoes. Bake for about 15 minutes, until the fish is cooked through. Cut each fillet in half and serve with the potatoes and any juices in the baking dish.

Editor's Note
This flavorful recipe makes an easy, satisfying midweek meal or a simple, elegant dinner party dish. The fish is the star here, so be sure to use the freshest fish you can find. Any mild, firm-fleshed variety would work.

All About Braising
Molly Stevens

Spice-Crusted Scallops with
Curry-Lemon Relish, PAGE 252

Go Fish

by Laurent Tourondel

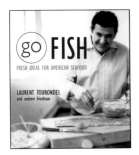

And Andrew Friedman, published by Wiley, 328 pages, color photos, $34.95

"It's a myth that restaurant chefs cook the same way at home as they do in their restaurants," admits Laurent Tourondel, a FOOD & WINE magazine Best New Chef 1998. "In reality, we cook recipes that are no more complicated than the ones you probably cook at home." So in his first-ever cookbook, Tourondel shows how to prepare fish the way he does when he's not working at his New York City restaurants BLT Steak, BLT Fish and BLT Prime. In addition to flavorful recipes, *Go Fish* includes a primer on types of fish, with buying and storing tips; it also gives useful advice on basic cooking techniques.

Featured Recipes Spice-Crusted Scallops with Curry-Lemon Relish; Lemon-Crab Risotto with Grilled Asparagus; Corn and Haddock Chowder

Best of the Best Exclusive Braised Swordfish with Olive and Caper Sauce

Spice-Crusted Scallops with Curry-Lemon Relish

To make this recipe, try to find scallops that are fresh out of the shell; they have to be dry to keep the spice mixture from becoming too wet. The relish is a new take on chutney, a spiced sweet-and-sour fruit puree that's usually served alongside curry dishes; here, the curry is part of the chutney.

6 SERVINGS

- 2 teaspoons coriander seeds
- 4 teaspoons cumin seeds
- 4 teaspoons fennel seeds
- 1 cup water
- ⅔ cup granulated sugar
- 4 lemons, peeled, seeded, and separated into segments
- 5 tablespoons olive oil
- 1 cup chopped shallots (about 5 shallots)
- 1 teaspoon curry powder
- ⅔ cup dry white wine
- 1 tablespoon rice wine vinegar
- 2 tablespoons chopped cilantro leaves

Fine sea salt and freshly ground black pepper to taste

- 2 fennel bulbs, shaved and kept in ice water
- 2 tablespoons extra-virgin olive oil
- 2 tablespoons freshly squeezed lemon juice
- 2 teaspoons mace
- 2 tablespoons plus 2 teaspoons confectioners' sugar
- 5 teaspoons ground star anise
- 2 teaspoons ground cardamom
- 1 pound medium dry sea scallops (about 18 scallops)

TOAST THE SPICES Preheat the oven to 200°F. Put the coriander, cumin, and fennel seeds on a baking sheet and toast until fragrant, approximately 5 minutes. Remove the baking sheet from the oven and set the spices aside to cool.

For more recipes by Laurent Tourondel go to foodandwine.com/tourondel. To access the recipes, log on with this code: **FWBEST05**. Effective through December 31, 2006.

MAKE THE CURRY-LEMON RELISH In a small saucepan, combine the water with the granulated sugar. Bring to a boil over high heat, stirring, until the sugar dissolves. Cut each lemon segment crosswise into 3 pieces. Put the lemon segments in a bowl. Pour the boiling syrup over the lemon segments; let cool. Heat 2 tablespoons of the olive oil in a pot set over medium-high heat. Add the shallots and curry, and cook, stirring, until the shallots are softened but not browned, approximately 3 minutes. Add the wine and cook until almost dry, approximately 4 minutes. Add the vinegar, cilantro, and cooled lemon pieces. Season with salt and pepper.

MAKE THE FENNEL SALAD Toss the fennel with the extra-virgin olive oil and lemon juice, and season with salt and pepper. Set aside at room temperature.

MAKE THE SPICE MIX In a blender, grind as fine as possible the toasted seeds, mace, confectioners' sugar, star anise, cardamom, and 2 teaspoons of fine sea salt. Strain the mixture through a fine-mesh strainer.

COOK THE SCALLOPS Heat the remaining 3 tablespoons olive oil in a wide, deep sauté pan set over high heat. Dip the lower half of each scallop in the spice mix. Add the scallops to the pan, coated side down, and cook, turning once, until golden brown, approximately 3 minutes per side.

TO SERVE Mound some relish in the center of each of 6 plates. Arrange 3 scallops around each mound of relish. Top the scallops with some fennel salad.

Go Fish
Laurent Tourondel

Lemon-Crab Risotto with Grilled Asparagus

6 SERVINGS

- 1 pound thin asparagus
- 4 tablespoons unsalted butter
- 4 garlic cloves, chopped
- 3 cups pea leaves or baby spinach

Fine sea salt and freshly ground black pepper to taste

- 3 tablespoons olive oil
- 1 medium onion, chopped
- 1 thyme sprig
- 2 cups arborio rice
- 1 cup dry white wine
- 5 cups canned low-sodium chicken broth
- 1 cup grated Parmigiano-Reggiano cheese
- ⅔ cup heavy cream

Grated zest of 2 lemons

Juice of 1½ lemons

- 1 pound jumbo lump crabmeat or Dungeness crabmeat, picked over; or 1 pound cooked, shelled, and deveined shrimp

BLANCH THE ASPARAGUS Bring a pot of salted water to a boil over high heat. Fill a large bowl halfway with ice water. Add the asparagus to the boiling water and blanch until tender, approximately 2 minutes. Drain, and add them to the ice water to stop the cooking and preserve their color. Drain again.

GRILL THE ASPARAGUS Prepare a hot fire in a barbecue grill or preheat an indoor grill. Grill the asparagus, turning, until lightly charred all over, 4 to 6 minutes, depending on the thickness of the asparagus. Cut off and reserve the tips. Cut the stalks into 2-inch segments; set aside.

SAUTÉ THE PEA LEAVES Melt 1 tablespoon of the butter with one of the garlic cloves in a sauté pan over medium heat. Add all but a small handful of pea leaves and season with salt and pepper. Cook just until wilted, approximately 30 seconds; remove and set aside.

MAKE THE RISOTTO In a heavy-bottomed saucepan, heat the olive oil over medium heat. Add the remaining 3 garlic cloves, the onion, and the thyme.

Cook, stirring, until the onion is translucent, approximately 4 minutes. Add the rice and stir to coat the rice with the oil. Cook for 3 to 4 minutes. Add the white wine and cook, stirring, until evaporated. Add about 1 cup of the broth and cook, stirring constantly, until it is completely absorbed by the rice. Then add another cup of liquid. Continue in this manner until you have used all the broth, which should take approximately 18 minutes. Stir in the grated Parmigiano-Reggiano cheese, remaining 3 tablespoons butter, cream, lemon zest and juice, asparagus stalk pieces, and sautéed pea leaves.

TO SERVE Mound some risotto in each of 6 bowls. Top with crabmeat and garnish with the reserved pea leaves and asparagus tips.

PEA LEAVES are a delicate, sweet spring green. They are available in some upscale supermarkets and in Asian markets and greengrocers.

Tourondel on His Favorite Snack
If I want to cook something quickly I make a Vietnamese omelet: shrimp, glass noodles, fish sauce, mushrooms, scallions and eggs. You can also make an omelet sandwich with a warm baguette and a little chili paste. The omelet's really good cold, too.

Go Fish
Laurent Tourondel

Corn and Haddock Chowder

Tourondel on Soups and Stock

Sometimes I make soup with water rather than stock. It might seem surprising, but it can actually have a *better* flavor that way because you taste more of what's in the soup rather than just the stock.

Made with finnan haddie (smoked haddock), this chowder has an understated smokiness. It isn't pureed or strained, so be sure to cut the vegetables uniformly for an appealing appearance. For a special occasion, replace half of the haddock with poached, diced lobster meat.

6 SERVINGS

2½ cups heavy cream

1½ medium onions, cut into small dice

4 garlic cloves, 2 left whole and 2 chopped

1 tablespoon black peppercorns

2½ cups water

1 pound finnan haddie (smoked haddock)

3 tablespoons unsalted butter

5 ounces bacon, finely diced (about 1¼ cups)

2 celery stalks, cut into small dice

3 thyme sprigs

2 bay leaves

1½ pounds corn on the cob (about 8), shucked and kernels scraped off

Pinch cayenne

2 fresh sage leaves, chopped

POACH THE FINNAN HADDIE Put the cream, one-third of the onion, 2 whole garlic cloves, and the peppercorns in a large saucepan and add the water. Add the finnan haddie, cover, and bring to a simmer over medium heat. Stop cooking 10 minutes from when you first put the pot over the heat. Let cool, then remove the fish from the liquid. Strain the liquid and set aside the finnan haddie and poaching liquid separately. Pick out and discard the garlic and peppercorns.

MAKE THE SOUP In a pot, cook the butter with the bacon over medium-high heat until the bacon is crisp, about 8 minutes. Add the remaining onion, chopped garlic, celery, thyme, and bay leaves. Cook until the onion is translucent, about 4 minutes. Add the corn and cook for 3 minutes. Add the reserved poaching liquid and cook until the corn is softened, 15 to 20 minutes. Season with cayenne and add the sage. Flake the poached finnan haddie into the pot.

TO SERVE Divide the soup among 6 bowls.

Go Fish
Laurent Tourondel

Braised Swordfish with Olive and Caper Sauce

Editor's Note

This stellar swordfish recipe was created by Tourondel for his BLT Steak restaurant in New York City. The capers and olives give the sauce a briny tang, which is excellent with the moist, slow-cooked swordfish.

6 SERVINGS

Six 8-ounce swordfish steaks, cut 1¼ inches thick

Kosher salt and freshly ground pepper

All-purpose flour, for dredging

2 tablespoons extra-virgin olive oil

6 garlic cloves, finely chopped

1 red bell pepper, thinly sliced

1 yellow bell pepper, thinly sliced

1 small white onion, halved and thinly sliced

1 cup dry white wine

One 28-ounce can peeled Italian tomatoes, chopped, juices reserved

¾ cup pitted green olives, halved

3 tablespoons drained capers

Pinch of sugar

Pinch of crushed red pepper

6 large basil leaves, thinly sliced

Steamed new potatoes, for serving

1. Season the swordfish steaks with salt and pepper, then lightly dredge them in flour, shaking off the excess. In a large skillet, heat the olive oil. Add the swordfish steaks to the skillet and cook over moderately high heat until golden brown, about 3 minutes per side. Transfer to a plate.

2. Add the garlic, bell peppers and onion to the skillet. Cover and cook over moderate heat until the vegetables begin to soften, about 5 minutes. Add the wine and simmer until reduced by half, about 5 minutes. Add the tomatoes and their juices, the olives, capers, sugar and crushed red pepper and bring to a simmer. Return the swordfish to the skillet, cover and simmer over low heat until very tender, about 30 minutes.

3. Using a slotted spoon, transfer the swordfish to a platter. Boil the sauce over moderately high heat until thickened, about 4 minutes. Stir in the basil and season with salt and pepper. Spoon the sauce over the swordfish steaks and serve with steamed new potatoes.

Go Fish
Laurent Tourondel

Wild greens for Spanakopita, PAGE 262

The Greatest Dishes!

by Anya von Bremzen

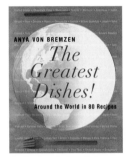

Published by HarperCollins, 368 pages, $27.50

"I have hundreds of cookbooks literally falling from the shelves of my apartment," says frequent FOOD & WINE magazine contributor Anya von Bremzen. "One day I just looked at them and thought—wouldn't it be nice to have the best recipes in the world in one book?" Von Bremzen's cookbook is a collection of 80 recipes that she describes as the world's "greatest hits," from American cheesecake to Indian Tandoori Murgh (Grilled Tandoori Chicken). Each dish comes with an explanation of its heritage and sometimes a tip on where to eat it at its best.

Featured Recipes Grilled Tandoori Chicken; Spanakopita with Wild Greens; Miso-Glazed Black Cod

Best of the Best Exclusive Braised Duck with Prunes, Olives and Pine Nuts

Grilled Tandoori Chicken

Test Kitchen Tip
The acid in the yogurt and lemon juice tenderizes the chicken and prevents it from drying out. But don't let the chicken marinate for more than 8 hours or it will turn mushy.

This is the recipe for the legendary *tandoori murgh,* in this case done on the grill. To make the chicken in the oven, roast it at 500°F in a shallow baking pan, turning occasionally, until cooked through, about forty minutes. Just before serving, pass it under a broiler for one to two minutes. The longer the chicken marinates, the more flavorful it becomes, so start ahead.

4 TO 6 SERVINGS

2 young chickens (about 3 pounds each), skinned and quartered

Salt

½ teaspoon chili powder, preferably Indian

Two large pinches of turmeric

⅓ cup fresh lemon juice

YOGURT MARINADE

1 tablespoon ground coriander

2 teaspoons ground cumin

2 teaspoons purchased garam masala

1 teaspoon chili powder, preferably Indian

Large pinch of freshly grated nutmeg

Large pinch of ground cinnamon

1½ cups plain whole-milk yogurt

½ cup chopped onion

2 tablespoons chopped fresh ginger

5 large garlic cloves, chopped

A few drops red Tandoori coloring, available at Indian groceries (optional) or 1 tablespoon sweet paprika

TO COOK AND SERVE

2 to 3 tablespoons melted ghee or butter, for brushing the chickens

Mint Chutney (recipe follows)

Lemon wedges and thickly sliced red onion

1. Make several ½-inch-deep diagonal slits in the thighs and breasts of each chicken. Place the chickens in a large nonreactive dish and rub them thoroughly with salt, chili powder, turmeric, and lemon juice. Cover with plastic and refrigerate for at least 2 hours.

The Greatest Dishes!
Anya von Bremzen

 For more recipes by Anya von Bremzen go to foodandwine.com/vonbremzen. To access the recipes, log on with this code: **FWBEST05**. Effective through December 31, 2006.

2. In a small skillet, over low heat, stir all the dry ground spices until fragrant and a few shades darker, 15 to 20 seconds. In a food processor or a blender, process the yogurt with the onion, ginger, and garlic to a paste. Stir in the toasted dry spices and the food coloring, if using. Pour this marinade over the chickens, toss to coat, cover with plastic, and refrigerate for at least 4 hours. Bring the chickens to room temperature before grilling.

3. Light a grill. Set an oiled rack 4 to 6 inches over glowing coals and brush the chicken pieces with ghee. Grill, in batches if necessary, until the juices run clear when you insert a skewer into the thickest part of the thigh, 10 to 15 minutes per side. Grill the chicken covered for a smokier taste.

4. Using tongs, transfer the cooked chicken pieces to a platter and serve with the Mint Chutney, if desired, lemon wedges, and sliced red onion.

Mint Chutney

MAKES ABOUT 1 CUP

1½ cups tightly packed fresh mint leaves

½ cup tightly packed cilantro leaves

1 long mild green chile, such as Anaheim, seeded and chopped

1 tablespoon grated fresh ginger

¼ cup chopped white onion

Small pinch of ground cumin

2 tablespoons fresh lemon juice, or more to taste

2 teaspoons distilled white vinegar

½ teaspoon sugar, or more to taste

2 to 3 tablespoons plain yogurt

Puree all the ingredients in a blender until fairly smooth. Scrape into a bowl, taste, and adjust the seasonings. Let the chutney stand for 30 minutes for the flavors to meld.

The Greatest Dishes!
Anya von Bremzen

Spanakopita with Wild Greens

If you prefer, you can use puff pastry or phyllo instead of the delightfully rugged village red wine pastry offered here. The wild greens used on Crete might include wild carrot, leek, wild fennel, beet tops, furry thistles, and edible chrysanthemum. At home, experiment with the likes of collard or turnip greens, chicory, dandelion, broccoli rabe, curly endive, beet greens, Swiss chard, or arugula—as long as you have a mixture of sweet and bitter greens. For a fluffier, more urban pie like those you know from Greek diners, you can add 1 or 2 beaten eggs to the filling.

8 TO 10 SERVINGS

RED WINE PASTRY

3½ cups all-purpose flour

¾ teaspoon salt

2 teaspoons baking powder

½ cup olive oil, plus more for greasing the pan

½ cup dry red wine

⅔ to ¾ cup warm water

OR 1 package frozen phyllo dough, thawed for 15 minutes; OR 1 (17½-ounce) package frozen puff pastry, thawed (see Variation on page 264)

FILLING

1½ pounds assorted greens (see above), tough stalks removed

1½ pounds spinach, tough stalks removed

3 tablespoons finely chopped parsley

3 tablespoons finely chopped mint

1 bunch firm, young scallions, including 2 to 3 inches of green, finely chopped

3 tablespoons finely chopped fennel fronds or tender dill

½ cup olive oil, preferably Greek

1 medium onion, finely chopped

¾ cup finely chopped fennel bulb

1 teaspoon sugar

Salt and freshly ground pepper

7 ounces good Greek feta, finely crumbled

1 or 2 large eggs, beaten (optional)

1 large egg yolk beaten with 1 teaspoon milk

1. MAKE THE RED WINE PASTRY In a large bowl, sift together the flour, salt, and baking powder. Gather the flour into a mound, make a well in the middle, and add the olive oil and wine. Swirl the flour in from the sides into the liquid ingredients, mixing in all the remaining flour. The dough will form in big, coarse crumbs. Knead in enough of the warm water to form a dough that sticks together. Turn the dough out onto a lightly floured surface and oil your hands. Knead the dough, adding a little more flour if it feels too sticky, until soft and smooth, about 7 minutes. Place the dough in an oiled bowl, cover with plastic, and let rest for at least 15 minutes. (The dough can be prepared the day before and refrigerated.)

2. MAKE THE FILLING Rinse the greens and the spinach well and squeeze out the water thoroughly with your hands. Chop them all finely and mix the greens and spinach in a bowl with the parsley, mint, scallions, and fennel fronds. In a large, deep skillet, heat the oil over medium-low heat and sauté the onion and fennel bulb until softened, about 5 minutes. Add the greens and cook, stirring until wilted, about 6 minutes. You might have to add the greens to the skillet in batches, letting the first batch wilt to allow for space. Season with sugar, salt, and pepper to taste. Transfer the greens to a colander and let drain for at least 15 minutes, pressing lightly to extract excess liquid and oil. Transfer to a bowl and stir in the feta and the eggs, if using. Adjust the seasoning as necessary. Let the filling cool completely. (The filling can be prepared up to a day ahead.)

3. Preheat the oven to 375°F. Divide the pastry into two balls, one slightly larger than the other. On a lightly floured surface, roll out the larger piece of dough into a rectangle about 12 by 15 inches.

4. Grease a 10-by-13-inch baking pan with olive oil. Line it with the dough and spread the filling on top. Roll out the second piece of dough slightly smaller than the first and lay it over the filling. With scissors, trim off some of the bottom edge if necessary and fold the bottom edge over the top crust, pinching tightly to seal. With a sharp knife, lightly score the top into serving portions and make a few small slits in the top for steam vents. Brush the top with the egg wash. Bake until the top is golden, about 50 minutes to 1 hour. Cover with a kitchen towel and let rest for 10 minutes. The pie is best slightly warm or at room temperature and tastes even better the next day.

Von Bremzen on Eating Out

As a restaurant critic, I've had so many extravagant meals that my dream is to have a simple, minimalist meal. Places with classics like the perfect roast lamb or chicken really work for me. My fantasy meal would be eating in a great-looking restaurant that serves one amazing dish. And I wouldn't mind a good glass of wine to go with it!

The Greatest Dishes!
Anya von Bremzen

VARIATION

To make the pie with puff pastry, which some Greek cooks prefer to commercial phyllo, you will need two sheets from a 17½-ounce package, defrosted. Roll out the pastry and assemble the pie as directed in steps 3 and 4 of the main recipe. Brush the top with the egg wash and bake at 350°F until golden brown, about 45 minutes.

If using phyllo, you will need 12 phyllo sheets, thawed in the package if frozen. To assemble the pie, oil a 10-by-13-inch baking pan and line it with four or five sheets of phyllo, brushing each sheet with a little olive oil. Spread the filling on top and cover with four or five more sheets of phyllo, folding over the bottom edges to form a rim. Brush the top with oil and bake at 350°F until golden brown, about 45 minutes.

The Greatest Dishes!
Anya von Bremzen

Miso-Glazed Black Cod

In an ideal world, this dish would be made with fresh black cod and white *saikyo* miso, a lightly fermented, sweet Kyoto miso, available at better Asian groceries or by mail. Fresh black cod can be found at fish markets in the Pacific Northwest or at gourmet fish shops in other regions from September to January.

   Lacking these ingredients, the dish is still incredible (and shockingly easy) with regular white miso (*shiromiso*) and almost any buttery fish. If using *saikyo* miso, cut the sugar to 2 or 3 tablespoons.

4 SERVINGS

- ⅓ cup sake
- ⅓ cup mirin (sweet Japanese rice wine)
- 1 cup *saikyo* miso or regular white miso paste (*shiromiso*)
- ½ cup sugar (see above)
- 4 unskinned fresh black cod, salmon, or halibut fillets, about 8 ounces each

Sea salt

- 1 tablespoon Asian (toasted) sesame oil

1. In a medium saucepan, bring the sake and mirin to a boil over medium heat and boil for 30 seconds to evaporate some of the alcohol. Turn the heat down to very low and add the miso, stirring constantly with a wooden spoon to prevent it from sticking. Add the sugar and stir until completely dissolved, about 2 minutes. Remove from the heat and cool to room temperature.

2. Pat-dry the fish with paper towels and rub lightly with salt. Place the miso marinade in a large nonreactive dish, add the fish, turn to coat with the marinade, and cover with plastic. The fish can be marinated anywhere from 6 hours to 3 days.

3. Preheat the oven to 400°F. Once the oven is hot, turn on the broiler. Place the fish skin side up on an oiled broiler pan, gently wiping off excess marinade. Brush the top lightly with the sesame oil and broil until the top is browned, about 5 minutes. Turn off the broiler, turn the oven back on, and bake the fish until it flakes easily when tested with a fork, about 10 more minutes. If you'd like to serve the marinade as a sauce, bring it to a simmer over medium-high heat while the fish is baking.

4. Divide the fish among 4 plates, adding a light drizzle of the marinade to each plate if you wish.

Test Kitchen Tip

If you can't find black cod, substitute regular cod or even salmon. Serve this dish with steamed white rice and bok choy sautéed with garlic and ginger.

The Greatest Dishes!
Anya von Bremzen

Braised Duck with Prunes, Olives and Pine Nuts

6 SERVINGS

 6 duck legs (about 4½ pounds total), fat trimmed

Kosher salt and freshly ground pepper

 1 large leek, white and tender green parts only, halved lengthwise and thinly sliced

 1 medium onion, coarsely chopped

 1 medium carrot, cut into ½-inch dice

 3 medium tomatoes, coarsely chopped

3½ cups chicken stock or low-sodium broth

 1 bay leaf

 1 thyme sprig

1¼ cups dry red wine

 1 cup pitted prunes, halved

 2 tablespoons whole almonds

 ¼ cup plus 2 tablespoons pine nuts

 2 Ritz crackers

 3 tablespoons chopped flat-leaf parsley

 2 garlic cloves

 ¼ cup vin santo or other sweet white wine, such as Moscatel

 ¾ cup pitted green olives, such as Picholine, halved

1. Preheat the oven to 325°. Season the duck with salt and pepper. Heat a large enameled cast-iron casserole. Add 3 of the duck legs to the casserole, skin side down, and cook over moderately high heat until well browned on the bottom, about 8 minutes. Turn the legs and brown for 3 minutes longer. Transfer to a plate and repeat with the remaining 3 duck legs. Discard all but 2 tablespoons of the fat in the casserole.

2. Add the leek, onion and carrot to the casserole and cook, stirring frequently, until browned, about 8 minutes. Add the tomatoes and cook until softened, about 5 minutes. Add the stock, bay leaf, thyme and ¾ cup of the red wine to the casserole. Return the duck legs to the casserole and bring to a simmer. Cover and braise in the oven for 2 hours, until very tender.

The Greatest Dishes!

Anya von Bremzen

3. Meanwhile, in a small bowl, cover the prunes with the remaining ½ cup of red wine. Microwave at high power for 1½ minutes, or until hot.

4. In a small skillet, toast the almonds over moderate heat, stirring constantly, until golden, about 4 minutes. Transfer to a plate to cool. Repeat with the pine nuts, toasting them for about 2 minutes. In a mini food processor, pulse the crackers with the parsley, almonds, garlic and 2 tablespoons of the pine nuts until finely chopped. Add the vin santo and pulse to form a loose paste.

5. Remove the casserole from the oven. Transfer the duck legs to a plate and cover with foil. Skim the fat off the braising liquid and strain the liquid through a fine sieve; return the liquid to the casserole. Add the prunes with their soaking liquid and the olives. Cover and simmer over low heat for 15 minutes. Season with salt and pepper.

6. Add the pine nut mixture to the sauce and simmer for 3 minutes longer, stirring occasionally. Return the duck to the casserole to rewarm for 2 minutes. Transfer the duck and sauce to a platter, sprinkle with the remaining ¼ cup of pine nuts and serve.

MAKE AHEAD The recipe can be prepared through Step 2 and refrigerated overnight. Remove the layer of fat and bring to a low simmer before continuing.

Editor's Note

This recipe will appear in von Bremzen's forthcoming book, *Celebrating Spain!* As with many Catalan dishes, the final boost of flavor here comes from the *picada*, a pounded mixture of garlic, parsley and nuts. Von Bremzen's trick is to add a couple of Ritz crackers to the mix to help thicken and enrich the sauce.

The Greatest Dishes!
Anya von Bremzen

Mama's Noodles with
Mushrooms and Ham, PAGE 270

The Breath of a Wok

by Grace Young

And Alan Richardson, published by Simon & Schuster, 256 pages, color photos, $35

This book is a paean to a powerful piece of cooking equipment: the wok. Grace Young, author of *The Wisdom of the Chinese Kitchen,* shows how to steam, deep-fry, boil, poach, smoke and braise in a wok, demonstrating its versatility far beyond the stir-fry. The opinionated Young also shows you how to pick the right wok. "These days everyone goes for nonstick cookware, and you simply don't get the same results," she writes, going on to praise the more traditional carbon-steel variety. To collect recipes for this book, Young traveled extensively through China, eating with friends, family and a host of food experts. She came back with fantastic recipes.

Featured Recipes Mama's Noodles with Mushrooms and Ham; Liang Nian Xiu's Moon Hill Corn and Beans; Scallop Siu Mai Spring Moon; Millie Chan's Chili Shrimp

Best of the Best Exclusive Scallion and Ginger Beef Stir-Fry

Mama's Noodles with Mushrooms and Ham

**Young on
Her Family's
Wok-a-Thon**

While I was writing the
book, my family agreed to
a wok-a-thon. Eighteen
family members decided
to cook stir-fries and other
dishes. Everyone showed
up at my Aunt Betty's
laden with ingredients but
not a single wok! Only
Aunt Betty had one. It was
indicative of how woks are
the endangered species of
cooking vessels.

Mama often makes this noodle dish for lunch. The Cantonese like using spare amounts of Smithfield ham [which requires steaming]; its flavor resembles that of a famous ham from Yunnan province in China. But for such a small amount, I use prosciutto to save time.

SERVES 4 AS PART OF A MULTICOURSE MEAL

- 6 dried shiitake mushrooms
- 8 ounces flat dried rice noodles
- 1 tablespoon vegetable oil
- 1 tablespoon finely shredded ginger
- 8 ounces mung bean sprouts (about 4 cups)
- 1 teaspoon salt
- ¼ teaspoon sugar
- 2 teaspoons sesame oil
- 3 teaspoons soy sauce
- 2 ounces prosciutto, julienned
- 1 scallion, thinly sliced

Cilantro sprigs

1. In a medium shallow bowl soak the mushrooms in ¾ cup cold water 30 minutes or until softened. Drain and squeeze dry, reserving the soaking liquid. Cut off and discard the stems and thinly slice the caps. Set aside. Soak the noodles in a bowl with enough warm water to cover 20 minutes or until they are soft and pliable. Drain and set aside.

2. Heat a 14-inch flat-bottomed wok over high heat until a bead of water vaporizes within 1 to 2 seconds of contact. Swirl in the vegetable oil, add the ginger, and stir-fry 10 seconds. Add the bean sprouts and stir-fry 1 minute. Add the mushrooms, ½ teaspoon of the salt, and the sugar and stir-fry 1 minute or until the sprouts are cooked but still crisp. Transfer to a shallow bowl and toss with 1 teaspoon of the sesame oil and 2 teaspoons of the soy sauce.

The Breath
of a Wok
Grace Young

3. Add ½ cup of the reserved mushroom soaking liquid, the remaining 1 teaspoon soy sauce, and 1 teaspoon sesame oil to the unwashed wok. Add the rice noodles and warm over medium heat, stirring constantly, 2 to 3 minutes until all the liquid is absorbed and the noodles are just tender. Add the bean sprout mixture and the remaining ½ teaspoon salt, and stir-fry 1 minute until combined. Transfer to a platter. Sprinkle on the shredded ham, scallion, and cilantro sprigs.

The Breath
of a Wok
Grace Young

Liang Nian Xiu's Moon Hill Corn and Beans

Young on Choosing a Wok

When you cook on a standard home stove, you can't cook with a traditional round-bottomed wok. You need a wok with a five- or six-inch flat bottom. When you are cooking meat in this style of wok, you don't want to crowd it; you shouldn't add more than 12 ounces at a time.

Liang Nian Xiu and I shopped for these vegetables in her local market in Moon Hill village in Guangxi province. Liang showed me a variation, adding a tablespoon or two of chopped pork with cilantro and Chinese chives, but I prefer the stir-fry without meat. In the summertime, with corn, beans, and tomatoes at their peak of sweetness, this delicious combination needs no additional ingredients.

SERVES 4 AS PART OF A MULTICOURSE MEAL

- 1 tablespoon vegetable oil
- 1 tablespoon minced garlic
- 1 tablespoon minced ginger
- 1 tablespoon minced mild fresh chiles
- 3 medium ears corn, kernels scraped off (about 2½ cups)
- ⅓ cup roughly chopped green beans
- ¾ teaspoon salt
- 1 ripe medium tomato, cut into thin wedges
- ¼ teaspoon sugar

Heat a 14-inch flat-bottomed wok over high heat until a bead of water vaporizes within 1 to 2 seconds of contact. Swirl in the oil and add the garlic, ginger, and chiles and stir-fry 30 seconds. Add the corn, green beans, and salt and stir-fry 1 minute. Add the tomato wedges and stir-fry 1 minute. Add 2 tablespoons cold water and the sugar and stir-fry 1 to 2 minutes more or until the tomatoes are just wilted and the vegetables are tender.

The Breath
of a Wok
Grace Young

Scallop Siu Mai Spring Moon

Chef Yip Wing Wah garnishes these exquisite dumplings with a dollop of crab roe, which can be substituted for the carrots.

MAKES 24 DUMPLINGS; SERVES 4 AS AN APPETIZER OR PART OF A MULTICOURSE DIM SUM LUNCH

- 8 dried shiitake mushrooms
- 8 ounces fresh sea scallops
- 10 ounces ground pork (about 1⅓ cups)
- 1 teaspoon cornstarch
- 1 teaspoon sesame oil
- 1 teaspoon salt
- ½ teaspoon sugar
- ½ teaspoon ground white pepper
- 24 round won ton wrappers
- ¼ cup minced carrots
- 4 large Napa cabbage leaves or cheesecloth

1. In a small bowl soak the mushrooms in ½ cup cold water 30 minutes or until softened. Drain and squeeze dry, reserving the soaking liquid. Cut off and discard the stems and mince the caps. Divide the scallops in half, putting the thickest on a plate; cover with plastic wrap and refrigerate. Mince the remaining thinner scallops. In a medium bowl combine the pork, mushrooms, minced scallops, cornstarch, sesame oil, salt, sugar, pepper, and 1 tablespoon plus 1 teaspoon of the reserved mushroom liquid.

2. Put the won ton wrappers on a work surface and lightly cover with a damp towel. Touch the tip of your left index finger to the tip of your thumb to form a small empty circle, or hole. Put one wrapper over the hole and put 1 tablespoon filling in the center of the wrapper. Let the filled wrapper drop halfway through the hole, and gently squeeze it closed with your fingers. Put on a work surface and carefully pleat the excess wrapper, pressing down the filling. Put the dumpling upright on a plate. Continue filling the rest of the wrappers. Cut the reserved scallops horizontally into 24 thin rounds. Put a slice of scallop on each dumpling. Put a pinch of carrot in the center.

The Breath
of a Wok
Grace Young

3. Line a 12-inch bamboo steamer with the cabbage leaves, or cheesecloth. Put half the dumplings on the leaves, ½ inch apart. Cover the steamer with its lid. Add water to a 14-inch flat-bottomed wok to a depth of ¾ inch and bring to a boil over high heat. Carefully put the steamer in the wok, and steam on high heat 5 to 7 minutes or until the pork is no longer pink and just cooked. Be sure to check the water level from time to time and replenish, if necessary, with boiling water. Carefully remove the steamer from the wok. The dumplings should be served immediately. Continue steaming the remaining dumplings, replenishing the wok with more boiling water.

Young on Creating "Wok Hay"

If you stir-fry correctly in a wok, you'll achieve what my father would call "wok hay"—the pristine, concentrated flavors and seared aromas that are prized in Chinese cooking.

The Breath
of a Wok

Grace Young

Millie Chan's Chili Shrimp

Young on Preparing Ginger

Before you shred ginger you need to peel it. The best way to do this is to scrape the skin off using the edge of a teaspoon. To create the most delicate shreds, cut the ginger with a chef's knife or cleaver.

Millie Chan uses chili bean sauce, a condiment made of capsicum, salt, and soybeans. If it is not available, chili sauce can be substituted, but the flavor is not as full. This shrimp has a wonderful balance of salty, sweet, peppery, and hot flavors and is an excellent appetizer served at room temperature.

SERVES 4 AS PART OF A MULTICOURSE MEAL

- 1 tablespoon salt
- 1 pound large shrimp, peeled and deveined
- 2 tablespoons soy sauce
- 1 teaspoon chili bean sauce
- ½ teaspoon sugar
- 3 tablespoons vegetable oil
- 2 tablespoons Shao-Hsing rice wine or dry sherry
- 2 tablespoons minced ginger
- 2 tablespoons chopped scallions
- 1 tablespoon minced mild fresh chiles, seeded

Cilantro sprigs

1. In a large bowl combine the salt with 3 cups cold water. Add the shrimp and let soak 1 hour. Drain the shrimp and set on several sheets of paper towels. With more paper towels, pat the shrimp dry. In a small bowl combine the soy sauce, chili bean sauce, and sugar.

2. Heat a 14-inch flat-bottomed wok over high heat until a bead of water vaporizes within 1 to 2 seconds of contact. Swirl in 2 tablespoons of the oil, add the shrimp, and stir-fry 1 minute or until the shrimp begin to turn pink. Swirl in the rice wine and immediately remove the wok from the heat. Transfer to a plate. Swirl the remaining 1 tablespoon oil into the wok over high heat, add the ginger, scallions, and chiles, and stir-fry 5 seconds. Stir the soy sauce mixture and swirl it into the wok. Return the shrimp to the wok and stir-fry 30 seconds to 1 minute or until the shrimp are just cooked. Garnish with the cilantro sprigs.

The Breath of a Wok

Grace Young

Scallion and Ginger Beef Stir-Fry

4 SERVINGS

1½ pounds flank steak, sliced lengthwise (with the grain) into 2-inch-wide strips

1 tablespoon cornstarch

2 tablespoons soy sauce

1 tablespoon Shao-Hsing rice wine

¼ teaspoon sugar

¼ teaspoon salt

¼ teaspoon freshly ground pepper

3 tablespoons vegetable oil

¼ cup plus 2 tablespoons finely chopped fresh ginger (3 ounces)

6 scallions, cut into 2-inch lengths

2 tablespoons oyster sauce

Cooked rice, for serving

1. Slice each flank strip across the grain ¼ inch thick. In a medium bowl, mix the cornstarch with the soy sauce, rice wine, sugar, salt, pepper and 2 teaspoons of the vegetable oil. Add the meat and toss to coat.

2. Heat a 14-inch flat-bottomed wok over high heat until a bead of water vaporizes within 1 to 2 seconds of contact. Swirl in the remaining 2 tablespoons plus 1 teaspoon of oil, add the ginger and stir-fry until very fragrant, about 15 seconds. Add the beef in one layer and cook undisturbed until it begins to brown, about 1 minute. Add the scallions and stir-fry for 2 minutes, until the meat is browned but still rare. Add the oyster sauce and stir-fry for 1 minute longer. Transfer to a platter and serve with rice.

Editor's Note

Flank steak is tasty, but it can be chewy. Young's quick way of preparing it in this recipe, however, results in tender beef. For perfect results, cut the steak lengthwise into long strips, then cut across the grain to create small strips.

The Breath of a Wok

Grace Young

Credits

All About Braising
The Art of Uncomplicated Cooking
From *All About Braising: The Art of Uncomplicated Cooking* by Molly Stevens. Copyright © 2004 by Molly Stevens. Used by permission of W. W. Norton & Company, Inc. Photographs copyright © 2004 by Gentl & Hyers.

Anthony Bourdain's Les Halles Cookbook
Strategies, Recipes, and Techniques of Classic Bistro Cooking
From the book *Anthony Bourdain's Les Halles Cookbook* by Anthony Bourdain with José de Meirelles and Philippe Lajaunie. Published by Bloomsbury USA. Copyright © 2004 by Anthony Bourdain. Reprinted by permission of Bloomsbury USA. Photographs by Robert DiScalfani.

Barefoot in Paris
Easy French Food
You *Can* Make at Home
From the book *Barefoot in Paris* by Ina Garten. Photographs by Quentin Bacon. Copyright © 2004 by Ina Garten. Photographs copyright © 2004 by Quentin Bacon. Published by Clarkson Potter/Publishers, a division of Random House, Inc. The Barefoot Contessa is a registered trademark of Ina Garten.

Bouchon
Excerpted from *Bouchon* by Thomas Keller with Jeffrey Cerciello, Susie Heller and Michael Ruhlman. Copyright © 2004 by Thomas Keller. Photographs copyright © 2004 by Deborah Jones. Used by permission of Artisan, a division of Workman Publishing Co., Inc., New York. All rights reserved.

The Breath of a Wok
Unlocking the Spirit of Chinese Wok Cooking Through Recipes and Lore
Reprinted with the permission of Simon & Schuster Adult Publishing Group from *The Breath of a Wok* by Grace Young and Alan Richardson. Copyright © 2004 by Grace Young and Alan Richardson. Photographs by Alan Richardson.

Celebrations 101
From *Celebrations 101* by Rick Rodgers. Copyright © 2004 by Rick Rodgers. Used by permission of Broadway Books, a division of Random House, Inc. Photographs by Mark Ferri.

Emeril's Potluck
Comfort Food with a Kicked-Up Attitude
From *Emeril's Potluck* by Emeril Lagasse. Copyright © 2004 by Emeril's Food of Love Productions, LLC. Reprinted by permission of HarperCollins Publishers Inc. William Morrow. Photographs by Quentin Bacon.

The Flavors of Southern Italy
From *The Flavors of Southern Italy*. Copyright © 2004 by Erica De Mane. Reprinted with permission of Wiley Publishing Inc., a subsidiary of John Wiley & Sons, Inc. Cover photographs by Damir Frkovic/ © Masterfile and Mitch Hrdlicka/ © Getty Images.

Fresh Food Fast
Delicious, Seasonal Vegetarian Meals in Under an Hour
From *Fresh Food Fast* by Peter Berley and Melissa Clark. Copyright © 2004 by Peter Berley. Reprinted by permission of HarperCollins Publishers Inc. ReganBooks. Photographs by Quentin Bacon.

Go Fish
Fresh Ideas for American Seafood
From *Go Fish* by Laurent Tourondel and Andrew Friedman. Copyright © 2004 by Laurent Tourondel. Reprinted with permission of Wiley Publishing Inc., a subsidiary of John Wiley & Sons, Inc. Photographs copyright © 2004 by Quentin Bacon.

The Greatest Dishes!
Around the World in 80 Recipes
From *The Greatest Dishes! Around the World in 80 Recipes* by Anya von Bremzen. Copyright © 2004 by Anya von Bremzen. Reprinted by permission of HarperCollins Publishers Inc. Cover design by Roberto de Vicq de Cumptich.

Jamie's Dinners
The Essential Family Cookbook
From *Jamie's Dinners* by Jamie Oliver. Copyright © 2004 Jamie Oliver. Reprinted by permission of Hyperion. Photographs copyright © David Loftus and Chris Terry.

The King Arthur Cookie Companion

The Essential Cookie Cookbook
Excerpted from *The King Arthur Cookie Companion: The Essential Cookie Cookbook*. Copyright © 2004 by The King Arthur Flour Company, Inc. Reprinted with permission of the publisher, The Countryman Press/W. W. Norton & Company, Inc. To order, go to www.countrymanpress.com or call 1-800-245-4151. Photographs by H/O Photographers, Inc.

Lobel's Prime Cuts

The Best Meat and Poultry Recipes from America's Master Butchers
By Stanley, Leon, Evan, Mark, and David Lobel with Mary Goodbody. Text copyright © 2004 by Morris Lobel & Sons Inc. Photographs copyright © 2004 by Rita Maas. Published by Chronicle Books.

Marcella Says...

Italian Cooking Wisdom from the Legendary Teacher's Master Classes, with 120 of Her Irresistible New Recipes
From *Marcella Says...*by Marcella Hazan. Copyright © 2004 by Marcella Polini Hazan and Victor Hazan. Reprinted by permission of HarperCollins Publishers Inc. Cover design by Roberto de Vicq de Cumptich.

The Middle Eastern Kitchen

75 Essential Ingredients with over 150 Authentic Recipes Published in North America by Hippocrene Books, Inc. Text copyright © 2001 by Ghillie Başan. Photography copyright © 2001 Jonathan Başan.

Nick Nairn's Top 100 Chicken Recipes

Quick and Easy Dishes for Every Occasion
Published by BBC Books, BBC Worldwide Ltd. © Nick Nairn 2004. Food photography © BBC Worldwide. Photographs by Philip Webb.

Nightly Specials

125 Recipes for Spontaneous, Creative Cooking at Home
From *Nightly Specials* by Michael Lomonaco and Andrew Friedman. Copyright © 2004 by Michael Lomonaco and Andrew Friedman. Recipes copyright © 2004 by Michael Lomonaco. Reprinted by permission of HarperCollins Publishers Inc. William Morrow. Photographs copyright © Shimon and Tammar Rothstein.

The Olive Harvest Cookbook

Olive Oil Lore and Recipes from the McEvoy Ranch
By Gerald Gass with Jacqueline Mallorca. Text copyright © 2004 by McEvoy of Marin LLC. Photographs copyright © 2004 by Maren Caruso. Published by Chronicle Books.

Olive Trees and Honey

A Treasury of Vegetarian Recipes from Jewish Communities Around the World
From *Olive Trees and Honey*. Copyright © 2005 by Gil Marks. Reprinted with permission of Wiley Publishing Inc., a subsidiary of John Wiley & Sons, Inc. Cover photograph © by FoodPix/Pavlina Eccless.

Pure Chocolate

Divine Desserts and Sweets from the Creator of Fran's Chocolates
From *Pure Chocolate: Divine Desserts and Sweets from the Creator of Fran's Chocolates* by Fran Bigelow with Helene Siegel. Copyright © 2004 by Fran Bigelow and Helene Siegel. Used by permission of Broadway Books, a division of Random House, Inc. Photographs by Sang An.

Raichlen's Indoor! Grilling

Excerpted from *Indoor! Grilling*. Copyright © 2004 by Steven Raichlen. Used by permission of Workman Publishing Co., Inc., New York. All rights reserved. Photographs copyright © 2004 by Susan Goldman.

Rick Stein's Complete Seafood

Text copyright © 2004 by Rick Stein. Photography copyright © 2004 by James Murphy. Published by Ten Speed Press.

The Spiaggia Cookbook

Eleganza Italiana in Cucina
By Tony Mantuano and Cathy Mantuano. Copyright © 2004 by Restaurant One Limited Partnership dba Spiaggia. Photographs by Jeff Kauck. Published by Chronicle Books.

The Weekend Baker

Irresistible Recipes, Simple Techniques, and Stress-Free Strategies for Busy People
From *The Weekend Baker: Irresistible Recipes, Simple Techniques, and Stress-Free Strategies for Busy People* by Abigail Johnson Dodge. Copyright © 2005 by Abigail Johnson Dodge. Used by permission of W. W. Norton & Company, Inc. Photographs copyright © 2005 by Gentl & Hyers.

Index

Page numbers in **bold** indicate photographs.

Page numbers in **bold** indicate photographs.

Page numbers in **bold** indicate photographs.